4/40

THE POLITICS OF HERESY

The Politics of Heresy

The Modernist Crisis in Roman Catholicism

LESTER R. KURTZ

UNIVERSITY OF CALIFORNIA PRESS
BERKELEY   LOS ANGELES   LONDON

University of California Press
Berkeley and Los Angeles, California

University of California Press, Ltd.
London, England

Library of Congress Cataloging in Publication Data
Kurtz, Lester R.
  The politics of heresy.
  Bibliography: p.
  Includes index.
  1. Modernism—Catholic Church. 2. Catholic Church—
History—20th century. I. Title.
BX1396.K87   273.9   85–1179
ISBN 0–520–05537–3 (alk. paper)

Printed in the United States of America

1 2 3 4 5 6 7 8 9

To Linda

Contents

Preface

The pages that follow constitute the culmination of a long-term effort to examine the fascinating and complex series of events known as the "modernist crisis" in the Roman Catholic Church. Those who wade into the troubled waters of that period will no doubt find themselves both enlightened and confused. The earthshaking issues of the nineteenth century—the conflicts between science and religion, between church and state, between Christianity and modern culture—were debated vigorously for decades, coming to a head in the papal condemnation of modernism in 1907. The turmoil did not end there, of course: the modernist crisis set the stage for the great religious and philosophical controversies of our own time. Because the modernist issues are also our issues, and because of their elusive nature, it is important to offer some caveats to the reader.

I must warn the reader of some major shortcomings of this study, in hopes that a critical evaluation of this work will further our understanding both of modernism and of the social construction of reality. First, an observation that has important implications and that should be explicit: this study is written by a scholar. This fact is important, because my work studies a struggle between scholars and their hierarchical superiors, who dislike the scholars' work and attempted to suppress it. Naturally, my sympathies tend to lie with the scholars, and I take for granted what I consider to be fundamental "rights" of free inquiry. This is not to say, however, that such rights do not have boundaries—no rights are absolute.

I would, for example, question the rights of another sociologist to teach a course on the genetic and social inferiority of a particular ethnic or racial group, because I would consider it not only empirically suspect but also extremely dangerous to the common good and a violation of my sense of justice: not only are rights and duties in tension but there are social boundaries around what is morally acceptable as well. Hence, despite my biases, I understand the Vatican's argument in defense of their suppression of modernist scholarship. The problem is compounded by the vastly disproportionate amount of primary source material available as data for this study from the modernist—rather than the Vatican—point of view.

A second problem is related to the first. This study is biased both because of my interests as a scholar and because of my broader cultural context. Most of us are, after all, now modernists—even those of us who hold strong religious beliefs despite the secular tone of modern culture. From the perspective of a sociology of knowledge, one might argue that just as Catholicism may have been in danger of capture by scholasticism in the late nineteenth century, so Catholicism is radically influenced by scientism in the late twentieth century. There is a fine line between science and scientism, and much that is valuable in an religious tradition can be seriously challenged by scientific studies—which may, however, simply replace one dogmatism with another.

Despite the fact that much is to be learned from science, it has a narrowness of purview that causes it to focus on select portions of the reality it examines. Much is lost when scientific methods replace rather than complement religious methods, with their rich, mythological analogies. When that prophet of the nineteenth century called for a "ruthless criticism of everything existing" (Marx [1843b] 1976), he helped to set in motion a great critical movement that constitutes a major contribution to the pursuit of truth. If we are to be true to critical and scientific methods, however (and my own work is guided by the scientific model), we must use criticism against our own ideas, including the critical method itself.

Finally, it may be significant that I do not come out of the Roman Catholic tradition, although I am active in the United Methodist Church. In the course of my research, I gained a new appreciation for the Catholic Church, but Protestant biases of which I am not aware may linger in the text.

Much that is valuable in the Catholic tradition could be swept away by a narrowness of vision. It is the heretic and the guardian of orthodoxy together who bring us the valuable treasures of our rich cultural traditions and reshape them for our time. We are thus indebted to the modernist scholars, to the ecclesiastical authorities, and to the conflict between them.

Acknowledgments

Although an author is finally responsible for what is published under his or her name, any work is a community project, from inception to completion. I am indebted to many individuals, notably the members of my dissertation committee: Terry Clark, Edward Shils (who first introduced me to the modernist movement), Teresa Sullivan (who commented insightfully on several drafts), and David Tracy. Others contributed at various points in the project, including Alec R. Vidler, John Root, Lawrence Barmann, Emile Poulat, Roger Haight, M. and Mme. Boyer de Saint Suzanne, Morris Janowitz, Donald Levine, Mary Jo Neitz, Carol Heimer, Arthur Stinchcombe, Michael Schudson, Steve Dubin, Robert Fowler, Andrew Weigert, Louis Zurcher, Gideon Sjoberg, Joe R. Feagin, John McCarthy, Charles Perrow, anonymous reviewers, and many others with whom I discussed these issues. Steve Lyng played a key role in the final version of this work, as a research assistant and, more importantly, as a colleague.

I would also like to thank the staff members at the British Library, the Bibliothèque Nationale, and the St. Andrews University Library for their assistance in consulting manuscript collections. I appreciate the permissions granted by Sr. Teresa, prioress of the Carmelite Monastery, St. Charles Square, London, and Mrs. Katherine Pirenne to copy materials at the British Library.

Victoria Scott smoothed many ragged edges with her superb editing; Laura Moore and John Dillard provided patient and competent assistance. Dereck Cooper translated French quotations into English and made many helpful suggestions. I am grateful to them, as well as to the many friends and colleagues at the University of Chicago and the University of Texas who provided encouragement. Finally, I could not have completed the research without financial assistance from the Danforth Foundation, the Sociology Department at the University of Chicago, the University Research Institute at the University of Texas at Austin, and Linda Scherbenske Kurtz.

1

Catholic Orthodoxy and the Dynamics of Heresy

> History is one long, desperate retching, and the only thing humanity is fit for is the Inquisition.
> —Msgr. Umberto Benigni, in Ernesto Buonaiuti, *Pilgrim of Rome*

Belief systems cannot be fully comprehended without some attention to the heresies that have emerged from within them. The role of heresy in the formation of orthodoxy is central, yet heresy is little understood by sociologists. Beliefs are most clearly and systematically articulated when they are formed *via negativa*—that is, when the boundaries of what is true and acceptable are marked out through a systematic identification of what is false and unacceptable. What people do not believe is often more clearly defined than what they do believe, and it is through battles with heresies and heretics that orthodoxy is most sharply delineated.

Definitions of heresy are also crucial in the maintenance and transformation of social institutions. Group solidarity is seldom strengthened by anything so much as the existence of a common enemy, and the heretic, as a "deviant insider," is close at hand. The identification of heretics shores up the ranks, enables institutional elites to make demands of their subordinates, and reinforces systems of dominance. As Georg Simmel put it, "the resistance which has to be eliminated is what gives our powers the possibility of proving themselves" (1971, 48).

My task, in this volume, is threefold. First, I attempt to develop some basic themes in the sociology of knowledge through the examination of a case study in the social construction of knowledge. I do so out of the conviction that our understanding of basic epistemological questions is dependent upon our grasp of the complex dialectical nature of the process of constructing worldviews, values, and beliefs. I try to outline aspects of the dynamic relationship between heresy and orthodoxy—particularly the ways in which orthodoxy is constructed through conflicts about heresy. Furthermore, I explore the dialectical relationship between ideas and belief systems on the one hand, and the interests of various groups, strata, and classes on the other, arguing with Weber that there are "elective affinities" between worldviews and personal and social interests.

A second goal of the study is to make a modest contribution to modernist studies. The reader who is unaware of the vast literature on Catholic modernism will soon recognize the wide variety of studies of modernism already carried out by numerous scholars, and might question the need for yet another study. I hope that my sociological approach to the topic—with an emphasis on the concepts of sociological ambivalence, social control, elective affinities, and deviant insiders—will shed some light on the modernist crisis by looking at it from a slightly different angle. I do not believe that my approach is substantially at odds with most of the historical and theological scholarship on modernism.

A third aim of the study is to delineate some of its implications for a sociological analysis of social change and social movements. For the most part, this means the advocacy of a dialectical model for such analyses—an approach which requires some major modifications of the prevailing paradigm for the study of social movements, which is known as the "resource mobilization" perspective. More specifically, the modernist movement can be examined as a case of what Zald and Berger (1978) have called "bureaucratic insurgency."

The series of conflicts surrounding modernism have proved to be one of the most important events in early modern culture, an important aspect of the conflict between science and religion, and a pivotal controversy in Roman Catholicism. In the course of the analysis, I hope to provide some insights into two important topics heretofore virtually ignored by sociologists: the broader problem of heresy, and the issue of Catholic modernism. The discussion that follows is based on an examination of various archival collections of letters and papers preserved by the modernists, as well as on published works and letters by both modernists and their opponents (see Bibliothèque Nationale, British Library, and St. Andrews University Library). My conceptualization of the nature of heresy was originally developed from a study of the modernists, but was subsequently broadened and then used as a conceptual tool for interpreting the modernist crisis.[1]

AN ANATOMY OF HERESY

In its formal sense in Roman Catholic Canon Law and moral theology, "heresy" refers to "a sin of one who, having been baptized and retaining the name of Christian, pertinaciously denies or doubts any of the truths that one is under obligation of divine and Catholic faith to believe" (Buckley 1967, 1069). The etymology of the term is instructive, since it is an English transliteration of the Greek αἱρεσις, which lacked the pejorative sense that the term has since acquired. It originally meant simply an act of choosing, choice, or attachment, then a course of action or thought, and finally a philosophical principle or set of principles and a party or sect (see Cross 1925, 614; McShane 1967, 1062). The idea of heresy as evil emerged in the bitter battles fought in the early church, which resulted in a series of councils that condemned various false doctrines and formulated fundamental aspects of traditional Christian orthodoxy (see Hughes 1961). The term as it has developed can provide a useful concept for studying the relation between belief systems and social organization. To elaborate on the concept, I would like to suggest several characteristics of heresy. It is simultaneously near and remote and it has social origins, yet it influences social arrangements as well. Moreover, the labeling and suppression of heresy and heretics serve as rituals for institutional elites, faciliating their dominance within the institution.

First, heresy refers to an intense union of both nearness and remoteness.[2] Heretics are within the relevant social circle or institution; consequently, they are close enough to be threatening but distant enough to be considered in error. In the Catholic tradition, a heretic is a baptized, professing Catholic. Unbaptized persons and non-Catholic Christians (e.g., a Protestant) are not guilty of "formal heresy," although they may be guilty of "material heresy," which is the outcome of ignorance but which is not defined as a sin "so long as there is no doubt in the heretic's mind regarding his false position" (Attwater 1954, 227). The heretic is also different from the schismatic (see Firey 1948) or the infidel, who are outside of the church. When the medieval scholastics developed catalogs of heresies, they were concerned not so much with abstract heresy as with guilty heretics (Lawlor 1967, 1063)—namely, persons within the community who were defined as a threat to the faith and to the institution.

Heresy thus has an important social dimension: the heretic is a "deviant insider." Every heresy implies a political stance and every heretic leads an insurrection, implicitly or explicitly. In 1890, Merry del Val, an ardent antimodernist who later became Vatican secretary of state, complained of "a group of traitors in the camp." He challenged their commitment to the church—a frequent charge against heretics—suggesting that one such suspect, William Gibson, "seems to be walking thro' the church on his way elsewhere, like people walk to and fro thro' S. Stefan's Cathedral in Vienna, going in by one door and out by the other to make a short cut."[3]

The combination of nearness and remoteness refers to belief systems as well as to the social relationship between heretics and the guardians of orthodoxy. As Dante observed in his *Divine Comedy,* "every contradiction is both false and true" (Paradise, canto 4). What makes heresy so potent is that it bears such a close resemblance to orthodoxy. It is developed within the framework of orthodoxy and is claimed by its proponents to be truly orthodox. Like the heretic, heresy itself is both near and remote at the same time.

A second characteristic of heresy is that it is socially constructed in the midst of social conflict. The interests of conflicting parties become attached either to a defense of the alleged heresy or to the refutation of it. Thus the problem of heresy is, at its root, a problem of authority. Battles between the orthodox and the heretic reveal the dialectical nature of the social construction of reality and the institutions within which reality is defined.

According to Catholic doctrine, a stubbornness of will is required for true heresy (Lawlor 1967, 1063). Saint Augustine pointed out that "not every error is a heresy" (Augustinus 1956, 59)—only those which are defined by authorities as being contrary to orthodoxy. Alleged heretics are thus allowed to recant; error is separated from sin by a behavioral test. The labeling of heresy is intimately tied both to self-interest and to group interest.

As social groups find an "affinity"[4] between their status interests on the one hand and a particular configuration of ideas or worldview on the other, they identify with that definition of the situation and use it to legitimate or enhance their social status. This does not imply that either the authorities or the heretics are necessarily malicious or self-serving, although they may be. The attempt to discern the motives of actors in a conflict is a risky business, and it is a necessary one if the nature of heresy and the conflicts between authorities and insurgents are to be understood. The difficulty appears, for example, in the fact that "duty" and "interests" may seem to imply differing motivations—the former presumably unselfish and the latter self-serving ones.

Actors usually perform duties because it is in their interest to do so. Authorities frequently defend what they perceive to be a genuine threat to what is considered sacred, sometimes at high personal cost. Similarly, insurgents frequently battle against aspects of orthodoxy which they consider destructive to the belief system and its institution. This is particularly true in religious institutions in which roles are defined so that interests include a considerable emphasis on altruism. Thus, when I speak of either the Vatican or the modernists pursuing their "interests," I do not necessarily mean to imply self-serving motivations; for the most part, both sides of the conflict, maintained a definition of the situation that identified their own personal and group interests with those of the Catholic faith and the church. As Goffman (1959) points out, a completely cynical view may be as inaccurate as one which accepts actors' statements of motivation at face value. "Sacred" doctrines and institutions require perpetual defense from destructive forces; institutional authorities are charged with carrying out that defense, whatever the cost. Yet heretics also play an important role in the formation of orthodoxy, and insurgents usually believe that they have the interests of the sacred institution and tradition at heart. Finally, one generation's heresy is frequently the next generation's orthodoxy.

A third characteristic of heresy is that it has social consequences as well as social origins. The conventional view of heresy emphasizes its divisive and disruptive nature as an affront to authority and the social order. The chancellor in Goethe's *Faust* who rails against heresy as an enemy of the social order exemplifies the attitude generally taken toward heresy and heretics (Goethe [1832] 1952, 203):

> Through Lawless men the vulgar herd
> To opposition have of late been stirred;
> The heretics these are, the wizards, who
> The city ruin and the country too.

Heresy is a two-edged sword, however: it is not only disruptive but can also be used for the creation of intragroup solidarity and for purposes of social control, as I have already suggested. Through the labeling and suppression of insurgents, institutional elites can rally support for their positions via battle with a common enemy. Ironically, then, elites may actually be involved, sometimes inadvertently, in the development of heretical movements. Such a perspective is at odds with much of the literature on social movements, in which, as Gamson (1975) argues, it is usually assumed that the probability of collective action is decreased by authorities' use of negative or "coercive" resources.[5]

Elites often evoke an insurgency as a self-fulfilling prophecy. They do this by beginning to portray a trend of thought in a particular way, so that it is defined as having a form, substance, and consistency that it might not have acquired had these aspects not been suggested by the elites. Adherents of the questionable views may then be driven together to form a movement for their common defense against the attack on those views by the institutional hierarchy. Having been labeled as dissidents, they may think that they have no choice but to define their interests in opposition to those of the established authorities.

A fourth characteristic of heresy is that the process of defining and labeling it has doctrinal as well as social consequences. It is in the heat of escalating conflicts that orthodoxy is formulated, often through explicit disagreement with a position held by "heretics." As positions polarize and persons within the conflict begin to choose sides, it becomes increasingly difficult to mix positions and beliefs that have conflicting political implications in the particular situation.

During the modernist controversy and throughout the century leading up to it, it became increasingly difficult to be both an advocate of scientific methods of inquiry, particularly scientific criticism, and an orthodox Catholic. Much of the "warfare of science with theology" (see White 1896–97) owes less to inherent differences between the two methods of seeking truth—although some do exist (see Barbour 1960)—than to conflicts concerning the authority of traditional Christian institutions, especially the Roman Catholic Church, in the modern world. To understand a particular set of orthodox beliefs, one must therefore examine the historical context in which they were formed and the types of heresies that arose in opposition to them.

A fifth defining characteristic of heresy is that the process of defining and denouncing heresy and heretics is a ritual. Like most rituals, the suppression of heresy has as one of its functions the relief of anxiety. Rituals serve to relieve social and psychological tensions and to focus anxiety on that which is controllable (see van Gennep [1909] 1960; Turner 1969). Anxiety over the weather is channeled into anxiety over the proper performance of weather-oriented rituals, such as the rain dance; anxiety over longevity can be translated into concern over keeping certain religious commandments.[6]

As with a rain dance, it is not clear that the denunciation of heresy is effective in fulfilling the explicit purpose of the ritual; nonetheless, such denunciations provide ritual occasions at which church authorities can deal with the difficulties the church is facing. Christian rituals for denouncing heretics began with the crises of church and state surrounding the first councils and were elaborated considerably in subsequent crises. They reached their apotheosis with the formation of the Inquisition and the use of the Augustinian formula *coge intrare*,[7] which gave infidels and heretics a choice between conversion and submission or extirpation.

The Vatican's condemnation of modernism, the elaborate system of control established throughout the church to root out modernist heretics, and the placing of books on the *Index of Prohibited Books* were all a response to the crisis in which the Catholic Church was embroiled in the modern era. A closer examination of that crisis and of the Vatican's response to it will help clarify the concept of heresy and the dialectical process of its development and suppression.

There is also a negative aspect to the affinities between ideas and interests—namely, that certain foes are ideal foes. Modernism was the ideal heresy for the Vatican to attack, just as the Vatican-sanctioned scholasticism was an ideal foe for the Catholic modernists.

HERESY IN MODERN CATHOLICISM

Although heresy has long been an integral part of religious life in all of the world's cultures, it has become particularly important in modern Western culture. So violent has been the conflict between "modern culture" and the Roman Catholic Church that Pope Pius X condemned "modernism" in 1907 as the "synthesis of all heresies." The full force of the Roman hierarchy was mobilized in an effort to destroy the "modernist movement" within the church. The Holy Office, successor to the Inquisition, placed numerous modernist books on the *Index of Prohibited Books*. Rome ruined the careers of Catholic clergy in order to punish and deter those labeled as modernist heretics. An antimodernist oath was administered to all clergy. A secret international organization (the Sapinière) and diocesan "vigilance committees" were instituted to detect and report heresy throughout the church. Countless individuals were harassed and censured, relieved of their posts, and stripped of their credentials.

Roman condemnations of modernism were an outgrowth of a crisis concerning definitions of Catholic orthodoxy which dominated nineteenth-century ecclesiastical history. Most threatening to the church were attempts to develop a "science of criticism." When the accuracy of the creation story in Genesis, the authorship of various parts of the Bible, the virgin birth, and the authority of the pope were attacked in the name of science, it was not just specific doctrines that were at issue but the entire body of Catholic dogma. Because of violent anticlerical attacks on the church by outsiders throughout the nineteenth century, such questions took on the aura of an internal attack on the very existence of Catholicism, even in cases in which they were not intended as such. Historical criticism was also used by external anticlericals, who saw scientific research as a valuable tool in their battle against Catholicism and its legitimating role in the ancien régime.

The Enlightenment philosophes of the eighteenth century paved the way for the French Revolution and set the tone for nineteenth-century intellectual debates. To be "enlightened" was to be at war with the ancien régime and consequently with Catholicism, the source of that regime's legitimation. Conflicts between Catholic tradition and modernist culture rose to a fevered pitch in the second half of the nineteenth century, exacerbated by Charles Darwin's theories of evolution and other scholarly works that challenged the validity of the account of creation found in Genesis. Ernst Renan's famous *Vie de Jésus* ([1863] 1965) contended that Jesus was no more than the pinnacle of human greatness—and "that," as George Sand remarked, "is the end of Jesus for all time."

Catholic intellectuals, especially in Europe, were exposed to critical currents in the secular intellectual milieu which created strains in their relationship with the Roman hierarchy, particularly for clerical scholars. Many felt that the answer to their intellectual difficulties lay in the formation of a scientific historiography within the Catholic tradition. But the very idea of such a development created a scandal in Rome and elsewhere, and the Vatican's response reveals much about the nature of heresy. Even more scandalous than anticlerical attacks from outside the church were attacks on the authority of Rome from clerics within the church. Moreover, those "deviant insiders" used the scientific methods of anticlericals in formulating works that they allegedly created to defend the church. Although Rome's war on modernism appeared to be waged against science itself, it was primarily a dispute over the boundaries of science and the incursion of scientific methods of inquiry into territory that was perceived by the Vatican as sacred ground. Due to the escalating conflict, many issues were swept into the debate which had not initially been involved, such as the efficacy of scientific method itself.

No reform movement per se actually developed until after ecclesiastical authorities had begun to suppress the work of a few relatively isolated scholars. A loose-knit network of relationships did begin to form toward the end of the nineteenth century, however, among Catholic intellectuals who were concerned with reconciling the church and modern culture. The chief intellectual figure in the movement was the young French priest and biblical scholar, Alfred Loisy. The major cultivator of the modernists' networks was the wealthy English lay scholar, Baron Friedrich von Hügel. Despite the networks that connected them, several divergent approaches emerged among those who were called modernists.

There were at least three distinct types of Catholic modernism, according to Alec Vidler (1934). The first was "doctrinal modernism," which is that part of the movement most commonly referred to by the term "modernism" alone. It was within this sector of the movement—under the leadership of Loisy, von Hügel, and the Jesuit priest George

Tyrrell—that attempts at an intellectual redefinition of the Catholic worldview took place, particularly through the use of critical methods and the articulation of implications for the church which grew out of the use of those methods.

France then witnessed the development of a group of "philosophical modernists," which included Maurice Blondel (although he had a fierce disagreement with Loisy and von Hügel), Edouard LeRoy, and Lucien Laberthonnière. Blondel, Laberthonnière, and especially LeRoy were concerned with the nature of dogma itself and questioned the narrow definitions of Catholicism developed by the scholastic theologians.

Finally, several movements organized around the issue of reconciling the church with democracy, particularly Marc Sangnier's Sillon ("The Furrow") in France and Don Romolo Murri's Lega Democratica Nazionale in Italy. The movements led by Sangnier and Murri were only loosely related to the doctrinal and philosophical modernists, and so will not be much discussed in this study. But some affinities did exist among the three groups—affinities which grew stronger when they were lumped together by the Vatican in its denunciations of all forms of modernism. Indeed, many traditional Catholic officials came to view all forms of modernism as different aspects of the same conspiracy to destroy the Catholic faith.

In the minds of such "integralist" Catholics as Msgr. Umberto Benigni, the church's enemies formed a unified whole that ran the gamut from anticlericalism to liberalism, antipapism, radicalism, feminism, republicanism, immanentism, interconfessionalism, socialism, syndicalism, individualism, and intellectual modernism (Poulat 1969, 121-123). The ecclesiastical elite defined its interests—and, eventually, Catholicism itself—almost exclusively within the framework of neo-scholasticism and a revival of the theology and philosophy of Thomas Aquinas. Thus the Roman hierarchy finally condemned modernism in a series of official decrees.

HERESY AS NEARNESS AND REMOTENESS

Members of the Roman hierarchy responded to the modernist crisis with a massive mobilization of the institution's defenses against an alleged international conspiracy, which was actually a caricature of the modernist movement. Modernism was in fact a movement primarily in the sense of a general, multifaceted direction of thinking precipitated by various scholars' attempts to apply "scientific methods" to the study of religious history and issues. To their adversaries, the modernists came to represent all that was wrong with the modern world. Modernism was perceived as a deliberate conspiracy to destroy the church, while at the same time those charged with heresy claimed that they, too, were attempting to defend Catholicism by creating a definition of their faith that was not repugnant to the modern intellect. An ethos or spirit of antimodernism so captured the imagination of many highly placed leaders in the church that the Roman hierarchy instituted a widespread "vigilance campaign" to wipe out the heresy. This antimodernist campaign created what many called a "reign of terror" within the church for a number of years.

What is puzzling at first glance is why so much concern arose on the part of a powerful institution over the work of a few somewhat isolated scholars and their sympathizers. Part of this opposition was due to conflicts that are inevitable between Christianity and intellectualism in all its forms. The Vatican hierarchy did not oppose all intellectualism or scholarship, however, and modernism was much more than an intellectual movement. Modernist scholarship represented an effort to free Catholic thought from the alleged straitjacket of late nineteenth-century scholastic intellectualism. Furthermore, a strong mystical element characterized the movement, evidenced particularly in the work of von Hügel, Tyrrell, and Fogazzaro. What disturbed the Vatican was not scholarship per se, but only those forms of scholarship that undermined a particular, narrow definition of Catholicism and thus subverted the hierarchy's authority.

The Vatican's war on modernism must be considered both within a context of the threat which modernism of all sorts presented to Rome and in terms of the relationship between the formation of dogma and conflict as a social form.[8] Any explanation must take into account not only the specific historical circumstances surrounding the controversy (notably the decades of anticlerical attacks on the church) but also the general characteristics of dissidence and of heresy. The effects of dissidence are relative; they involve both the intellectual content of a given protest and the social relationship between the critic and the criticized, the orthodox and the heretic.

THE RELATIVITY OF DISSIDENCE

Ideas and interests are dialectically related: the way in which belief systems are formulated and articulated is largely shaped and influenced not only by their actual content but also by the interests of the groups adhering to them, particularly in times of social conflict. Particular religious beliefs, worldviews, and political orientations are chosen both because they make sense to people intellectually and because those definitions of reality have an affinity with the interests and life-styles of those who choose them. Both the "modernists" and the ecclesiastical hierarchy defined Catholicism and science in ways that served their respective interests, and then surrounded their definitions with an aura of objective truth and universality.

Responses to heterodoxy within an institution are a function both of the "social distance" between dissidents and institutional authorities and of the "ideational distance" between them—that is, the degree of divergence between the beliefs of dissidents and those of the authorities. In other words, a "relativity of dissidence" is analogous to the dynamics of relative deprivation, as conceptualized by Tocqueville ([1856] 1955) and Merton (1968).[9] The relativity of dissidence leads to two propositions that are examined in this study:

1. Criticism from within a social organization may be more intellectually offensive than external criticism.
2. Mechanisms of control will be activated by elites only when social distance, as well as ideational distance, reaches but does not exceed a critical level.

With regard to the first proposition, modernist criticism cut to the heart of the Catholic belief system. Although the modernists adhered to some of the standard criticisms of the anticlericals and nonbelievers, they claimed to be Catholic defenders of the faith. Church authorities identified the modernists as deviant insiders and linked them with external critics, especially "rationalists," Protestants, and modernists of all sorts. External critics, unlike the modernists, used non-Catholic standards and non-Catholic terms and imagery, which could be more easily ignored by the faithful and by members of the hierarchy alike. Outsiders were also less likely to mislead the unsuspecting faithful because they made no claims to orthodoxy. Ideational distance is crucial in the dynamic situation that evolves whenever a heresy develops, because heresy is more dangerous to those in power than are critiques which operate from extrinsic assumptions. thus some members of the Roman hierarchy complained that Loisy was more threatening to the Catholic faith than was the Protestant Adolf von Harnack ([1903] 1958), just as the priest Luther had been perceived as more threatening than the secular King Henry VIII. Loisy's *L'Evangile et l'Eglise* ([1903*b*] 1976) was in fact an effort to demonstrate the historical legitimacy of the Roman Church in the face of arguments to the contrary by Harnack and others.

Although the work was praised by many, it drew criticism from Protestants and Catholics alike. If the book was an antiprotestant polemic, why did it create such a storm among the Catholic hierarchy and evoke a tirade in the Catholic press? The answer lies in the fact that its antiprotestant sentiments were less important to the Roman hierarchy than was the neo-Catholicism outlined in the book. Whereas Loisy genuinely disagreed with Harnack's Protestant definitions of Christianity, his work implicitly challenged scholasticism and official Catholic theology (Loisy [1913] 1968, 229).

The second proposition just listed states that mechanisms of control will be activated by elites only when social distance, as well as ideational distance, reaches but does not exceed a critical level. Thus the relationship between social distance and suppressive activities by elites is curvilinear, as is the relation between ideational distance and suppression. If the ideational or social distance is either too high or too low, the critique may well be ignored. At a critical point between the two extremes, however, the ideas of dissidents will become defined as dangerous. Because the dissidents themselves are within the sphere of the elites' institutional authority, the elites demand action. Dissidents working in an organization are within its networks and authority structure, and hence are more likely to attract followers than are external critics, who can make no legitimate claims.[10]

Thus deviant insiders pose a more direct threat than do external critics who, as "outside agitators," can be "defined out of the scene" and fairly easily dismissed. Critics within an organization are more susceptible to control by its elites than are those outside of the circle; immediate sanctions are often available and effective. Deviant insiders may also be used as "scapegoats," when they can be linked to external critics who make no effort to be considered orthodox but who constitute a threat both to the institution and to its belief system.

Critics outside of the church were not under the Vatican's control, but the modernists—particularly the clergy—were subject to the authority of the hierarchy. After the labeling of modernist heretics, Catholicism could be defined not only on the basis of papal and traditional authority but also in terms of a common enemy. The Catholic faithful at all levels of the institution could be called on to oppose the heresy in their midst. The issue of modernism was, fundamentally, a conflict between ecclesiastical authority and the authority of independent scholars. In an effort to control the alleged heresy, the Roman leadership and the Catholic press cultivated a spirit of antimodernism that pervaded the church. In the process, both the heresy itself and the orthodoxy from which it was alleged to deviate were socially constructed.

THE SOCIAL CONSTRUCTION AND CONSEQUENCES OF HERESY

Heresies and efforts to define and suppress them are not created ex nihilo, but through responses to situations of social conflict. As belief systems become institutionalized, those in power begin to attach their interests to certain definitions of orthodoxy and become convinced that the belief system itself would be endangered if their definitions of orthodoxy were challenged. In times of social conflict, those on each side of a conflict construct belief systems and definitions of those systems that have an affinity with their perceived interests, and those belief systems in turn help to shape the way in which parties to the conflict define their interests.

Within the Catholic Church, the power to define orthodoxy was gradually limited to the offices of the pope and to the ecumenical councils which he convened. Doctrines of papal supremacy and infallibility were not official Catholic doctrine until the First Vatican Council in 1870, and were constructed as a direct response to the institutional crisis of the church. The philosophical system of scholasticism, which was used to legitimate the notion of the apostolic succession of authority, became in effect a "status ethic"[11] for the hierarchy of the Roman Church. The interests and status of the bishops—and even more so those of the burgeoning clerical bureaucracy of the Vatican—became attached to and associated with the prestige of the papacy and the doctrines on which it was based. The development of such definitions of the situation leads almost inevitably to the persecution of heretics.

The growth of modern science was accompanied by countless conflicts between scientists and church officials, in part because the organized skepticism required by the norms of science[12] frequently led to refutations of the established doctrines of the church. It was the combination of anticlerical movements in western Europe (during the eighteenth and nineteenth centuries) with popular theories of evolution and the development of scientific criticism that posed the greatest threat to the Roman Church. The antagonism between the advocates of science and the defenders of traditional Christianity was so intense that it became a key issue in late nineteenth-century social thought and a central theme in the work of such thinkers as Durkheim, Weber, Pareto (Aron 1970, 2:2), and Freud. As Marx put it, "the basis of all criticism is the criticism of religion" ([1843a] 1972, 11–12).

ELECTIVE AFFINITIES

Scientific arguments became weapons for anticlericals who attacked the church not so much because of its cultural traditionalism as because it was a symbol of the hated ancien régime (Tocqueville [1856] 1955, 6). Anticlericals began to recognize an affinity between their hatred of the church and the ideas of science, which could be used to attack the church's doctrines, thereby weakening the latter's hold on the populace.

Nineteenth-century political battle lines were frequently drawn so that affinities were defined between particular approaches to scientific and religious thought on the one hand, and various political and social alliances on the other. If one supported the replacement of the monarchy with a republic, especially in France, one was expected to oppose Catholicism and to favor the expansion of scientific research, while most who elected to be defenders of the Catholic faith also tended to oppose republicanism and science and to defend the monarchy. Monarchical models of authority were used by clericals to defend Catholic orthodoxy, just as scientific models of inquiry were used by anticlericals to attack that orthodoxy and the monarchy which it legitimated.

The ecclesiastical elite defined its interests within the framework of neo-scholasticism and a revival of the theology and philosophy of Thomas Aquinas. The orderly, hierarchical thought of that famous theologian was consistent with the ethos of ecclesiastical absolutism developed in defense against anticlerical attacks. Scholasticism legitimated the monarchical model of ecclesiastical government that had been taken to its extreme in the doctrine of papal infallibility. Notions of papal authority developed in the fourteenth century were further elaborated, and Catholic orthodoxy was defined within the boundaries of scholasticism and papal authority. For many in Rome, all was heresy outside the boundaries of scholastic theology, and all were heretics who defied the authority of the pope.

In addition to political and nationalistic divisions and genuine theological differences, and despite the increasing centralization of ecclesiastical authority, the Roman Church underwent considerable structural differentiation throughout the nineteenth century. Within the Vatican and elsewhere, the bureaucratization of various tasks resulted in competing institutional centers within the church (e.g., the Catholic universities, which were created to exercise the teaching functions of the church). Revolutions in transportation and communication, coupled with the expansion of the church through missionary efforts and migrations to the New World, brought heterogeneous demands to bear on the central ecclesiastical structure. This increasing centralization was accompanied by a mounting resistance to that centralization. However, little visible resistance to Rome appeared in the period immediately following the First Vatican Council of 1870, when any rebellion would have been futile. These developments paralleled those which Durkheim ([1893] 1933) discerned in society at large as a consequence of the division of labor—namely, increasing individuality and a simultaneous increase in the unity of the entire society, due to the interdependence of various specialized parts.

The specialization of academic research created a world of scholars in which members of the church hierarchy were often unwanted strangers. The basic problem that emerged from structural changes in the church was that the pope, who was given authority to interpret scripture and tradition for the church, did not function in that capacity on a day-to-day basis. He relied increasingly on a professional staff, like the head of any large organization. The institutionalization of specialized scholarship meant that the pope became far removed from the experts actually performing the task of study and interpretation. When radical disagreements arose between scientifically oriented scholars and church authorities, that division of labor became problematic, and was complicated even further by internal debates within the scholarly community.

For a number of scholars, scholasticism was a distortion of reality, but the Vatican defined the two worlds of scholasticism and science as mutually exclusive. Much of the modernist controversy concerned the nature of religious truth. The scholastics and Vatican authorities contended that Christian truths were universal and unchanging, and that they were to be interpreted through the teaching authority of the Church. Modernist historical scholarship, on the contrary, suggested that religious dogmas evolved and changed over time. Each party to the conflict sometimes elaborated its definitions of the situation so as to exclude parts of its opponents' definitions, simply because those opponents believed in them.

Trapped between the culture of the Vatican and the demands of a secular intellectual culture, the modernists experienced considerable "sociological ambivalence" (Merton and Barber 1976). They were in a situation in which they confronted contradictory normative demands from scientific scholarship on the one hand, and the ecclesiastical hierarchy on the other. They denied the pope's authority to limit their research, and so struck a sensitive nerve within the Vatican. Not only were the modernists using suspect "scientific methods" in their research but they were also defying the authority of the pope, which had been used by clericals to defend the church against scientific scholarship.

Catholic officials found affinities both between their interests and scholasticism and papal absolutism and with the spirit of antimodernism, which saw in modernism a symbol of all that threatened the church. A group of Jesuits who were organized around the review *Civiltà cattolica*, published in Rome, provided the core of the neo-Thomist movement from the middle of the nineteenth century on, and they exerted a powerful influence within the Vatican. Their unqualified opposition to everything "modern" was part of a well-organized drive to defend the church from the modern world by developing a Thomist revival. The work of Loisy, Tyrrell, Fogazzaro, and others did not fit into their plan: for the Jesuits, all modern systems and methods of intellectual inquiry were intrinsically unsatisfactory. Yet Catholic modernism at the end of the nineteenth century was not an organized movement, but simply the work of a few relatively isolated scholars. Gradually, through a series of book reviews and articles, an image of the modernists as a heretical conspiracy began to take shape (see Ranchetti 1969), culminating in denunciations. Unintentionally, these attacks forced the modernists to seek out one another and form a more solidified position for their common defense, although the effort was not a successful one.

The *Civiltà cattolica* Jesuits were opposed to modernist ideas not only from an intellectual and religious point of view but also because their privileged position in the ecclesiastical hierarchy was threatened by any group with rising popularity and an ability to operate in the sphere of doctrinal interpretation. Vatican officials themselves joined in the campaign against the modernists and finally took over the direction of that campaign.[13] As in all cases of heresy, the question of authority was at the core of the controversy. Once developed, such controversies have a dynamic of their own that precipitates further escalation and polarization. The social construction of heresy, carried out by both the orthodox elites and the heretical dissidents, has radical social consequences as the conflicting parties fight for authority within the institution.

By campaigning against the modernists and their ideas, those concerned about the church's crisis were able to defend the institution. Little could be done to silence the anticlericals who attacked the church in the French parliament and elsewhere, but Loisy, Tyrrell, von Hügel, Fogazzaro, and the other deviant insiders could be reprimanded and, if necessary, silenced. What began as an unofficial, fragmented campaign of innuendo and public charges developed into a full-scale attempt by the hierarchy to defend the church against modernism. Once the institutional mechanisms for the control of heresy were set in motion, there was no room for compromise on either side; the drama had to be played out to its bitter end.[14] A series of official proclamations against modernist ideas culminated in the decree *Lamentabili,* issued 2 July 1907, and the encyclical *Pascendi* of 8 September 1907, which contained an extensive systematization of the alleged doctrines of the modernists and a plan for the suppression of the movement, respectively.

Much of the framework of current debates over the relationship between scientific inquiry and Catholic doctrine derives from the modernist crisis, since both the modernists and the Vatican defined the controversy as a conflict between science and orthodox Catholicism. The nature of scholarship and doctrinal definition in Catholicism was profoundly affected by the controversy, as the Vatican proposed a series of remedies to deal with the crisis.

THE RITUAL OF THE HERESY HUNT

Both the extent of the antimodernist campaign and the later suppression of the antimodernists by the Vatican show that the real issue surrounding modernism, at least by the time of its condemnation, was much more than a series of specific objections to particular modernist ideas, or even to use of scientific methods for historical and textual research. The real issue that Pius X addressed in his pronouncements was a broadly perceived challenge to the authority of Catholic orthodoxy, to the Roman Church, and to those who ran the institution. This challenge exemplified both the dialectical character of conflict in cultural institutions and the dynamics of the heresy hunt.

It was not, however, simply the conflicts between science and scholastic theology that precipitated the modernist crisis. Ironically, it was also the Vatican's posture of heresy hunting which elicited a reform movement among scholars who might otherwise never have created one. Why, then, did church authorities bother with the modernists and their scholarship, if by doing so they were actually provoking the formation of a reform movement? In part, it may have been because the authorities were not cognizant of the consequences of their actions. More importantly, however, the existence of the modernist movement was not only a threat but a source of strength as well. The modernists were a symbolic focus for the hierarchy's attack on subversive forces, which it held responsible for the church's many problems. This curious development is less baffling when one recognizes the central role that heresy plays in the process of belief formation, and in mobilizing people in voluntary religious institutions. Heresy and orthodoxy are opposite sides of the same coin: they are twin aspects of the same social process, within which belief systems are defined. Belief systems are created not by people contemplating the universe (although passive contemplation may play an essential role) but by groups of people interacting with other groups of people— talking, debating, and sometimes fighting. Of particular importance in the process is the interaction between the so-called heretics and the orthodox, between heresy and orthodoxy itself.

People tend to act in a routine fashion, operating within boundaries established by the normative requirements of their roles. In times of crisis, however, both structures and beliefs are shifted, transformed, and re-created. People break the rules and redefine their situations, and unanticipated consequences inevitably result. It is important for sociologists to examine these processes of change and redefinition, and to recognize the importance of conflict in the formation of beliefs and values.

2

The Modernist Crisis

In the nineteenth century the notion of "dogma" acquired a negative connotation for many European intellectuals, and "criticism" acquired a positive one. A dogma originally referred to an affirmation of beliefs, ideas, and doctrines, but the concept evolved until it referred to unbending, narrowly held opinions. In the age of the Enlightenment and the period that followed, to be dogmatic was to be unenlightened and closed to alternative interpretations of the truth.

Members of the Catholic hierarchy were not novices at fighting heretical dogmas,[1] but now the notion of dogma itself was under attack. A growing tradition of "scientism"[2] was used by anticlericals and even by a number of religious scholars to deny the validity of traditional doctrine, the idea of dogma, and the authority of the ecclesiastical elite as an arbiter of truth. The methods and conclusions of the positive sciences—which insisted on direct, firsthand observation—seemed to be antithetical to the notion of dogma and were used as tools for attacking the church.

In France, where anticlericals mounted a vociferous and extended campaign against the church, two somewhat distinct camps emerged: the Republicans, who stood for the creation of a democratic polity, the end of monarchical and ecclesiastical rule, and the hope for humanity's gradual perfection through scientific rationalism; and those who defended the church and the monarchy, lamenting the Revolution's destruction of the social fabric of French life. Attempts to synthesize elements of these two polemical positions were met with resistance by both the Vatican hierarchy and the anticlericals. The history of nineteenth-century Europe provides a preeminent opportunity for scrutinizing the dialectics of conflict. A series of movements and countermovements, suppressions by authorities and rebellions by insurgents, influenced one another in reciprocal fashion throughout the century.

A key religious issue in the nineteenth century was the development of higher criticism, or scientific historiography, in the study of the church's scriptures and documents of church history. The Council of Trent (1546) proclaimed that the divine truth is contained "in the written books and the unwritten traditions which have come down to us." It was therefore essential that no contradictions be found between the church's doctrine and the scriptures. Challenges concerning the most minute portion either of the scriptures or of church doctrine constituted a radical challenge to the entire Catholic belief system, because one of the central dogmas of the church was the infallibility of scripture and tradition.[3]

In this chapter, I briefly review the development of scientific criticism and Vatican responses to the crisis of the time. Of central importance is the fact that conflicts surrounding criticism were exacerbated by anticlericalism throughout the nineteenth century. The Catholic hierarchy responded by articulating an official theology based upon the work of the neo-Thomist, or scholastic, theologians. By giving all Catholic doctrine a scholastic cast, ecclesiastical authorities aimed at developing a comprehensive theology that would defend Catholic orthodoxy against anticlericalism and other threats posed by the modern world.

SCIENTIFIC CRITICISM AND CATHOLIC DOCTRINE

Rumblings of the conflict between the modern sciences and the Roman Church emerged in classic form with Galileo Galilei's seventeenth-century encounter with the Inquisition. In refuting Ptolemaic astronomy, Galileo contended (with Copernicus) that the universe consisted of a heliocentric system, and was promptly denounced by the Jesuit Melchior Inchofer, who alleged that Galileo was undermining the church. Galileo's research called into question both the scriptures and the church's interpretations of the scriptures. "The opinion of the earth's motion is of all heresies the most abominable, the most pernicious, the most scandalous," Inchofer contended. "The immovability of the earth is thrice sacred" (quoted in White 1896–97, I;139).

Other seventeenth-century scientists also resented restrictions imposed by religious authorities. Francis Bacon complained that in the universities "everything is found to be opposed to the progress of the sciences" and that nothing "out of the common track scarcely enter[s] the thoughts and contemplations of the mind" ([1605] 1952, 124). He charged that the advancement of learning had been impaired by those who "have proceeded to mingle an undue proportion of the contentious and thorny philosophy of Aristotle with the substance of religion"—a complaint that foreshadowed the modernists' critique of scholasticism. Throughout the seventeenth and eighteenth centuries, a new ethos emerged among European intellectuals, an ethos scornful of orthodox Christianity.

THE ENLIGHTENMENT AND RELIGIOUS AUTHORITY

The exploration of the world's frontiers in the sixteenth and seventeenth centuries precipitated a recognition of common threads in all of the world's religions. In England, Lord Herbert of Cherbury posited a natural religion implanted in all humans. His 1624 *De Veritate* was a classic statement of the deism which attracted a great deal of attention, first in England, and later in France, Germany, and the United States. A wide range of deist "creeds" existed, but most contained a new appreciation of global religious diversity and an affirmation of religious toleration that contradicted post-Reformation Catholicism.

Much of the conflict between the deists and Christians focused on the importance of reason as a source of truth. There was never complete agreement within the church, as the famous twelfth-century debate between Peter Abelard, professor at the University of Paris, and Bernard of Clairvaux had shown. Christianity was based upon both reason and revelation. If the two appeared to be in conflict, Roman authorities usually defended revelation as the more reliable source. But the deists affirmed the superiority of reason, and some thinkers of the time, such as David Hume, believed that no reasonable person could believe in Christianity.

The development of textual criticism—particularly investigations into questions of authorship, historical development, and composition of biblical writings—was of great interest to those questioning orthodox Christianity. The most provocative applications of critical methods came first from political philosophers like Thomas Hobbes, who questioned the Mosaic authorship of the Pentateuch in his 1651 *Leviathan*, and from Baruch Spinoza. In his famous *Tractatus Theologico-Politicus* ([1670] 1883), Spinoza claimed that theologians simply used the Bible for their own purposes. Spinoza examined historical contradictions and inconsistencies in the biblical texts, and called for a criticism of the scriptures independent of theological assumptions.

Spinoza's methods were later adopted and developed by other scholars. In *The Reasonableness of Christianity, as Delivered in the Scriptures* (1695), John Locke contended that one must differentiate the Gospels and the Acts of the Apostles from the Epistles, which were too far removed from the simple gospel (see Locke [1705–1707] 1824, VII:xvi).

In the eighteenth century, deist controversies subsided somewhat in England, but were influential in France, where a number of the Enlightenment philosophes were deists. Rousseau's *Emile* (1762), for example, included a deist profession of faith which affirmed the supremacy of reason in religious matters. Rousseau continued to believe in the "immortality of the soul" and the idea of a beneficent Providence,[4] but a number of the philosophes, including Voltaire, attacked Christianity and the church. Several important works appeared, such as Voltaire's *Candide* (1758), Montesquieu's *Esprit des lois* (1748), and David Hume's *Natural History of Religion* (1757), as well as the first volume of the irreverent and popular *Encyclopedie* (1751). Dissatisfaction with the ancien régime gave strength to a growing movement of "incrédulité" in France. In Germany, one of the most influential *Aufklärung* (Enlightenment) philosophers was Pierre Bayle, whose *Dictionnaire historique et critique* (1697) was read and supported by a wide range of influential eighteenth-century figures, from Rousseau, Voltaire, and Montesquieu, to David Hume, Frederick II of Prussia, Benjamin Franklin, and Thomas Jefferson.

In France, Enlightenment influences and deism were decisive in the growth and spread of Freemasonry, long perceived by the Vatican as a threat to Catholicism. Most of the Freemasons were not explicitly anti-Christian, but their lodges, rituals, and beliefs in the "Great Architect of the Universe" often provided a secular, communal alternative to participation in the church. One wing of the Grand Orient of France became a center of violent anticlericalism; in 1738 a papal condemnation of Masonry was issued, partly because of the initiation vow, and Catholic masons were later threatened with excommunication. The campaign against Masonry symbolized the Vatican's efforts to delegitimate all threatening modern movements.

Enlightenment philosophes set the agenda for intellectual activity in the eighteenth century and paved the way for the scientific rationalism of the nineteenth. Yet it was not rationalism that the nineteenth century inherited from the Enlightenment, but the revolt both against church authority and against the ancien régime with which the church had been so intimately associated. Many nineteenth-century intellectuals made "a political demand for the right to question everything, rather than the assertion that all could be known or mastered by rationality" (Gay 1966–1969, I:141). Reason was merely a tool of the critic. The philosophes' criticism of the church inspired efforts to destroy the church's influence

in France at the time of the 1789 Revolution. It also precipitated scientific
and anticlerical disputes over the use of historical criticism.

DEVELOPING CRITICAL METHODS

Controversies surrounding higher criticism centered on the contention
that the sacred texts of Christianity had a history—namely, that they
were human products, the development and transformations of which
could be analyzed scientifically, like any other text. Meanwhile, the
emergence of left-wing Hegelianism and historiography stimulated scholarly developments that continued the rationalistic trends of deism and
the Enlightenment. The earliest critical investigations of the scriptures
focused primarily on the Old Testament, such as sixteenth-century studies
by Elijah ben Asher and Louis Cappel of changes in Hebrew texts to
which vowel points and accents had been added long after the consonantal
texts were written.

The French Oratorian Richard Simon, usually acknowledged as the
father of biblical criticism, used the methods of rationalist critics to defend
Catholicism. By showing the Bible to be unreliably transmitted, Simon
reasoned, he would discount the Protestant doctrine of *sola scriptura*
("scripture alone"), thereby making it clear that the tradition of the
Catholic Church was a necessary supplement to the Bible (see Simon
1693). The problem with Simon's argument was his failure to recognize
that the church's tradition itself affirmed the infallibility of the scriptures.
To suggest the possibility of error in the scriptures was to imply error in
the tradition. Although Simon's *Critical History of the Old Testament*
(1678) was approved by the censor, it was greeted with fury by the
famous French bishop and theologian Jacques Benigne Bossuet, who
stopped its publication.

Bossuet continued his campaign against Simon and succeeded in
driving him from the Oratory and in degrading his reputation. Because
of Bossuet and his collaborators, the lack of religious pluralism in the
country, and (more importantly) the lack of an institutional base from
which to develop it, scientific criticism was brought to a halt in French
Catholicism until after the founding of the Catholic universities in 1875.
After Simon, literary and historical analyses of the Bible developed primarily in Germany, but also in England under the influence of the deists. In
Germany, critical studies of the New Testament were advanced by Protestant scholars Johann Salomo Semler and Johann David Michaelis, both
of whom adopted Simon's critical methods but opposed his conclusions
about the necessity of the Catholic Church.

In a series of developments throughout the eighteenth century, historical problems of the Bible became increasingly apparent. Challenges to church doctrines concerning scripture were made with increasing frequency. Criticism moved from the task of simple exegesis to historical and philosophical criticism with Johann Gabler, and to hermeneutical discussions with Karl Keil. The level of controversy escalated with the studies of Jesus' life that proliferated during the nineteenth century.

"LIFE OF JESUS" STUDIES

In 1819 Friedrich Schleiermacher began delivering his popular lectures on the life of Jesus at the University of Berlin. He had a profound influence on liberal Protestantism throughout the nineteenth century, applying the critical methods to several important texts and drawing theological implications from them. David F. Strauss's *Das Leben Jesu kritisch bearbeitet* (1835–36) precipitated lively debates over the implications of critical methods and had a radical impact on the world of scholarship. He called into question the entire traditional conception of Jesus and the gospels, and questioned the sources and interrelationships of the gospels.

Attempts to reconstruct the life of Jesus brought biblical scholarship back to the fore in France. The most popular work of the genre was Ernest Renan's famous *La Vie de Jésus* (1863), which expounded a rationalist interpretation of Jesus as nothing more than the pinnacle of humanity. Renan was a young seminarian at Saint Sulpice, the only French Catholic institution in the mid-nineteenth century where biblical studies were carried out in earnest, but where the strictest orthodoxy was used to combat critical methods. Renan's *Vie de Jésus* evoked a clamor on all sides. Although not himself an anticlericalist, Renan's work did much to convince the Catholic authorities that scientific criticism was injurious to the faith. Renan claimed that, contrary to the opinion of the theologians, the Bible should be seen as a collection of texts for which the common rules of criticism are just as appropriate as with any other historical documents ([1863] 1965, 12).

Twenty years after the publication of *Vie de Jésus*, the young Alfred Loisy began attending Renan's lectures at the Collège de France. Loisy first intended to refute Renan, but was eventually won over to the methods of criticism. Loisy maintained that it was his own study of the Bible and not the ideas of any other scholar, even those of Renan and the German critics, that precipitated his own controversial conclusions (1930–31, II:16).[5] There is no need to assume—as Loisy's archbishop, Cardinal Richard, did—that the same or similar conclusions reached from critical

studies of scriptures were necessarily the consequence of German influences. Renan's work—and, more importantly, the creation of the Catholic
Institutes in France—did much to cultivate an alternative to the narrow
orthodoxy imposed in France from the time of Bossuet.

THEORIES OF EVOLUTION

Yet no piece of biblical criticism created as much widespread skepticism
about the literal truths of the Bible as did the theories of evolution, which
took intellectuals throughout Europe by storm in the latter half of the
nineteenth century. Charles Darwin's *The Origin of Species* (1859) and
Descent of Man (1871) elicited a vociferous public debate on evolution,
despite Darwin's claim that there was "no good reason why the views
given . . . should shock the religious feelings of anyone" ([1859] 1952,
239; cf. [1871] 1952, 593).

Darwin's theories of evolution and natural selection seemed to contradict the creation account in Genesis and to degrade the importance of
the human species and its relationship to the Creator.[6] As *The American
Church Review* put it in a July 1865 article, if Darwin's hypothesis is
true, "then is the Bible an unbearable fiction; . . . then have Christians
for nearly two thousand years been duped by a monstrous lie. . . . Darwin
requires us to disbelieve the authoritative word of the Creator." Roman
authorities went to great lengths to combat Darwinian theories.

Anticlerical affinities with Darwin's evolutionism—and the church's
opposition to it—made sense in the context of nineteenth-century intellectual debates. Church authorities argued that notions of change, progress,
and evolution within human history contradicted the immutable, eternal
truths of Christian dogma. Scientific criticism of the scriptures posited
the historical and changing character of human perceptions of God. Few
Catholics even dared to venture into the field until the end of the
nineteenth century; liberal Catholics earlier in the century, such as Felicité
de Lamennais, were concerned primarily with political rather than
theological liberalism.

Political liberalism was an important element in the historical process
leading up to the modernist crisis, not because of any direct influence of
liberal Catholics on the modernists, but because it was in fighting anticlericalism and political liberalism both within and outside of the church
that the Vatican developed its strategies for coping with the modern
world—strategies which later proved fatal to the modernist movement.
Thus it is important to develop a brief sketch of anticlericalism in Europe
and of the Vatican's response to it.

ANTICLERICALISM AND THE CONSERVATIVE
CATHOLIC ALLIANCE

In recent times, few phenomena have been more important to the life of the Roman Church than the growth of anticlericalism, which opposed clergy influence in secular affairs, in the eighteenth and nineteenth centuries. Attacks on the church came from virtually every corner of the Western world. These controversies are germane to an understanding of the modernist crisis for three reasons. First, anticlericalism exacerbated the Catholic hierarchy's conflicts with the modern world, and it was largely in response to anticlericalism that Vatican policies were formulated. Every new development was viewed through the eyes of a Vatican elite which had been persecuted, and in some instances physically threatened, by the anticlericalism that emerged in the eighteenth century and erupted during the French Revolution.

Second, the methods of scientific criticism were used by anticlericals to attack the church and its doctrines. Consequently, the ecclesiastical hierarchy defined anticlericalism and biblical criticism as two aspects of the same enemy. Finally, the anticlericalism of the nineteenth century inadvertently led to the creation of an institutional base for the development of critical methods. Catholic clericals were driven out of institutions of higher education, particularly in France, leaving the church without a foothold in the educational sphere.

Two of the most decisive phenomena leading to anticlericalism were the rapid growth of Enlightenment rationalism among the intelligentsia and the close association between the hierarchy of the church and the power structure of the ancien régime. It is far too simplistic to view proponents of the Enlightenment as uniformly opposed either to the church or to the ancien régime (see Darnton 1980), but they became the driving force in revolutionary movements of the eighteenth century. The confidence that the enlightenment philosophes had in the power of human reason, and their aversion to "superstition" of all sorts, placed them in direct opposition to much of the teaching of orthodox Catholicism. The Enlightenment became the source of much revolutionary fervor.

THE FRENCH REVOLUTION

When advocates of the French Revolution attacked the ancien régime, they were relentless in their assault on the Gallican church, the leadership of which was recruited largely from the hated aristocracy. The French Revolution marked the beginning of a new era in political and religious history (see MacCaffrey 1910, vii). Yet some efforts of the revolution to eliminate traditional religious practices provoked considerable irritation among the *citoyens* (see Bodley 1906, 26-27). For example, the revision of the calendar resulted in the division of months into three ten-day periods; the last day of each period, called the "decadi," was declared a day of rest. This disrupted social habits and reduced the number of rest days per month.

Wielding the power of the ecclesiastical institution, the pope anathematized the French church's relationship with the Republic and refused to consecrate any bishops for it. Radical positions consolidated on both sides, the church was polarized, and the French clergy were cut off from Rome. The aim of the revolution was to destroy the church as a political force in France, although the thrust of its anticlericalism was political and social rather than religious (see Tocqueville [1856] 1955). Pope Pius VI was driven from Rome by French forces in 1798, and captured the following year and hauled off to France, only to die in exile at Valence (see Pastor 1891–1953, XL:332 ff.). It is not surprising, then, that when Napoleon Bonaparte came to power as a champion of social order, the papacy signed the Concordat of 1801, thus aligning the Roman Church with conservative forces—a move which dominated nineteenth-century ecclesiastical policy.

Bonaparte saw the church as an important factor in unifying the divisive French society. The church was used as an instrument of legitimation for the state, in exchange for restoration of its central position in French society, although many of the church's losses in the revolution were never regained. Confiscated church property was not returned, and the pope was forced to acknowledge its ownership by hundreds of thousands who had acquired titles to church land. Nevertheless, Catholicism was to be the state religion to the exclusion of all other sects, and religious truth was again "absolute." Church and state were to be partners in the enterprise of maintaining the social order.

The revolution was not over, however, and the church's alliance with the empire was costly. Political order in France was extremely fragile throughout the century, as the state vacillated between republics and empires. A number of events—such as the Congress of Vienna in 1815, which reestablished the papal states in Italy—solidified the church's alliance with conservative political forces. The restoration of the Bourbon monarchy in France in 1814 was probably the most decisive event, not only in cementing that alliance but in precipitating violent anticlericalism as well.

The French Charter of 1814 defines the Catholic religion as the "Religion of the State," and legal protection of the church was reinstituted. Members of the ecclesiastical hierarchy were given seats in the House of

Peers, and "the nation was governed, or thought that it was governed, by the priests—their influence was felt everywhere" (Tocqueville [1856] 1967, 133). Control over other social institutions, such as education and the family, which had been taken from the church during the revolution, was once again placed under its aegis. Catholic schools were granted government subsidies, and monks and sisters were placed in the public elementary schools.

During the early nineteenth century, participants in clerical and anticlerical movements articulated much of the earlier debate about the relationship between church and society. Even the terms "clericalism" and "anticlericalism" were not part of the general vocabulary until the mid-nineteenth century.[7] Joseph de Maistre (1753–1821), for example, combined his belief in the church with support for the monarchy in a radically reactionary position that became normative for many influential Catholics. As the first of the French "traditionalists," he envisioned a society within the Romantic organic model, as opposed to a more individualistic, mechanistic Enlightenment model (see McCool 1977, 37 ff.).

Maistre contended that the pope, as creator of the absolute monarchy, was therefore responsible for its restoration. He provided much of the intellectual content of the restoration and of "ultramontanism,"[8] a movement advocating papal supremacy. Along with Bonald, Chateaubriand, and others, Maistre advocated the reestablishment of strong hierarchical control that would provide the church with both political and religious authority. This position reinforced the fears of those who despised the church as a political institution bent on the destruction of republicanism in France.

Appalled by the chaos created by the revolution and its aftermath, Maistre warned that only a return to subjection by the pope could provide hope. "Every European nation," he contended, "when withdrawn from the Holy See, will be inevitably borne towards servitude or rebellion."

Because of the hatred which so many felt toward the Bourbon monarchy, anticlerical forces began to consolidate during the period, playing upon the antichurch sentiments so ubiquitous at the time. Anticlericalism raised some of the most critical issues of the century and was an extremely complex movement, a multiplicity of forces rather than a united front. Some anticlericals were republicans, some were not; some were anti-Catholic, while others differentiated between clericalism and Catholicism. Some were practicing Catholics themselves, who objected only to ecclesiastical influence in the polity.

Most anticlericals were united in their adherence to Positivism or some form of philosophical naturalism (see Reddick 1950, 339) that was influenced by the growth of science, historiography, and evolutionism. Furthermore, they had a common political stance in progressive republicanism and opposition to the monarchy, although agreement even on those issues was not monolithic. Anticlericalism focused on the separation of church and state for the purpose of eliminating ecclesiastical political hegemony, but anticlericals fought to mitigate ecclesiastical influence in other spheres as well. Many of them were concerned about church control of educational and familial institutions, contending that Catholic hegemony should be eliminated in favor of state regulation (although much of that controversy did not come to a head until later in the century).

Charles X (1824–1830) perceived anticlericalism as a threat to the crown and took an extremist clerical position, only to precipitate renewed opposition. Monarchists and conservatives, repelled by the radical destruction of the social fabric by democratization, saw the church as an instrument for defending the ancien régime, while the hierarchy of the church saw an alliance with the conservatives as the only hope for preserving the church itself.

Popes Gregory XVI and Pius IX opposed all forms of political liberalism and associated themselves with ultramontanism. They cultivated a revival of the papacy based upon doctrines of the papal monarchy of the Middle Ages. Unanimity in such a diverse organization as the Roman Church was virtually impossible, however. A liberal Catholic movement was growing in a number of countries—particularly in France, but also in Belgium, Italy, Germany, England, and elsewhere (see Aubert 1952, 236 ff.). The classic expression of liberal Catholicism in the period was in the work of Felicité de Lamennais (1782–1854), a French traditionalist who became dissatisfied with the Bourbon monarchy and aligned himself with republican forces.

LIBERAL CATHOLICISM

"Liberal Catholicism" waxed and waned through the nineteenth century, receiving virtually no official encouragement from Rome. Pope Gregory XVI's condemnation of it in 1834 was a key event in the series of actions the Vatican took to provide a coherent strategy in its opposition to anticlericalism. Precipitated by the July Revolution of 1830 in France, the short-lived liberal Catholic movement tried to undermine the alliance between Rome and the conservatives. The July Revolution did not have the radical impact of the Revolution of 1789, but it did significantly change the status of the church in French society. In 1831, Prime Minister Casimer Perier remarked to an ecclesiastic: "The time is coming when you will be supported by only a handful of old people" (Dansette 1961, I:208).

The major figure in the liberal Catholic movement was Felicité de Lamennais, who had a strong commitment to the church as a priest and a devout Catholic, but who was also a scholar with strong commitments to the intellectual community and to secular educational institutions. He applied his keen intellectual powers to dilemmas on both sides of the conflict between the church and the newly established republic. "The world is in a great crisis," he said. "Everywhere it is trying to detach itself from a past out of which the life is gone, and to begin a new era. Nothing will stop this magnificent movement of the human race—it is directed from on high by Providence—" (1967, 134). He sought to bring about a separation of church and state that would disentangle the church from what he thought was an unhealthy and perhaps fatal alliance with the ancien régime.

Lamennais' *Essay on Indifference in Religious Matters* (1817–1823) received wide attention throughout Europe, and in 1830 he founded the daily journal *L'Avenir* ("The Future"), with a masthead slogan that read "God and Liberty." Lamennais and his followers—notably Lacordaire and Montalembert—attempted to reconcile the causes of the church and the revolution, and supported the movement toward political and individual liberty. The policy of *L'Avenir* included complete religious liberty, educational liberty, liberty of the press, liberty of association, universal suffrage, and decentralization (see Vidler 1954, 164 ff.). The controversies surrounding the journal grew so intense that it was forced to suspend publication after little more than a year. In 1832 the pope issued the encyclical *Mirari vos* condemning the general policies of the paper without mentioning it or its editors specifically.

In *Paroles d'un croyant* (1834), Lamennais denounced competitive capitalism on religious grounds and called upon the working classes to demand their God-given rights. But his arguments were no more welcome among the liberals in France than within the Catholic hierarchy, because Catholicism was out of favor among political progressives. The rejection of liberal Catholicism by both ecclesiastical elites and republicans indicates the extent to which the polarized political climate required individuals to choose between liberalism and Catholicism. Gregory XVI, preoccupied with disorder in the papal states and his opposition to the building of railroads there, finally moved to condemn Lamennais' work. His encyclical *Singulari nos* described *Paroles d'un croyant* as "small in size but immense in perversity," and as encouraging ideas that were "false, calumnious, rash, inducing to anarchy, contrary to the Word of God, impious, scandalous, and erroneous." The pope charged Catholics with "the submission due to authority" rather than "the horrid conspiracy of the upholders of every erroneous doctrine against church and state."

The Revolution of 1848 revived republicanism among French Catholics, and a significant segment of the church appeared for the first time to be on the side of the revolution. Priests joined the revolutionaries, and liberal Catholics were elated over the replacement of the Bourgeois monarchy with the Second Republic. Liberal Catholic movements were developing in Prussia under the leadership of Ignace Döllinger, and in Italy around Rosmini and others.

Elected to the papacy in 1846, Pius IX was liberal in his thinking at the beginning of his term and quickly moved to reform the ecclesiastical structures. In a few short months, however, the climate at the Vatican changed once again. Revolution spread rapidly throughout Europe after the French Revolution of 1848, and the pope was forced to flee from Rome. Once again the church took the side of order, and Pius IX, "now cured of all liberalism, gave a triumvirate of cardinals a free hand to restore absolute government" in Rome (Dansette 1961, I:263). Under the guidance of Pius IX, whose papacy encompassed one of the most tumultuous periods in the church's history, the papacy grew to the epitome of its power within the church, but lost a great deal of authority in the larger political environment of Europe.

New waves of anticlericalism followed the restoration of the empire under Napoleon III in 1851, and Ernest Renan's *Vie de Jésus* (1863) became a symbol of the French intelligentsia's dissatisfaction with orthodox Catholicism. There is some evidence that large segments of the populace were not active in the church (see Marcilhacy 1962), although many of them clung to rituals of Catholicism as a matter of custom. In *Madame Bovary* (1857), for example, Flaubert presented a picture of people who were anticlerical most of the time, but who continued to have their children baptized and to receive last rites from a priest. Religious practices were associated with the nation and the family.

THE CHURCH AND THE SCHOOLS

Anticlericalism became most threatening to the Roman Church in France, where much of the controversy concerned the secularization of the school system, particularly in the latter quarter of the nineteenth century. The debate over church control of and influence on the French educational system was important to the development of the modernist crisis for two reasons. First, the debate became a battleground for which clerical and anticlerical strategies were formulated, and it exacerbated the Roman hierarchy's sense of despair about the modern world. The vast ecclesiastical school system, and the presence of large numbers of religious teachers in the secular schools, had been a bulwark of religious influence within the broader population. To lose the schools was a major blow to ecclesiastical influence. The French intelligentsia were deeply concerned about the issue, and the polarization of clericals and anticlericals affected school teachers at all levels of French society, from elementary schools in isolated French villages to the Sorbonne in Paris.

Second, because the church was driven out of educational institutions throughout France (and elsewhere in Europe), Catholic universities were established in 1875 in an attempt by the church to recover some of its losses. The new Catholic Institutes then provided critical scholars with an institutional base, and it was in them that modernist scholarship evolved. The Roman Church had emphasized the importance of education for centuries, and had monopolized the educational process under the ancien régime. The conflict between clericals and anticlericals was fought at the local level on the issue of schools; with two sides represented by the priest and the schoolteacher, respectively: "Parents would side with one faction or another by entrusting their children either to the secular, state school or the clerically operated school" (Clark 1973, 34).

Religious control of the schools was defined as the major obstacle to the formation of a new order by many republicans, who questioned the appropriateness of clerical education within a secular republic (see Durkheim 1961). Republican reformers were quick to recognize the importance of such institutions for the formation of a particular form of government. If the schools could be used to "indoctrinate" students into the Christian life, why could they not be used to teach future generations the principles of "liberty, equality, and fraternity" and the civic virtues necessary for the maintenance of a democratic society?

Ecclesiastical control of the schools meant continued training of the young by antirepublican priests and nuns. In the Third Republic, however, toward the end of the century, a comprehensive national system of public education was finally developed. The moderate architects of the Third Republic believed that a "loyal army of schoolteachers" could carry the message of republicanism to every hamlet in the nation (Talbott 1969, 23). The *parti radicale* demanded educational reform, and they got it. Responsibility for the reforms went to the new Minister of Education, Jules Ferry. Like his mentor, Auguste Comte, Ferry believed that theological and metaphysical eras were past and that the positivistic sciences should provide the basis of a new order. Condorcet's dream of making science the basis of French education was finally to come true. "My goal," Ferry declared, "is to organize society without God and without a king" (quoted in Dansette 1961, I:405).

Ferry's first reform was to rid the French schools of the thousands of teachers from various religious orders through a process known as "laicization" (secularization). He forbade all "nonauthorized" religious orders—especially the Jesuits, Dominicans, and Marists—from teaching in state or private schools. Eight or nine thousand men and 100,000 women were affected by the decrees issued 29 March 1880, which required that the orders be dissolved and the premises vacated. Three months later, a police superintendent went to the Jesuit house in the Rue de Sèvres in Paris and sealed the door of the chapel. The priests were turned out the following day, after the locks of their rooms had been picked (Dansette 1961, II:44).

Vigorous protests followed, but without success, and Ferry's reforms produced widespread, long-term changes in the French educational system.[9] In 1881, school laws passed the Chamber of Deputies and the Senate, making primary education free; in 1882, education was made obligatory for all children between the ages of six and thirteen. The religious neutrality of the schools was proclaimed, and an 1886 decree required that all teaching in public schools be carried out exclusively by the laity. Ferry also ousted the clergy from a Superior Council formed during the Second Republic to control the public elementary schools.

The complete secularization of the schools did not occur, but the church had lost its educational monopoly. In a counterattack in 1875, the church established the Catholic Institutes in Paris, Lille, Lyon, Angers, and Toulouse, with the primary aim of providing high-quality education for secondary-school teachers and those in the liberal professions. The secularization of the schools gave a great impetus to the development of the institutes, and thus provided an institutional setting for the growth of critical Catholic scholarship at a time when the intellectual life of the church was at a low ebb (see Battersby 1968, III:43 ff.). Although the modernists came from and worked in a variety of institutional settings, the Catholic Institutes—particularly the one in Paris, at the center of French scholarship—were a crucial factor in the rise of Catholic modernism.

At the request of the Vatican, the Catholic Institutes created theological faculties that were independent of the state universities. Their purpose was to foster a response to the major challenges of modern scholarship and anticlericalism. The new pope, Leo XIII (successor to Pius IX in 1878), thought that the new French theological faculties could refine and disseminate scholastic theology in France as part of his program to create a modern Catholic apologetic within the framework of scholasticism.

THE VATICAN'S RESPONSE TO THE CRISIS

Throughout the first half of the nineteenth century, the Vatican leadership was embroiled in a series of political and theological controversies. Anticlericals recognized an affinity between their interests in attacking the church and the newly developing science of criticism. Ecclesiastical leadership, in contrast, sought to reestablish the Vatican's authority and the position of the church in European society, which were called into question by both criticism and anticlericalism. The Vatican followed a threefold strategy. First, it defined Catholic orthodoxy within the bounds of scholastic theology, thereby providing a systematic, logical response to the probing questions of modern scholarship. Second, it elaborated the doctrines of papal authority and of the *magisterium* (the teaching authority of the church), claiming that the church and its leadership alone had inherited authority in religious matters from the apostles of Jesus. Finally, it defined Catholic orthodoxy in terms of what it was not—and provided a point around which to marshal the Catholic faithful in defense of the church—by constructing the image of an heretical conspiracy among deviant insiders.

As Max Weber points out in his study of Confucianism, it is when both cherished beliefs and the interests of a particular social group are threatened that a heresy is labeled as such. In the case of Confucianism, the religion "was a status ethic of the bureaucracy educated in literature," and when the interests of that bureaucracy appeared to be threatened, the "instinct of self-preservation in the ruling stratum" reacted "by attaching the stigma of heterodoxy" (1968, 213).

The doctrines of papal supremacy and infallibility, the system of scholastic theology and philosophy, and the doctrine of the apostolic succession of authority became attached to the interests of the Roman Church's leadership, providing a carefully constructed system of thought appropriate for the status of the church's leadership. The interests of the bishops—and even more so those of the burgeoning clerical bureaucracy at the Vatican—became attached to and associated with the prestige of the popes and the doctrines upon which that prestige was based.

A picture of a heresy gradually emerged in the conservative Catholic press (notably the Jesuit publication *Civiltà cattolica* in Rome and *La Verité* in Paris), in a series of papal edicts (the 1864 *Syllabus of Errors,* 1879 *Aeterni Patris,* and 1893 *Providentissimus Deus*), in the condemnation of Americanism (*Testem benevolentiae,* 1899), and, finally, in the condemnation of modernism (1907–08). In these pronouncements and others, the Vatican and its collaborators developed a strategy which enhanced both the status of the papacy and the papal bureaucracy and that of scholastic theology and theologians.

A major aspect of the Vatican's strategy was its characterization of the enemy as a conspiratorial group that was endangering the church while masquerading as its friend. This construction of heresy by Vatican intellectuals became a central part of the defensive efforts by church authorities, and it reveals the dialectical process of identifying and labeling deviant insiders. In this process, the hierarchy takes the ideas of a real movement (or quasi-movement) and synthesizes and exaggerates them for purposes of defining orthodoxy. Official doctrines are legitimated by contrasting them with alleged heresies. Because the doctrines of the real dissidents are caricatured in the condemnation, the dissidents themselves sometimes exaggerate their lack of relationship to condemned heresies.

"The establishment" thus has a more clear-cut case for its arguments than it would if those arguments adhered strictly to the complex doctrines of the heretics. This also leaves open the possibility that the heretics will themselves denounce the teachings identified as heretical—an act which would defuse any insurgent movement. Hence a process of negotiation frequently follows the condemnation of heresy, after which dissidents make appropriate submissions to the authorities, who must then decide what symbolic acts the insurgents must perform to prove their faithfulness. Only when all other channels have been exhausted will the authorities condemn individuals by name, since this might backfire by making martyrs out of the insurgents, and thus adding to their list of grievances (see G. Marx 1979). Thus it is not uncommon for both authorities and dissidents to define the condemned doctrines, at least in public, as not representative of the works of any real individuals within the institution.

The real enemy of the Vatican at the time of the modernist crisis was not Alfred Loisy or Baron von Hügel or George Tyrrell, or any other individual within the church, but the widespread attack on the Vatican's authority. Roman authorities decided that the only way to avert danger and to save the faith was to identify the interests of the Vatican—and of Catholicism itself—with scholastic theology and the doctrines of papal authority.

DOCTRINES OF PAPAL AUTHORITY

In responding to the crisis of the nineteenth century, the Vatican leadership did what it had done in past crises: it accentuated the authority of the church, particularly that of the pope. This strategy was carried to its extreme in the doctrine of papal infallibility, which was declared for the first time by the First Vatican Council, convened in 1870.

Nineteenth-century Catholicism was dominated by two pontiffs, Pius IX, who served from 1846 to 1878, and his successor, Leo XIII (1878–1903). Pius IX encouraged the elaboration of doctrines of papal authority, and Leo XIII provided support for the revival of scholastic theology, which provided a sophisticated rationale for earlier doctrines of papal authority.

The Vatican hierarchy identified an affinity between its interests and monarchical theories of governance, both within and outside of the church. Although Leo XIII accepted the legitimacy of the democratic government in France, urging French Catholics for the first time to rally around the republic, he continued to differentiate between authority in government and in the church.[10] In his condemnation of Americanism, he insisted that secular government might be democratic, but that the church required an absolute authority which could guard the infallible tradition from heresy. Catholic advocacy of monarchism was affirmed in the Roman Catholic Church at least as early as the tenth century, when Leo IX (949–954) and Gregory VII (973–1011) elevated the papacy as a means of removing the church from the control of the laity.[11] Pius IX reinforced notions of papal authority in his encyclical *Quanto Conficiamur,* which evoked the doctrine of papal supremacy from the papal bull *Unam Sanctam,* issued by Boniface VIII in 1302.

Throughout the nineteenth century the papacy was challenged on one side by Gallicanism and Febronianism,[12] and on the other by anti-clericalism and criticism, leaving it in a precarious political situation by the middle of the century. In the aftermath of the Revolution of 1848, anticlericalism became a significant movement for the first time in Italy, where many subjects of the papal states resented the autocratic papal government. The government of the prosperous Italian state of Piedmont initiated several secularizing measures, and the Italian unification movement gathered strength. Pius IX, concerned with the general erosion of papal authority, refused to submit to international pressure to abdicate his temporal powers, responding instead by reorganizing the pontifical army. He also issued an apostolic letter, *Aeterni Patris* (1868),[13] calling for the First General Council of the Vatican. Its purpose was to seek a resolution of the crisis and to review questions of faith raised by anticlerical and critical attacks on the church.

> It is at this time evident and manifest to all men in how horrible a tempest the Church is now tossed, and with what vast evils civil society is afflicted. For the Catholic Church, with its saving doctrine and venerable power, and the supreme authority of this Holy See, are by the bitterest enemies of God and man assailed and trampled down; all sacred things are held in contempt, ecclesiastical possessions spoiled, and the ministers of holy things harrassed in every way. (Pius IX, in Butler [1868] 1930, I:88)

The Vatican Council was calculated to provide a show of unity, although there was hesitation from some papal advisors, who thought that there would be opposition from various governments that would compromise the church's unity. Political overtones surrounded the council from its beginning, heightening the sense of crisis. Even as preparations for the council were under way, political events threatened its very existence—notably the temporary withdrawal of French troops protecting Rome from Italian nationalist forces, and the Seven Weeks War between Prussia and Austria.[14]

Documents issued by the Vatican Council emphasized the sacred nature of the church and of the pope's leadership. "It is an article of faith," declared the council, "that outside the Church no one can be saved" (First Vatican Council [1870*a*] 1967, 216). Furthermore, the church "is the pillar and foundation of truth, free and untouched by any danger of error or falsehood" (ibid., 218). It is, therefore, "absolutely necessary . . . to defend it against human error and sustain it against the controversies of false science" (ibid., 219).

If that infallible deposit of faith was to be guarded from heresy, the legitimacy of the ecclesiastical hierarchy had to be recognized: "The Church of Christ is not a community of equals in which all the faithful have the same rights." Rather, some are given "the power from God . . . to sanctify, teach and govern" (ibid., 219–220). In a moment of crisis, "seeing that the gates of hell with daily increase of hatred are gathering their strength on every side to upheave the foundation laid by God's own hand" (ibid., 221), the council reaffirmed the pope's authority. In its most controversial declaration, it thus stated:

> We teach and define that it is a dogma divinely revealed: that the Roman Pontiff, when he speaks *ex cathedra*, that is, when in discharge of the office of Pastor and Doctor of all Christians, by virtue of his supreme apostolic authority he defines a doctrine regarding faith or morals to be held by the Universal Church, by the divine assistance promised him in Blessed Peter, is possessed of that infallibility with which the divine Redeemer willed that his Church should be endowed for defining doctrine regarding faith or morals. (First Vatican Council 1870*b*, 229)

Ironically, the notion of papal infallibility had been declared the work of the devil by Pope John XXII (1316–1334) in *Qui quorandam* (1324). The council's declaration fanned the flames of anticlericalism outside of the church, precipating attacks against the church and the pope,[15] but within the church, opposition was quite discreet. Many of the so-called minority bishops[16] opposed the declaration. Most of them believed in the doctrine but were fearful of its political implications; some felt that it would widen the schism between Catholics and Protestants. Those who disagreed with the doctrine itself were a very small minority.[17] The bishops were, after all, the institution's elites, and centralization of power at a time of crisis was in their own interests as well as in the pope's. The majority of the council advocated a bold action that would demonstrate the strength and unity of the church and reinforce its hierarchical structure. There was pressure throughout the conference to foster an impression of unanimity.[19] Pius IX reportedly commented to the editor-in-chief of the *Civiltà cattolica* that "my mind is so made up that if need be I shall take the definition upon myself and dismiss the Council if it wishes to keep silence" (Hasler 1981, 81).

The First Vatican Council thus made papal infallibility an article of faith for the first time in the history of the church. There was only scattered resistance, the most important of which was that organized by the well-known ecclesiastical historian, Ignaz Döllinger, and his former British student, Sir John Action (Lord Acton), editor of *The Rambler*. Although one group of individuals from Döllinger's movement in Germany broke with the Roman Church, creating the Old Catholic Church, Döllinger himself did not join them, and the movement had little impact on the Roman Church (Butler 1936, II:190). Those who disagreed knew it was best to remain silent.[19] What was unique about the council's action was its affirmation of a broad consensus within the church's hierarchy—and the extent to which the exercise of absolute papal authority had become a reality.

Even at the height of papal hierarchy in the late Middle Ages there had always been considerable diversity within the institutional structure, with strong pockets of resistance to papal hegemony. Although the secular power of the papacy was radically reduced during the nineteenth century, the pope became the supreme authority within the church. Effective administration of a global institution was becoming a possibility because of technological revolutions in communications and transportation. The telegraph, railroads, and newspapers linked the church's networks together in a way never dreamed of in medieval Europe, when a crisis in northern Germany might be resolved long before the pope's decision on the matter could reach the parties in conflict. The ecclesiastical elite took advantage of these new opportunities to strengthen the church in its battle with secularizing forces, both by broadening the scope of the pope's authority and by creating a highly centralized institutional apparatus. Bishops from throughout the church, harrassed in countless situations by rulers of the modern world, called for the creation of a modern institution based on medieval principles.

It was not just the model of church governance that the church's leadership borrowed from the Middle Ages, however; it also took a model for articulating and elaborating doctrine from the work of the thirteenth-century scholar, Thomas Aquinas.

THE THOMISTIC REVIVAL

From the beginning of his papacy, Leo XIII (1878–1903) had been anxious to promote the use of scholasticism as a unifying philosophy for Catholic intellectual statements in the modern world. Less than a year and a half after his term of office began, he issued *Aeterni Patris* (1879), which assigned Thomistic thought the dominant role in modern Catholic thought, and which has been called the "Magna Carta of official neo-Thomism in Catholic philosophy and theology."[20] Neo-Thomism was part of a broader nineteenth-century movement, the neo-scholastic movement, and was favored by the pervasive antirevolutionary mood, the Romantic movement, and ultramontanism (Hartley 1971, 1).

AETERNI PATRIS AND LEO XIII'S STRATEGY

Scholasticism, like Romanticism, involved a return to the pre-Enlightenment and pre-Reformation thought of the Middle Ages, and was an apt historical symbol of Catholic cultural unity (see Reardon 1975, 175 ff.). The historical tendency of the nineteenth century could in this instance be used by, rather than against, the Roman establishment, by legitimating the re-creation of the ancien régime.

Scholastic theology had been the subject of scathing attacks by eighteenth-century philosophes. According to Voltaire, it was the bastard daughter of Aristotle's theology. But a great theological fervor in Europe, accompanied by an increasing consciousness of history, stimulated interest in the medieval period, and Roman leaders rediscovered the master of medieval philosophy. By the middle of the nineteenth century, Romanticism and German Idealism had subsided, and Pius IX had denounced modern movements in religious and philosophical thought. The Jesuit Joseph Kleutgen was the most influential theologian of the period, having drafted the final version of *Dei Filius*[21] adopted by the First Vatican Council. He was also the primary author of *Aeterni Patris* (McCool 1977, 2).

Neo-Thomism emerged out of a late nineteenth-century debate between Thomism on the one hand and ontologism and German theology on the other. Ontologism was largely a Catholic movement represented by Antonio Rosmini Serbat and Vincenzo Gioberti, while the metaphysical dualism developed by the German Anton Gunther was a post-Kantian approach to philosophy and theology inaugurated by moderate traditionalism (McCool 1977, 86). Jesuit neo-Thomists attacked both systems; Matteo Liberatore and Kleutgen attacked Gunther, the Tübingen theologians, and Georg Hermes. The outlines of neo-Thomism thus began to appear.

Following the Revolution of 1848, the Holy See initiated a campaign of intervention in Catholic theology. Between 1855 and 1866, almost every variant of modern theology that had presented a challenge to the Catholic hierarchy's definition of theology had been condemned—traditionalism, ontologism, Gunther's dualism, and Jakob Frohschammer's rationalism. Whereas condemnations earlier in the century had been against individual theologians, by the time the First Vatican Council convened, virtually every major force in Catholic theology except scholasticism had been condemned. Ultramontanism was growing rapidly, supported by mass movements among workers, farmers, and middle-class professionals.

Church officials were trying to replace as many bishops and theology faculty members as possible with ultramontanists and, eventually, neo-Thomists. The Vatican also expressed considerable concern over the growth of universities and scholarly professionals independent of the church's control. Thibault (1972) argues that the Thomist revival was a triumph of the Catholic hierarchy over university learning. Precipitated by a fear of modern political and intellectual freedom, the neo-Thomists advocated suppression rather than open discussion in theological matters. The clerical establishment thus facilitated a scholastic revival in order to rescue the church from the throes of its critics—and also to maintain its hegemony.

Growing centralization of authority in the Roman Church made it possible for Pius IX to grant Jesuit theologians considerable power in the formulation of Catholic theology; the most influential of these were the founders of the *Civiltà cattolica,* a journal created in 1849 at the request of the pope, as a response to the events of the Revolution of 1848.[22] The *Civiltà cattolica* Jesuits played a significant role in ecclesiastical politics in the years following; they facilitated the neo-Thomist revival[23] and were decisive in constructing pictures of heretical conspiracies, notably Americanism and modernism.

Taparelli d'Angelo, one of the two founders of the journal, was a driving force in the development of a program to replace all systems of Catholic theology with neo-Thomism. One of Taparelli's students at the Roman College, Gioacchino Pecci, paved the way for the final triumph of Thomism. A promising disciple of Taparelli's, Pecci became the archbishop of Perugia and worked with his brother, Giuseppe Pecci, to transform the diocesan seminary into a center of Thomistic studies (see Hartley 1971, 2-6). In 1878 Cardinal Pecci was elected to the papacy, assumed the name Leo XIII, and quickly moved to establish neo-Thomism as the official approach to Roman Catholic theology and philosophy. Thomist studies at Perugia were complemented by a similar revival of Thomism in Naples, particularly by Gaetano Sanseverino, and in Spain by Salvatore

Roselli and others. The Thomists were unequivocally opposed to developments in modern thought, holding that modern intellectual developments
could not be reformed and adapted, but must be discarded altogether.
Catholicism and modern thought, argued the neo-Thomists, were
antithetical.

This is not to say that the neo-Thomists rejected "science" or the
rhetoric of science. On the contrary, they tried to show that they were
practicing true science. Kleutgen and Liberatore[24] argued—as St. Thomas
had—in favor of a science of faith (*scientia fidei*) that was not the same
as the modern sciences but the science of Aristotle. One of the most
important distinctions between the Thomistic, deductive, Aristotelian science of faith and the emerging sciences of nineteenth-century Europe was
that the neo-Thomists did not have the sense of historical development
that was the landmark of nineteenth-century thought. Kleutgen, like the
post-Reformation scholastics Cano and Suarez, had little interest in history or community, in cultural development or changes in conceptual
frameworks over time (McCool 1977, 187, 202). The Catholicism of
timeless truths affirmed by the Vatican was legitimated by scholastic
thought, in opposition to the evolutionary approach of the historical
critics.

Neo-Thomism thus provided a radical alternative to modern thought
and a broad philosophical and theological basis for the pronouncements
made at the First Vatican Council. Drafted primarily by scholastic theologians, *Dei Filius* defined the limits of faith and reason. It rejected virtually
all nonscholastic alternatives and approved of the arts and sciences only
insofar as they followed their own methods within the proper sphere of
their competence. When conflicts arose between scientific research and
the teachings of the church, they were to be explained as due to an
erroneous interpretation of the church's teaching, or to false conclusions
drawn by scientific reasoning:

> If any one shall say that human sciences are to be so freely treated that their
> assertions, even if opposed to revealed doctrine, may be held as true, and cannot
> be condemned by the Church; let him be anathema.

> If any one shall assert it to be possible that sometimes according to the
> progress of science, a sense is to be given to dogmas propounded by the Church
> different from that which the Church has understood and understands; let him
> be anathema. (First Vatican Council [1870] 1967, 40)

Leo XIII's *Aeterni Patris* (1879) made neo-Thomism official. Apparently the original schemata for the encyclical was written by Liberatore
and Kleutgen. This document included a number of strategies for the

institutionalization of Thomism. For example, bishops were instructed to appoint seminary teachers who would recognize the clear superiority of the Thomist philosophical system. Future priests could thus be instructed in "the wisdom of St. Thomas" from the spring of Thomistic thought, learning from the "streams which . . . in the certain and unanimous opinion of learned men run pure and undefiled," rather than from those streams which "are in reality swollen with alien and unhealthy matter" (Leo XIII [1879] 1931, 159–161; cf. Alexander 1979).

Leo thus provided in the intellectual community what the Vatican Council's proclamation of papal infallibility had created in the ecclesiastical institution—a unitary, undifferentiated, and authoritative system designed to combat the divisive subjectivity and individualism of modern social and intellectual movements. Neo-scholasticism and a renewed emphasis on institutional authority were emphasized together in the magisterium.

THE MAGISTERIUM

Based upon the insights and methodologies of neo-scholasticism, the boundary between orthodoxy and heterodoxy was clearly drawn. That which was not within the boundaries of scholastic thought and the doctrine of papal infallibility was not legitimately Catholic. The legitimacy of intellectual enterprises was linked to their approval by the hierarchy.

Positions taken by the Vatican Council and Leo XIII's *Aeterni Patris* redefined the Catholic doctrine of the magisterium. The papacy, according to Congar (1967, 178), "until modern times, rarely exercised the active magisterium of dogmatic definition and constant formulation of Catholic doctrine in the way it has been exercised since the pontificate of Gregory XVI and especially since that of Pius IX." In the early church, doctrinal disputes were resolved by "immediate reference to Scripture and to a series of patristic, conciliar or canonical texts, in short a kind of magisterium of tradition itself" (ibid.). In a series of developments, the Curia became increasingly involved in the definition of doctrine, in part as a response to antiecclesiastical spiritual sects (from the twelfth century on) and various theological controversies, as well as to changes in conceptions of authority in the broader society. Furthermore, with the emergence of canonical studies there was an "invasion of theology by juridical ways of thinking," and the canonists were generally sympathetic to the Curia (ibid., 179).

In *Authority in the Church: A Study in Changing Paradigms* (1974), Sanks notes that there are three paradigms[25] involved in the theology of the magisterium: one relating to the sociopolitical structure of the church, one defining the authority within that structure, and a paradigm of truth and its mode of communication (teaching), or the "epistemological model" (1974, 109). The paradigm which guided notions of the sociopolitical structure of the church was informed by the model of a pure (rather than constitutional) monarchy. The pope is to have supreme and unquestioned God-given authority—that authority which is the very foundation of the church and which is defined in sharp contrast to democratic liberalism. There are clear hierarchical lines of this authority, at least in theory, from the pope through the bishops to the priests, and finally to the laity.

The paradigm of Catholic truth was thus based upon the "deposit" model, a scholastic notion of truth which implied that the truths of revelation "were given complete, unified, consistent, absolute and immutable from the beginning." Because there can be no contradictions in God, there can be none in the truth which God has revealed to humanity through the apostles and the church. Thus the pope's teaching authority is, by definition, infallible.

Pope Leo moved quickly to implement the program implied in *Aeterni Patris*. Neo-Thomists replaced their less enthusiastic colleagues in key positions in ecclesiastical institutions. The Roman Academy of St. Thomas was revived, and neo-Thomist Tommaso Zigliara was appointed prefect of the Congregation of Studies. There was a shake-up in the faculties of the Apollinaire and the Propaganda. Perhaps the most far-reaching changes occurred with Leo's effort to make the Gregorian University, which had become the most important university in the Catholic world, a major center for Thomistic studies. Long before the encyclical was issued in 1879, there were numerous heated controversies surrounding the Gregorian University and the neo-Thomists. Despite—or perhaps because of—the generally cool attitude of the Gregorian faculty toward neo-Thomism, several new faculty were appointed whose commitment to neo-Thomism was "above suspicion" (McCool 1977, 238).

The Thomist revival was to be a period of "routinization" and popularization of an adequate intellectual system more in need of dissemination than of perfection. This strategy was consistent with the entire tenor of the Roman establishment, which was more concerned with guarding and perpetuating old truths, believed to be sufficient, than in discovering new ones. What was needed, from the Vatican's perspective, was not so much a cadre of scholars and researchers involved in developing a critical science, but a group of effective teachers. From the standpoint of the scholastic theologians, the call for a science of criticism simply made no sense. On the contrary, it played right into the hands of the church's critics.

Despite the pope's vigorous attempts to unify all Catholic thought within the boundaries of scholastic theology, acceptance of his program was far from unanimous, especially from among those involved with the development of scientific criticism. A few years after *Aeterni Patris*, Pope Leo moved to channel biblical studies into a more acceptable line of inquiry with *Providentissimus Deus* (1893).

PROVIDENTISSIMUS DEUS AND THE BIBLICAL COMMISSION

Leo XIII's polemical rejection of scientific criticism in *Providentissimus Deus* foreshadowed the later antimodernist wrath of Pope Pius X. This encyclical was the first skirmish initiated by the Vatican against the modernist heresy. "We admonish, with paternal love," the encyclical read,

all students and ministers of the Church always to approach the Sacred Writings with reverence and piety; for it is impossible to attain to the profitable understanding thereof unless the arrogance of "earthly" science be laid aside, and there be excited in the heart the holy desire for that "wisdom which is from above." In this way the intelligence . . . will acquire a marvelous facility in detecting and avoiding the fallacies of human science. (Leo XIII [1893] 1967, 337)

The encyclical was provoked by the publication of a controversial article on "La Question biblique" by Monsignor d'Hulst, the open-minded rector of the Institut Catholique in Paris, in which he clumsily attempted to cultivate a milieu that would be more open to Loisy's work. Although a more detailed discussion of the events surrounding the encyclical appears in chapter 3, it is helpful to note the impact of the edict as part of the Thomistic revival.

There is some indication that the original draft of *Providentissimus Deus* was written in conciliatory terms, but that it was quickly revised to convey an opposite meaning by the Jesuit Cardinal Camillo Mazzella, one of the neo-Thomist appointments at the Gregorian (Fawkes 1913, 55). Although the pope avoided explicit condemnation of any individuals, the encyclical made a clear statement of the Vatican's opposition to scientific criticism and cautioned those who advocated such a science that they were the enemies of the papacy. "Now, we have to meet the Rationalists," the encyclical warned,

true children and inheritors of the older heretics, who, trusting in their turn to their own way of thinking, have rejected even the scraps and remnants of the Christian beliefs which have been handed down to them. They deny that there is any such thing as revelation or inspiration of Holy Scriptures at all; they see, instead, only the forgeries and falsehoods of men; they set down the Scripture narratives as stupid fables and lying stories. . . .

These detestable errors, whereby they think they destroy the truth of the divine books, are obtruded on the world as the preemptory pronouncements of a certain newly-invented "free science," a science, however, which is so far from the final truth that they are perpetually modifying and supplementing it. (Leo XIII [1893] 1967, 329)

The publication of this encyclical dampened the hopes of Catholic scholars who had been encouraged by the pope's somewhat conciliatory policies concerning intellectual activities.[26] Particularly disturbing to some scholars was the apparent connection between the Biblical Commission (see below) and the pope's scholastic revival (see Briggs and von Hügel 1906, 23). Although single-minded in his attempts to establish neo-Thomism in the church, Pope Leo was aware of the necessity not to close the door on modern scholarship. He encouraged cautious investigation of the scriptures in their original languages at the level of advanced studies, but decreed that the (Latin) Vulgate be used as the text for classroom study ([1893] 1967, 1, 330), thereby ensuring that textual disputes would not arise within the classroom.

Leo XIII claimed to advocate "true criticism" but to oppose "higher criticism," lest "the enemies of religion" be made "more bold and confident in attacking and mangling the sacred books" (ibid., 334). He was anxious to encourage intellectual life within the church and may have thought that scholasticism was so superior to the intellectual alternatives that all Catholic scholars would eventually see the light, if given proper guidance. Pope Leo also appointed a Biblical commission in 1902, which institutionalized the direction outlined in *Providentissimus Deus,* and in his apostolic letter "Vigilantiae," he announced the formation of a "commission of men of learning whose duty shall be to effect that in every possible manner the divine text will find . . . the most thorough interpretation which is demanded by our times, and be shielded not only from every breath of error, but also from every temerarious opinion."

At first, it seemed as though the commission might allow (if not facilitate) the development of biblical criticism, but within a year, its original twelve members were overshadowed by the addition of twenty-eight more. According to von Hügel, the new members were either scholastic-trained, noncritical scholars or men without scholarly reputations at all.[27] The Biblical Commission's real task, it seemed, was to guide biblical studies away from critical historiography and toward methods more compatible with neo-Thomist presuppositions. Although it is not clear why the composition of the commission was changed, the pope may have been under pressure to alter his original strategy.

Pope Leo's attempts to revitalize Thomistic scholarship, and his creation of the Catholic universities and Biblical Commission, indicate that he was in a position of considerable ambivalence. On the one hand, he was repelled by Pius IX's heavy-handed solutions to the church's confrontations with the modern world and modern scholarship. He respected the world of scholarship and had confidence in the renewal of Catholic doctrines through a revitalization of Thomistic philosophy and theology. On the other hand, Leo XIII stepped into a role that was not of his own making and that placed constraints upon his options. There were innumerable pressures to conform to the definitions created by his predecessor. Leo XIII thus encouraged scholarship, but only within the boundaries of a narrow scholasticism; he encouraged biblical studies and established a commission of scholars to evaluate its progress and direction, but then added scholars who were opposed to scientific criticism.

Similar ambivalence can be seen in his handling of the "Americanist" controversy, in which he attempted to avoid outright condemnation of a "heresy" attacked by a number of conservative forces within the church. Those who favored the conservative alliance—such as Abbé Charles Maignen and Cardinal Mazzella, and the Jesuits of the *Civiltà cattolica* in Rome and *La Verité* in Paris—rejected modern thought, scientific criticism, and democracy, lumping them together into one unified, systematic heresy. Yet Leo XIII did identify certain trends as dangerous, using the Americanist controversy "to point out certain things which are to be avoided and corrected" and to promote scholasticism.

THE CONDEMNATION OF AMERICANISM

Leo XIII's apostolic letter *Testem benevolentiae* (1899) denounced Americanism as a heresy. The controversy centered around the degree to which the church should adapt its doctrines and practices to new social circumstances.[28] Curiously, the letter was not so much a condemnation of what was occurring in the United States as it was an attempt to discourage certain European (especially French) interpretations of how American Catholics felt about the ubiquitous conflict between democracy and monarchism. Those who regarded republicanism as inherently anti-Catholic accused some members of the American Catholic elite of seeking to undermine the church and its authority by supporting "liberals, evolutionists, Americanists" and by "talking forever of liberty, of respect for the individual, of initiative, of natural virtues, of sympathy for our age" (Klein 1951, 119).

Leo XIII's decision not to side with either party but to suppress the public debate was indicative of the diplomatic leadership which he frequently offered, seeking a *via media* in deliberate contrast to his predecessor, Pius IX, and his successor, who took Pius's name.

Those who were in favor of the *ralliement* (rallying) in France began to point to the American Catholic Church as a model for friendly relationships between the Catholic Church and a democratic government. The French controversy came to a head with the publication of a French translation of a biography of Father Isaac Hecker, founder of the Congregation of St. Paul the Apostle (the Paulists) in the United States, and a progressive who called for a limited adaptation of the church's approach to the modern world (Elliott 1898; cf. McAvoy 1963, 113; Hecker 1887).

Hecker became a symbol of a new type of religious leader and was the subject of much admiration among a number of young French clergy—notably Félix Klein, a professor at the Institut Catholique in Paris, who helped to edit the French translation of the biography. Klein wrote a preface to the work telling the French that he was introducing an important leader in the church, a self-made man comparable to Benjamin Franklin and Abraham Lincoln, a model of the modern priest (Klein 1951, 811). Archbishop John Ireland of St. Paul, Minnesota, wrote an introduction for the volume, which was released with great fanfare, creating both enthusiasm and controversy.

Most of the Americanist controversy developed not in the United States but in Paris and Rome, although many of the developments in the American church were quite out of step with the political climate of Rome.[29] There was very little coverage of the controversy in the American press, and what created a great deal of excitement in Europe was little known in the United States. In *Justice Sociale,* Abbé Naudet wrote that "if Americanism is a body of doctrine, we confess having found it in the books of Abbé Maignen, and in diverse articles published in 'La Verité,' but we have not seen it elsewhere" (quoted by Ireland [Etheridge] 1900, 305).

Opponents to the *ralliement* used the Americanist controversy as a way of mitigating progressive influences within the church. They pressed for the condemnation of Hecker's biography and the ideas associated with it. At the Catholic Congresses, held in Chicago in connection with the World Columbian Exposition in 1892 and 1893, there was much discussion of the relationship between Catholics and the United States—an event which disturbed antirepublican Catholics because of its openness to democratic forms of government and the independence of spirit that seemed to pervade the discussion. Surprisingly, Archbishop Francis Sartolli, the Apostolic delegate, charged the congressional participants to "go forward! in one hand bearing the Book of Christian truth and in the other the Constitution of the United States" (1893, 46).

In France, the most enthusiastic opponent of Americanism was Charles Maignen, a member of the Brothers of St. Vincent de Paul. He attacked the *Life of Father Hecker* with a series of articles in the conservative *La Verité,* later published in a book entitled *Etudes sûr l'Américan-isme, Le Père Hecker est-il un Saint?* (1899; cf. Houtin 1904, 295 ff.). In the *Life of Father Hecker,* Maignen saw all of his worst fears about the dangers inherent in the combination of Catholicism and democracy. The book was, for him, "a complete synthesis of contemporary errors," and he proceeded to outline what he saw as the elements comprising that synthesis.[30]

Archbishop Ireland, writing under a pseudonym (Ireland [Etheridge] 1900), claimed that "M. Maignen, as a critic and theologian, is . . . adept in all the devices of the heresy hunter. He puts upon the rack the thoughts of the simple priest whom he is pursuing, and strives to extort from them by hook or crook matter for the condemnation of the Inquisition." Canon Delassus of Cambrai (1899) claimed that Americanists and Jews were conspiring to destroy Catholicism, and a battle ensued in the French press.

In Rome, Maignen's position was supported by the Jesuits at *Civiltà cattolica,* Cardinal Mazzella, and others. Archbishop Ireland contended that the *Civiltà cattolica* had "done immense harm to the best interests of religion by the narrowness and intolerance of its views. "Its bigotry, political and theological, its truculent methods of controversy, and its impatience of liberty and progress in every form are contributing much to alienate the intellectual element of Europe from the Church" (Ireland [Etheridge] 1900, 305).

In *Testem Benevolentiae* (1899), the pope proclaimed his affection for the American people and their bishops, but stated that he wished "to point out certain things which are to be avoided and corrected." First, efforts to adapt the church's teachings to the modern world are misguided because, as the Vatican Council made clear, the Catholic faith is not a philosophical theory that human beings can elaborate, but a divine deposit that is to be faithfully guarded and infallibly declared. Similarly, there is a difference between authority in the church and governmental authority, because of the divine nature of the church: whereas the state exists by the free will of those associated with it, the church is based upon its own infallible teachings. To be preserved from private error, members of the church must thus submit to that infallible authority.

The condemnation, mild as it was, was somewhat contrived. The doctrines summarized were not from American writings, but from their opponents' characterizations of them. Archbishop Ireland charged that the Jesuits, Dominicans, and Redemptorists fought for their lives to have Americanism condemned. Nonetheless, he claimed that "the words of the letter allow us to say that the things condemned were never said or written in America not even by Hecker—but were set afloat in France—as 'Americanism'. . . . Fanatics conjured up an 'Americanism'—& put such before the Pope" (in McAvoy 1963, 237).

The Jesuits of the *Civiltà cattolica,* however, claimed that they were
not surprised that those who had taught Americanism were now disclaim-
ing it. "Just so the Jansenius, the proposition condemned in the celebrated
bull 'Inigenitus', . . . and the Rosminianists read nothing of the works of
Rosmini except what was in the Summa of Saint Thomas." Exaggerations
on both sides, in the heat of the conflict, made it difficult to sort out the
truth in the midst of the historical complexities of the situation. Yet the
condemnation of the Americanists does provide some important insights
into the process by which the Roman leadership formulated and carried
out a strategy for responding to the crisis of Catholicism in the modern
world—strategy that reached its apex in the modernist crisis.[31]

CONFLICTING DEMANDS IN THE CHURCH

In attempting to understand the social sources of ambivalence for Catholics at the end of the nineteenth century, it is helpful to compare some
of the situations that they faced and their various responses to them.
First, one can see the importance of the sociohistorical context in which
decisions were made by the three popes who were most important in
forging the church's early response to the modern world—Pius IX, Leo
XIII, and Pius X. Congar (1967, 214–215) suggests that the modernist
crisis emerged from the conjunction of two factors: the lack of correspondence between church doctrine and the conclusions of critical studies,
and elements of religious philosophy in a post-Kantian, post-Schleier-
macherian context. The first factor led to an opposition between dogma
and history, and the second justified the separation, while suggesting a
link between the two. Throughout the nineteenth century and well into
the twentieth, Roman pontiffs were pressured to take a firm stand on
the conservative side of the debates of the period. The three popes in
question differed somewhat at the beginning of their respective terms,
but all three eventually arrived at similar policies.

Pius IX began his papacy as a reforming pope, and was finally forced
by the events of the period and by ultramontane forces within the church
to take a rigid position against what he defined as the errors of the
modern world in his *Syllabus of Errors* (Pius IX [1864] 1968). He helped
to promote papal authority through various proclamations and his advocacy of the doctrine of papal infallibility. Leo XIII inherited Pius IX's
authority and his problems. Pope Leo attempted to resolve the church's
crisis by reviving scholastic theology, promoting an intellectual renaissance within the church, and supporting what he considered to be the
legitimate grievances of the working class. His diplomatic course was

fraught with difficulties, and he vacillated between enabling reforms on the one hand, and drawing the line against change on the other. Pius X picked up where Pius IX had left off, taking a hard line against reformers, defining modernism as heretical, and amplifying the power of the papacy.

When Mastai Ferretti was elected to the papacy in 1846 and took the name of Pius IX, there was considerable celebration among progressive Catholics. It seemed that Pius IX would reverse the conservative policies of his predecessor, Gregory XVI, and these hopes were not disappointed. The problem created by the new pope's reforms lay not in the reforms themselves, but in the way in which they were interpreted. In the polarized climate of the period, there were no moderate political factions. As a consequence, the liberal pope unintentionally became the champion of the revolutionary populace and helped to hasten the Revolution of 1848. Demands for the independence of the papal states grew, and in November of 1848, while a "Committee of Public Safety" ruled Rome, the pope fled the city disguised as a priest. Pius IX's hopes of implementing Gioberti's program for reform were ended. He stopped accommodating simultaneous demands to promote both papal authority and movements for change. By the autumn of 1850, many who had heralded his reforms considered him a tyrant.

One of Pius IX's first acts to encourge ultramontanism and bolster the authority of the papacy was his definition of the dogma of the Immaculate Conception,[32] an idea that was gaining widespread popular support and that was stimulated by visions of Mary reported in Lourdes and in Paris. A decade later, Pius IX issued a *Syllabus of Errors,* which condemned the proposition that "the Roman Pontiff can and should reconcile himself with and accommodate himself to progress, liberalism and modern civilization." He also turned to the Jesuits for assistance, providing the financial assistance and support necessary to establish the fortnightly review, *Civiltà cattolica,*[33] later a central component in the campaign against modernism.

Finally, Pius IX convened the First Vatican Council in 1870, which pronounced the doctrine of papal infallibility. At the time of his death in 1878, Pius IX was forced by hostile anticlericals to remain within the Vatican, where he died a virtual prisoner. His earlier attempts to balance the demands of both traditional Catholicism and the democratic revolution had faded well into the background.

The new pope, Leo XIII, found his ambivalence exacerbated by his interest in scholarship—especially the work of Thomas Aquinas and the scholastic scholars—as well as by his concern for the poor and working classes (see Moody 1961). His strategy was to facilitate an intellectual renaissance and to provide a Catholic alternative to socialist proposals for the alleviation of the plight of the workers, an alternative outlined in his *Rerum novarum* of 1891. Pius IX's confrontation politics were replaced by Leo XIII's conciliatory diplomacy, which proved a difficult task.

Pope Leo's attempts to accommodate contradictory demands were not entirely successful. He encouraged scholarship in order to promote his Thomistic revival, loosening the tight reign Pius IX had imposed upon scholars and establishing Catholic universities. What resulted was not just the anticipated scholastic revival but also the creation of an independent base for scholars within the church. Pope Leo thus inadvertently created an institutional context for the development of the modernist movement, and so was attacked by progressives and traditionalists alike. Times of great polarity do not easily accommodate diplomatic policies.

A good example of Leo XIII's dilemma was his creation in 1902 of the Pontifical Biblical Commission to guide scholarly studies of the scriptures—although, as already noted, he appeared to vacillate between the liberation and suppression of scholarship within the church. Another example of the pope's difficulty in maintaining a balance between conflicting demands was his condemnation of Americanism. Leo was unwilling to endorse the strong charges pressed by some of his advisers, but he did think it necessary to do something. In the end, he delivered a rather mild condemnation of what he called Americanism, which was directed toward no particular individuals or identifiable movements.

Progressive American leaders were told privately that this condemnation did not apply to them, so Leo was in effect sending mixed signals to the church. Believing in the importance of a strong papacy, he was forced to turn for support and advice to ultramontane forces within the church, particularly the *Civiltà cattolica* Jesuits. There was continual pressure for leaders of the church to get "out of the diplomatic mists of confusion" and rely upon "a plain declaration of truth,"[34] as British Cardinal Vaughan put it.

Ironically, the diplomatic Leo was forced to move closer and closer toward papal absolutism—the point at which his successor, Pius X, began his papacy. Pius X was horrified by most aspects of the modern world and operated from an acute sense of crisis. He was convinced that "the number of the enemies of the cross of Christ has in these last days increased exceedingly" (1907), and that only those who were on the side of God could be "on the side of order and have the power to restore calm in the midst of this upheaval."[35]

There was never any question of where Pius X stood on the issues. He confronted the ambivalence of his office with firm intransigence from the outset, and acted consistently throughout his term, increasing the authority of the Biblical Commission (see his *motu proprio, Praestantia Scripturae Sacrae*), further defining biblical and doctrinal matters within the bounds of scholasticism, bolstering papal authority, condemning modernism, and establishing a series of institutional mechanisms to wipe it out (see chap. 6). Yet the modernists against whom Pius X fought were not the malicious enemies of the church that he thought them to be; for the most part, they were sincerely religious Catholics seeking to resolve the ambivalence of the situations in which they found themselves. The problem was that their solutions were different from those of the pope.

3

From Scholarship to Scandal

It was the best of times, it was the worst of times, it was the
age of wisdom, it was the age of foolishness, it was the epoch
of belief, it was the epoch of incredulity.
                    —Charles Dickens, *A Tale of Two Cities*

Ambivalence is always a significant aspect of human life, but is particularly
acute during periods of social and political upheaval. The end of the
nineteenth century, like the previous century as described by Dickens,
was an era in which "some of its noisiest authorities insisted on its being
received, for good or for evil, in the superlative degree of comparison
only" (Dickens [1859] 1957). Passionate commitment to extremes was
more frequent than mediocrity or indifference. Efforts to view the universe
or to develop the merits of a doctrine as a seamless whole, without
contradiction or inconsistency, were usually the efforts of those who tried
too hard to deny ambivalences that could not be eliminated by mere
rhetoric.

Any age of turmoil and conflict is characterized by polarization.
Harsh conflicts over anticlericalism and the separation of church and
state marked the last decade of the nineteenth century, and people were
expected, more often than not, to be either anticlerical republicans or
clerical antirepublicans, anti-Catholic scientists or antiscientific Catholics.

From the *Syllabus of Errors* through the declarations of the First Vatican Council and *Aeterni Patris,* the Vatican strove to eradicate doubts and ambivalences. A systematic scholastic theology would interpret the faith once and for all, providing definitive answers for all generations.

Similarly, anticlericals, such as Ferry, and members of the *parti radicale* in France were constructing a comprehensive view of the world in which Catholicism seemed not only anachronistic but reactionary and dangerous as well. It is always easier to rally the troops when the enemy is perceived as unequivocally evil (see Coser 1956; Douglas 1966), and the exaggerated rhetoric on both sides of the debate over clericalism and anticlericalism was calculated to eliminate doubts and hesitancy. Furthermore, the growth of newspapers in the nineteenth century may have exaggerated the tendencies toward simplification already present in public debates of such issues (see Chadwick 1975).

Throughout the nineteenth century, conflicts between scientific and religious world views were frequently acute. Many clericals and anticlericals alike defined science as antithetical to traditional Catholicism. Scientism was associated with the interests of individuals who were attacking the Catholic Church as a social and political force, just as the scholastic system became associated with the interests of the Roman establishment. Yet large numbers of Catholics refused to shed their traditional religious beliefs, even if they believed in the efficacy of scientific inquiry and democratic forms of government. They combined anticlerical rhetoric with continued participation in the church's rituals. Intellectuals, seminarians, and clergy often found themselves trapped between the polarities of the time.

Two new factors emerged in the nineteenth century: the tremendous growth in the number of students and academic posts, and the suppression by anticlerical forces of the church's traditional hegemony in education. In France, the church–state alliance in education ended under the Third Republic in the last quarter of the century. It was a victory for anticlerical forces, but created unanticipated benefits for the church. The law of 1875 abolished that alliance's monopoly, and in return for relinquishing its partial control over public education, the church was given the freedom to establish its own schools. Consequently, a revival of ecclesiastical studies took place in France, centered in the establishment of the Catholic Institutes and the separation of the theological faculties from the state-controlled University of Paris (see MacCaffrey 1910, II:492).

The creation of educational systems to revitalize the church in times of crisis was nothing new to Catholicism. European educational systems after the Reformation resulted from the Vatican's Counter-Reformation, particularly through the efforts of the Jesuits.[1] European universities were originally developed primarily by the church. Important cosmopolitan centers of learning emerged in such places as Rome and Paris. The Jesuits were mainly responsible for the education of the Catholic clergy, establishing the first modern seminary, the Gregorian University, in 1551. Through their efforts, the theological disciplines flourished until the suppression of the Society of Jesus in 1773.

An international community of scholars emerged as revolutionary changes in transportation and communication facilitated communication over long distances. Scholars gathered for such meetings as the International Catholic Scientific Congresses and congresses of French clergy. There was a mood of reform at these congresses, combined with agreement on the intellectual mediocrity of the French clergy and on the urgent need to remedy the situation. Scholars within the new Catholic faculties belonged to two competing groups: a scholarly community whose interests had become associated primarily with the scientific world view, and an ecclesiastical institution in which there was strong opposition to modern science. Consequently, many of the scholars of the period were torn by ambivalence.

THE SOCIAL CONSTRUCTION OF AMBIVALENCE

Many studies of the modernist movement have focused on the inner turmoil faced by modernists, pointing to personality and psychological factors. It is also crucial, however, to recognize the social-structural components of modernism and the social context in which it developed, an aspect that has not received sufficient attention. Although cultural orientations are not directly determined by social structures, and social movements are not automatic results of certain social configurations, the patterned arrangements and normative expectations surrounding various roles and statuses usually provide the conditions necessary for the creation and suppression of insurgent movements. Cultural orientations and social movements have an elective affinity with social structures and configurations, and that is the subject of the analysis which follows.

Individuals are frequently faced with contradictory demands for the fulfillment of a given social role, or have to choose between fulfilling demands from one role and those from another. A social role consists of a dynamic organization of norms and counter-norms, in a tension identified by Merton and Barber (1976) as "sociological ambivalence." Ambivalence in a role is not only a matter of social psychology;[2] it is also the result of a particular role structure and of the set of expectations surrounding that structure. Ambivalence is especially observable in professional roles—most acutely when those roles are embedded in institutions and networks that are in turmoil.

The concept of sociological ambivalence, as Merton and Barber develop it, does have some deterministic tendencies that obscure variations in responses to ambivalence which result from personality differences, psychological factors, and matters of personal and social choice. When combined with Weber's concept of elective affinity, however, the concept can be an invaluable tool for understanding the modernist crisis. Both the modernists and the Vatican hierarchy were responding to their entrapment in situations of radical ambivalence—ambivalence arising out of contradictory demands and expectations associated with their social roles; conflicts among various social institutions, interest groups, and social networks; and larger cultural conflicts between scientific and religious worldviews.

Both the modernists and the church hierarchy constructed worldviews and definitions of their roles to resolve those ambivalences, while at the same time preserving cherished beliefs and definitions. Their respective attempts to resolve the conflicts had unanticipated consequences and moved them in opposite directions, toward mutually exclusive positions. The ecclesiastical hierarchy finally decided that the modernist position could not be tolerated within the institution of the church. Furthermore, ecclesiastical elites recognized and capitalized on the possibility of fortifying their own position by constructing a caricature of the modernists' position through weaving their opponents' views into a coherent whole and condemning modernism as a heresy.

The modernists were responding both to the conflict within the intellectual culture of western Europe and to the manner in which the Roman hierarchy had defined that conflict. Secular intellectual culture was dominated by questions of authority, and the growing prestige of scientific research involved efforts to break away from the authority of medieval institutions in matters of intellectual inquiry (see Mead 1936). The modernists were influenced by that culture; although they did not share the Enlightenment's anticlericalism, they shared its distaste for papal absolutism.

Roman ecclesiastical culture was increasingly insulated from the outside world. Just as secular intellectual stances were often defined in reaction to Catholicism, so the positions of persons within the ecclesiastical culture were often a reaction to what was perceived as heresy. The elaboration of cultural codes excluded elements of the secular culture which the authorities found dangerous.

The modernists responded with a neo-Catholicism that rejected the extremes of both scientism and scholasticism, and a modernist program of intellectual activity gradually emerged. The modernists extracted from official Catholicism what they defined as the "true Catholicism of the future," with roots in the Catholicism of the past. Historical studies, which informed many of the modernists' intellectual tasks, guided their scientific-religious search; Loisy said of his *L'Evangile et l'Eglise,* for example, that "it was an apology for the Catholicism that should be, a discreet criticism of actual official Catholicism" (1930–31, II: 321).

THE MODERNISTS AND THEIR ISSUES

> Some among you, puffed up like bladders with the spirit of vanity, strive by profane novelties to cross the boundaries fixed by the Fathers, twisting the meaning of the sacred text . . . to the philosophical teaching of the rationalists, not for the profit of the hearer but to make a show of science. . . . These men, led away by various and strange doctrines, turn the head into the tail and force the queen to serve the handmaid.
>
> —Pope Gregory IX, in Pius X, *Pascendi*

Nineteenth-century science "symbolized the triumph of comprehensive theoretical systems" (Ben-David 1977, 256). For the Roman establishment, the growth of the sciences was a matter of great consternation because science was so frequently linked with the destruction of ecclesiastical hegemony. The Vatican's attempted resolution of the Catholic crisis—namely, the use of scholasticism as the only authoritative science in religious matters—was far from satisfactory for many Catholic intellectuals. Murmurs of discontent grew stronger in intellectual centers throughout Europe in the final decades of the nineteenth century. What was emerging, however diffuse and unorganized, was a modernist response to sociological ambivalence.

Facing Ambivalence

The modernism defined by the papal condemnations was never a reality; some scholars, in fact, have hesitated even to talk about the existence of a movement per se, because the term connotes the existence of an organized structure. For example, Alec R. Vidler, an established authority on Catholic modernism, chose to write about "modernists" rather than "modernism" (1970, 15).[3] From a sociological point of view, however, "modernism" existed in three senses. First, modernism existed as a group of people in the Roman Church who attempted to reform it, particularly its "intellectual regime." Although they had frequent disagreements, they wrote to one another, read one another's work, and had some sense of "we-ness," albeit in a fragmented form. Second, an image of modernism formulated by the Roman theologians, although it did not directly correspond to the reality of the first modernism, was nonetheless profound in its consequences.

Third, there was a broader modernism in the general cultural climate of the modern world—a style of cultural expression. We can speak of modernism in literature, science, technology, or political thought, and this modernism was distinct from but related to Catholic modernism. Both secular modernism and the official definition of modernism by the Vatican had an impact on how Catholic modernists defined their own ideas, albeit by way of contrast at times. The Vatican's definition of Catholic modernism failed to distinguish between Catholic and secular modernists; it grouped together Catholic modernists and a variety of secular modernists and anticlericals, defining them all as enemies of the church.

Catholic modernism differed from the broader meaning of the term, in that most of its adherents maintained a rigorous belief in the Catholic faith and the Roman Church, at least until a series of condemnations and excommunications killed the movement. Underlying all of the various types of modernism was a belief that the modern world was somehow different from the ages preceding it— a belief that was often an exaggerated picture of the changes brought about by such phenomena as the Industrial and French Revolutions. Modernists also shared a concern about the relationship between the Roman Church and the modern world's secular institutions, a marked dissatisfaction with the Roman establishment's response to nineteenth-century culture, and a dislike for the authoritarianism of the papacy.

The situation of those performing scholarly roles within the Catholic Church constituted an institutional crisis of major proportions. As long as intellectual life was effectively monopolized by the church, ambivalence resulting from a combination of priestly and scholarly roles could be effectively minimized, although the marriage of priesthood and scholarship has always been a stormy alliance. Within limits, ambivalence serves a creative function. It was the tension between orthodox Catholic theology in thirteenth-century Paris and the philosophy of Aristotle, for example, that motivated Thomas Aquinas to develop his powerful intellectual system, which was condemned by the Vatican. Modernism was largely a response to the ambivalence created by the institutionalization of two roles (priest and savant) in the same status—that of a professor in a Catholic university or of a scholar in a religious order like the Jesuits.

A number of Catholic scholars faced profound ambivalence, most notably Loisy and Tyrrell. Other priestly savants who will be discussed here are the French clergymen Charles Denis, Albert Houtin, Joseph Turmel, Jacques Chevalier, Paul Lejay, Hippolyte Renaudin, and Marcel Hebert; Don Amelli, Giovanni Genocchi, Giovanni Semeria, Ernesto Buonaiuti, Alessandro Casati, Brizio Casciola, Germane Morin, Romolo Murri, and others in Italy; and Alfred Fawkes, Christian van den Biesen, and others in Britain; as well as Henri Bremond in Belgium, Hyacinthe Loyson in Switzerland, and others, all of whom were Catholic clergy as well as scholars (see the appendixes for summary lists).

The world of modern secular scholarship was quite different from the medieval Catholic world in which the normative expectations for the role of Catholic priests were defined. Because the church was the subject of so much abuse in the modern culture, even in Rome itself, efforts were made to insulate the ecclesiastical world.[4] Catholics in cosmopolitan urban centers like Rome, Paris, and London could not help but pass back and forth between curious mixtures of the two cultural orientations, which existed in tension with each other. Priests were somewhat insulated from modern secular culture by a number of factors, not the least of which was the soutane, the traditional priestly garb that set the clergy apart from the laity. Those wearing the soutane were defined as people with certain kinds of attitudes (see Burke [1945] 1969, 16), from whom one could expect particular types of behavior.

Life was only slightly less difficult for Catholic laity engaged in scholarly activity. The most important example was Baron von Hügel, around whom most modernist networks formed, a matter discussed in some detail below. Other important modernists include Petre, Ward, and Bishop in England; Laberthonnière, LeRoy, Blondel, Chevalier, Fonsegrive, François Thureau-Dangin, Augustin Leger, and other laity in France; and in Italy, the group of lay scholars associated with the modernist journal *Il Rinnovamento*—especially Fogazzaro, Alfieri, Scotti, Gallavresi, and others.[5]

Also associated with the modernists—and facing some of the same issues—were non-Roman scholars such as the Anglican clergyman A. L. Lilley; Oxford scholars F. C. Burkitt, Percy Gardner, and Clement Webb; German scholars Ernst Troeltsch and Heinrich Holtzmann; and the French Protestant Paul Sabatier. Although subject to some of the same tensions created by conflicts between scientific and religious worldviews which were faced by the Catholic modernists, their situation was different because of less stringent institutional constraints.

Another significant group facing ambivalence consisted of clergy and laity like Archbishop Ireland and Cardinal Newman who, although not scholars themselves, were well educated and well versed in the critical scholarly debates of the period. For example, French bishops Eûdoxe-

Irénée Mignot of Albi and Lucien La Croix of Tarantaise were quite sympathetic to the modernists, but were under considerable pressure to oppose them because of their episcopal positions. Similarly, British journalists E. J. Dillon and Robert Dell were involved, as were other educated Catholic laity, such as Adeline Chapman, G. B. Coore, H. C. Corrance, Cesare Foligno, Eveline Lance, and Ida Taylor in England; publishers Picard and Nourry in France; and Concetta Ginntini and Contessa Lillian Priuli-Bon in Italy.

Finally, there were a number of students, often difficult to identify by name, who became involved with the modernist movement when they encountered the implications of modern scholarship in their studies. Many of the most visible modernists first encountered the ambivalences of their culture in their student days, often after migrating to urban settings from the more orthodox settings of their childhood. Writing about his migration from a rural French village to Paris, Loisy referred to that city as a "Babylon where one's head is so easily turned" ([1913] 1968, 91). Minocchi spoke of Rome as a place where "we studied theology like we never had in the provinces" (quoted in Ranchetti 1969, 81). There were others, including students in Oxford, Cambridge, and Rome, who read and admired Loisy.

Before examining the ways in which these various groups of people constituted a reform movement, a sketch of the ideas and concerns of the modernists is in order. Although their purposes and methods were somewhat diverse, at the core of Catholic modernism (and many other modernisms) was the development of historical criticism as a tool of scholarship. The most important critical scholar in the movement was Alfred Loisy.

"LOISYISME" IN FRANCE

> In its catechism and in its customary utterances from the pulpit particularly, the Catholic Church . . . is in daily and hourly contradiction with the most elementary results of modern science.
> —Alfred Loisy, *My Duel with the Vatican*

From early in his career, Loisy became increasingly frustrated with the lack of intellectual freedom within the Roman Church. In the last two years of the nineteenth century, he penned the draft of what he called his "Livre inedit," which included a chapter on "The Intellectual Regime of the Catholic Church" that "was having the effect of arousing the contempt of the entire learned world, of all enlightened spirits" ([1913] 1968, 182). For Loisy, scholasticism prevented the growth of the religious sciences and impeded the development that he felt was necessary for the church. Modernism—especially what was in France called "Loisyisme"— was part of a "historicist crisis of culture," and Loisy's efforts to develop the Catholic religious sciences anchored the controversy. He was the leading figure in the movement until about 1904, when he lost faith in its future (see Vidler 1934, 68).

Born in 1857 in the small rural French village of Ambrière, Loisy grew up in an agricultural family. He would probably have been a "cultivateur" himself, had not the war of 1870 and his bad health led to his being kept at home by his parents (Loisy [1913] 1968, 51–52). There he was instructed by a priest who noticed his promising intelligence. The milieu in which he matured encouraged Catholic orthodoxy, and there were occasional suggestions that he might become a priest.[6] Loisy entered the diocesan seminary at Châlons-sur-Marne in 1874, where he excelled at his studies and was noted for his fervent piety.

An intellectual movement against dogmatism in religious thought was under way, and the head of Loisy's seminary was the open-minded Guillaume Meignan, formerly a professor of holy scripture at the Sorbonne. Abbé Ludot, professor of church history at the seminary, had come from a liberal Catholic background. He spoke with sympathy of Lacordaire and Montalembert and abstained from taking part in action against his bishop, who had opposed the Vatican Council's stance on papal infallibility. After having some of his students prepare topics on the Concordat of 1801, Lamennais, liberal Catholicism, and the Vatican Council, Ludot was relieved of his teaching duties and given a series of unimportant parish posts. He was replaced by a devotee of scholasticism (see Loisy [1913] 1968, 63–66). As a seminarian, Loisy became dissatisfied with the scholastic approach to religious questions (see Loisy 1930–31, I:50). His study of Thomas's *Summa Theologica* did not quiet his internal turmoil but worsened it, and he turned to the study of the scriptures, learning Hebrew and Greek so that he could read them in their original languages.

After a brief period serving rural parishes near his home, Loisy migrated to Paris, where an association with the eminent church historian Louis Duchesne at the newly established Institut Catholique moved the young priest toward the intellectual odyssey that precipitated his modernism.

HISTORICAL STUDIES AT THE INSTITUT CATHOLIQUE

Wishing to remain firm in his faith, and having already had his orthodoxy badly shaken in seminary, Loisy at first resisted Duchesne's urging that he move to Paris to work on his doctorate. Loisy's suspicions about the effect of the Parisian intellectual milieu on his thinking were correct. Not being inclined toward scholastic orthodoxy, he chose other directions of inquiry. At the time he returned to Paris, scholastic theology was not being taught at the Institut Catholique, where there was cautious resistance to the Vatican's attempts to make scholasticism the exclusive theology of Catholicism.[7]

In contrast, the nearby Seminary of Saint Sulpice, where Loisy attended the lectures of Abbé Vigouroux, was a center of impeccable orthodoxy. In the meantime, Duchesne had given Loisy Tischendorf's classical edition of the New Testament, which led Loisy to the astounding discovery of contradictions in the gospel narratives. He soon became convinced that "these writings require to be as freely interpreted as they were freely composed. It is vain to treat, as rigorously historical, texts that are obviously not so in the least" ([1913] 1968, 87). At the same time, Vigouroux was condemning in his lectures the critical exegesis that Loisy was savoring, and Loisy found the professor's arguments superficial and unconvincing. "His instruction," Loisy later wrote, "and his writings did more to turn me away from orthodox opinions . . . than all the rationalists put together, Renan included" (ibid., 88). In 1882, under Vigouroux's influence, Loisy acknowledged in his notes the ambivalences that were to plague him throughout his career. He found himself confronted with two opposing attitudes:

> On the one hand, routine calling itself tradition; on the other, novelty calling itself truth. The former no more stands for faith than the latter authentically for science. These two attitudes are in conflict as to the Bible, and I wonder if anyone in the world is able to hold the scales even between faith and science. If so, he shall be my master. (Loisy [1913] 1968, 90; 1930–31, I:84)

The conflicts between his religious orthodoxy and his intellectual inquiry plunged Loisy into a depression. He asked himself if he shouldn't return to the country. But the illness of Abbé Martin left the institute without anyone to provide instruction in Hebrew, and upon Duchesne's recommendation, Loisy was appointed to teach the course.

Loisy was soon fully immersed in the Parisian intellectual milieu; he entered the Ecole Pratique des Hautes Etudes to take lectures in Assyriology from Arthur Amiaud, a step which led in 1886 to a lectureship in that field at the Institut Catholique. Feeling somewhat uneasy about his sudden lectureship in Hebrew, Loisy began attending the Hebrew course of the controversial Ernest Renan at the Collège de France in 1882. Renan's lectures were extremely significant for Loisy's career (see Loisy 1930–31, III:98–99), introducing Loisy to the textual criticism of the

Old Testament. Renan's sharp and controversial style caused Loisy to question whether he should risk entering the lecture room, but his confessor advised him that to take lectures at the renowned Collège de France was a patriotic duty. Loisy was not the only priest attending the lectures from time to time, but many were even more suspicious than he, sometimes sitting by the door and leaving in disgust when Renan presented an objectionable argument.

Loisy learned scientific methods of historical criticism from Duchesne, but their application to the scriptures Loisy learned from Renan. Even so, he clung adamantly to his intellectual independence, insisting that it was from his own study of the scriptures and not from the "rationalist critics" that he drew his conclusions.[8] As Loisy found himself drawn into biblical studies, the distance between him and Duchesne grew. Although the Italian translation of Duchesne's own *Histoire ancienne de l'Eglise* was placed on the *Index of Prohibited Books* in 1912,[9] and students at Saint Sulpice were eventually forbidden to attend his courses, Duchesne avoided the ambivalence surrounding biblical criticism by avoiding the subject altogether in his published works. Loisy later wrote that Duchesne always "had a horror of what is called modernism" and that he never attacked the dogmas of the church ([1913] 1968, 120).

Duchesne was not the only person to warn Loisy that his studies were fraught with danger. Monsignor Meignan, the former head of the seminary at Châlons, reminded Loisy of the fate of Richard Simon, advising him that if he exposed himself to danger, "those who think as you do will not come to your rescue." Given that climate within the church, what is remarkable is not that the modernist movement failed, but that it fared as well as it did. Meignan cautioned Loisy to stay on good terms with the Jesuit fathers, who "give us the measure of what is possible to print on Biblical questions"—an important comment on the position of the Jesuits within the power structure of the church (ibid., 134).

Loisy could not accept the advice, however, and his difficulties were exacerbated by the pressures of his career. He was required to publish his doctoral thesis in order to obtain a promotion, but as he later observed, it was only after he began to publish that the "persecution for heresy" was instigated in the Catholic press (ibid., 116). Loisy was faced with conflicting demands from the two aspects of his role as scholar-priest; on the one hand he was required to publish, but on the other to refrain from publishing, lest he offend his superiors.

Intellectual production was, for Loisy, closely related to his teaching, and his students inspired his early efforts to overcome the ambivalence of his inquiries, since Loisy hoped that somehow he could help his students escape "the painful crisis by which I had been overhwelmed" (ibid.,

112–113). His role as a scholarly priest was both the source of his troubles and the driving force behind his creative work.

LOISY'S DISMISSAL AND "EXILE"

In the fall of 1892 Loisy began publishing a review entitled *Enseignement biblique,* in which he proposed to print a summary of his lectures (see Loisy [1913] 1968, 108–109). The journal gained about two hundred subscribers in less than a year, but the controversy surrounding his course grew more quickly than his subscription list. When Loisy arrived to present his first lecture in the fall of 1892, there were no students from Saint Sulpice: although a large majority of his students were usually from that seminary, the rector, M. Icard, had forbidden his students to attend Loisy's lectures. As Loisy himself correctly observed, he and the orthodox Icard had quite different definitions of how the church could best be served. Each sought in his own way to serve the interests of the church, but they defined their responsibilities quite differently.

D'Hulst was concerned about protecting the fragile reputation of the Institut Catholique, but was also impressed with Loisy and hoped that the institute would become a center for the new biblical methods. He himself was not familiar with the complex issues involved, but prepared an article on "The Biblical Question" for publication. He sent the proofs to Loisy, explaining that it was "primarily a stroke of diplomacy, intended to gain a gradually enlarging measure of tolerance, then full freedom" (in Loisy [1913] 1968, 138). But rather than opening the way for Loisy's work, as he had intended, d'Hulst touched off a violent polemic in the Catholic press, and thus was persuaded that he must relieve Loisy of his instructorship in scriptures. Loisy was replaced by Abbé Fillion of Saint Sulpice, an irreproachably orthodox scholar, and was confined to teaching Hebrew and other oriental languages.

The controversy culminated in the issuing of *Providentissimus Deus,* an encyclical which condemned the "école large" of d'Hulst's article, and which for the moment put an end to Loisy's growing popularity at the Institut Catholique. Loisy's defense of his position, written in response to the charges brought against him, also created an unexpected furor. Both Loisy and d'Hulst miscalculated in their definitions of the situation, incorrectly thinking that the climate in the church would allow them to advance their positions openly. Loisy's article was never attacked by the Catholic press or condemned by the church (ibid., 151), but the Board of Bishops that had jurisdiction over the institute denounced Loisy, on the recommendation of Cardinal Richard.[10]

As the polemic unfolded, the scholastics interpreted the scriptures with increasing rigidity, whereas the modernists interpreted them with increasing freedom. D'Hulst was caught between the two parties, being required by his roles of scholar and administrator to protect the interests of both sides. Cardinal Richard accused d'Hulst of allowing himself to yield to the "seductions of science," and Loisy claimed that d'Hulst had created the controversy that deprived him of his teaching post. The rector was forced to choose between saving his institution and defending Loisy. The hierarchy of the church, bound as it was by the prevailing scholastic definitions of orthodoxy, left neither the bishops nor Monsignor d'Hulst with much choice, nor could Loisy refute what he felt to be the obvious and necessary implications of his research. From that time on, Loisy charged, there was a "reign of terror" that weighed down the intellectual life of Catholicism (ibid., 164–165).

In 1894, Loisy was relieved of his teaching duties and promptly sent off to rusticate as the chaplain of a Dominican girls' school in Neuilly. Once again, Loisy found his intellectual life nurtured by his teaching duties. At the Institut Catholique, he had been "nearly confined in the purely scientific order, studying the rapport of criticism with theology on the terrain of exegesis. Now it was the ensemble of the religious problem and the general conditions of ecclesiastical ministry that came to be the daily object of my experience" (Loisy 1930–31, I:358).

Official Catholic interpretations of traditional dogmas became increasingly unsatisfactory to Loisy as he worked on them in a systematic manner.[11] He broadened the scope of his thinking, began working out the plan for his further studies, and kept in touch with his previous interests. He became a collaborator with the *Revue critique,* and its editor, Abbé Chuquet, sent him current books on the history and philosophy of religions, the history of the church, and the history of Christian dogma. Loisy founded the *Revue d'histoire et de littérature religieuses* to replace his ill-fated *Enseignement biblique,* which had been lost in the turmoil of his 1893 dismissal from the institute. A number of distinguished scholars were recruited to publish in the review, and Loisy himself contributed a large number of articles, sometimes using pseudonyms for the purpose of "throwing inquisitors off the scent" (Loisy [1913] 1968, 199). From the time of his dismissal in 1893 until his excommunication in 1908, Loisy was constantly in trouble with church officials, and he sought wherever possible to gain a measure of independence.

Following a breakdown of his health in 1899, Loisy took up residence in Bellevue, a Parisian suburb. With Mignot's assistance, he was granted an *indult*—that is, an exemption from the usual regulation binding the clergy—which allowed him to say mass in his own room. Loisy left Cardinal Richard's diocese and gained a new freedom from episcopal

supervision. But his troubles were far from over, due to continued opposition to his published work. In 1900 Cardinal Richard denounced an
article published by Loisy, under the pseudonym Firmin, in the *Revue
du clergé français*. Leo XIII, however, was not induced to intervene.
Loisy's interpretation of this decision was that the pope wished as much
as possible to have the conflict viewed as a "French affair"; but although
the pope did not commit himself publicly, "he was entirely capable of
suggesting privately to his bishops what measures they should take"
(ibid., 204).[12]

To increase his independence, Loisy sought and received an appointment as a lecturer in the section of the religious sciences at the Ecole
Pratique des Hautes Etudes. The prestige afforded to Loisy by his new
position reportedly troubled Cardinal Richard, who had intended that
Loisy never again teach publicly in Paris (ibid., 109).[13] The position
increased Loisy's autonomy because "to censure instruction given at the
Sorbonne appeared too daring a venture, and it was not dreamed of, at
least under Leo XIII" (ibid., 213). Mignot wrote to Loisy that some of
his adversaries would not fail to say "he passes to the enemy," but that
the "wise and moderated spirits" would regret that he had been forced
to leave the Institut Catholique and enter the university.[14]

Richard did not interfere with Loisy's courses at the Sorbonne, and
in January of 1902 Prince Albert of Monaco let it be known that he
wished to present Loisy's name as a candidate for the episcopacy. Loisy
objected to Prince Albert that he had the habits of a hermit and that he
did not have the strength for a public life (1930–31, II:93). Mignot,
however, counseled Loisy to accept the nomination: "It would be excellent
for your health, first of all, for the honor of science, and for the rehabili-
tation of your person and your ideas."[15] Loisy consented to the candidacy
and, through the effort of a Parisian priest, was placed on the French
Director of Worship's list of candidates (Loisy [1913] 1968, 218–219).
But there were too many obstacles to Loisy's candidacy in Rome, even
though the influential Cardinal Mathieu supported him and wrote a note
to Loisy to that effect.[16]

According to Loisy, Rome's efforts to prevent his becoming a bishop
provided part of its motivation for condemning his *L'Evangile et l'Eglise*,
which took the Catholic world by storm the following year (ibid., 223–
224). *L'Evangile et l'Eglise* was something of a manifesto of the modernist
movement, and its publication, "more than any other single event," precipitated the conflicts over modernism in the church (Vidler 1934, 101).
If Loisy's speculations were correct, his candidacy for the bishopric had
precisely the opposite effect from that for which Mignot had hoped—it
accelerated the hierarchy's efforts to suppress his work.

A Modernist Manifesto

If *L'Evangile et l'Eglise* was a manifesto for modernism, it is appropriate that there was not complete agreement with it even among the members of the movement, although it did provide a focus for many modernist ideas. Loisy's chief aim in the book was to

sketch the history of Christian development, beginning with the Gospels, in order to show that its essence, in so far as it could be said to have any, had historically perpetuated itself in Catholic Christianity, and that its successive transformation had been as a matter of fact anything but a continuous decadence

as the Protestant scholar Adolf von Harnack had argued in his important work of 1900, *Das Wesen des Christentums* (Loisy [1913] 1968, 227). Loisy's work was intended as an apology for the Roman Church, and as a response to liberal Protestantism's claims that the essence of Christianity had been only recently rediscovered, having been lost for eighteen centuries (Vidler 1965, 40).

Loisy contended that Catholicism was in need of extensive reform, but that it was a legitimate development of the work of Jesus. The church was a human product, but also a valid outcome of Christ's work:

To reproach the Catholic Church for the development of her constitution is to reproach her for having chosen to live, and that, moreover, when her life was indispensable for the preservation of the gospel itself. There is nowhere in her history any gap in continuity, or the absolute creation of any system. (Loisy [1903*b*] 1976, 165)

In attacking Harnack's interpretation of the scriptures, Loisy developed a twofold argument (see Fawkes 1913, 60). First, one cannot separate the Christian idea from the Christian community. For Loisy, the social element was a constitutive part of religion: "It is necessary . . . to insist on this social character from which religion draws its force and which is the guarantee of its endurance" (Loisy 1899, 200; see Scott 1976, xxxvi). Harnack's individualistic interpretation is Loisy's initial target, because for Loisy Christianity has an existence that is independent of the individual (Loisy [1903*b*] 1976, 8).

Second, Loisy argues that one cannot represent any one feature of Christianity as the invariable essence of the whole. Harnack's work, a classic statement of liberal Protestantism, was an ostensible search for the essence of Christianity, stripped of its institutional trappings and "perversions." In Harnack's model, the essence of Christianity is the kernel, the *kerygma* (apostolic proclamation), while the husk is that which was added over time, resulting in a break from Jesus's teachings by the early church. For Loisy, a more appropriate model for the church is the tree that grows from an acorn (ibid., 16). For Harnack, change threatens the loss of an unchanging essence, whereas for Loisy, when there is no change, the tree is dead. Harnack's method of interpretation of the scriptures had, in Loisy's opinion, a close affinity with the scholastic approach. To examine the facts of history, one could not ignore the institutionalization of Christianity; as Loisy put it, "Jesus announced the kingdom, and it was the Church that came" (ibid., 166). Thus the evidence does not show a break between Jesus and primitive Christianity.[17]

According to Loisy himself, half of *L'Evangile et l'Eglise* was "calculated to awaken opposition" ([1913] 1968, 228). And that it did. Abbé Gayraud, a clerical member of the French House of Deputies, published a series of violent articles in *L'Univers.* "He knew nothing at all about criticism," Loisy charged, "but he wielded a trenchant pen and was not even abashed when it was proved to him that he had taken citations from Harnack for the expression of my own ideas" (ibid., 229).

There were two problems with *L'Evangile et l'Eglise* from the Roman hierarchy's point of view. First, Loisy's aim was to interpret the scriptures from an historical rather than a theological point of view. More specifically, he refused to work within the boundaries of scholastic theology, and that separation of history from theology was unconscionable to the Catholic authorities. A second objection concerned the status of the Roman hierarchy. If the Catholic Church is legitimated because of a process of historical development from the gospel to the church, then the ecclesiastical establishment of any given historical epoch is never safe; Christianity would by necessity evolve continually throughout history.

Loisy's legitimation of Catholicism was based upon its innate propensity for adaptation and change. A study of the origin and history of the church revealed for him not an "absolute, abstract doctrine," but "a living faith linked everywhere to the time and circumstances that witnessed its birth" ([1903*b*] 1976, 177). Adaptation is essential to the preservation of Catholicism, and the authority of the institution is legitimated only if it is responsive to the changing needs of different sociocultural milieux. The early church was a legitimate outcome of the adaptation process, and the modern church must adapt to the culture of the modern world. In a subtle *coup de plume,* Loisy struck at the Roman establishment by striking at Harnack: "If the Church were entirely a political institution, such as Herr Harnack conceives and represents her, it is certain that she would have nothing in common with the gospel, and would simply have to be regarded as the successor of the Roman Empire" (ibid., 197).

Loisy's "petit livre rouge" (little red book) contained an implicit call for a further process of adaptation in light of a "great religious crisis in the modern world":

The best means of meeting it does not appear to be the suppression of all ecclesiastical organization, all orthodoxy, and all traditional worship . . . but to take advantage of what is, in view of what should be, to repudiate nothing of the heritage left to our age by former Christian centuries, to recognize how necessary and useful is the immense development accomplished in the Church, to gather the fruits of it and continue it, since the adaptation of the gospel to the changing conditions of humanity is as pressing a need today as it ever was and ever will be. (Loisy [1903*b*] 1976, 276)

Loisy's friends and admirers were as enthusiastic about the work as the hierarchy was scandalized. In an article on the book in the *Verité française,* Abbé Maignen reported that in Rome, when the professor of holy scripture at the important Apollinaire gave a lecture on the condemnation of Loisy by Cardinal Richard, "a certain number of students rose, crying 'Vive Loisy!'"[18] Some of the positive reaction is recorded in the letters received by Baron von Hügel,[19] Loisy's English supporter who facilitated the book's positive reception, sending copies to various people and soliciting reviews for it. Loisy inspired admiration among many in von Hügel's wide circle, including the Jewish scholar Claude Montefiore and the eminent Protestant church historian Ernst Troeltsch.[20]

In the furor that followed, however, the positive voices were drowned out by official opposition, and by those who clamored to denounce "the scandal."[21] Loisy was quite right in contending that the book might not have created such a widespread scandal if it had not been for "the clamor of my adversaries that had made it known" ([1913] 1968, 232). Ironically, efforts to silence Loisy simply brought attention to his work.

The book was not intended for the public at large, Loisy argued, but for an audience of young Catholics who read Harnack (Loisy 1903*a*, 20). It was intended for intellectuals who had experienced ambivalences similar to those Loisy himself had faced. "For good or ill," Loisy argued, "there are and have been for too long in French Catholicism, too many people who are not frightened enough to scandalize the experts. Each to his own audience. The good honest folk don't read" (ibid., xxxii). Because the populace could not read or understand Loisy's work, it was to the advantage of the hierarchy to spread the scandal that it created. By extracting selected passages from the book, the hierarchy could evoke the sentiments of those who defended the church, thereby reinforcing scholastic Catholicism.

L'Evangile et l'Eglise sold 20,000 copies in France and throughout Europe in little more than a year.[22] The success of the manifesto was not entirely Loisy's doing, although his lucid arguments and sharp style were important. The work was, rather, an appealing statement that entered a volatile context, with a largely rigid Roman hierarchy searching for heresies to denounce on one side, and an undercurrent of discontent among young lay Catholics and clergy on the other. Loisy had not foreseen the scandal his book would create. Although not naive about its controversial nature, Loisy claimed that Tyrrell, von Hügel, Mignot, and himself

> never suspected that we were on the eve of a Seven Years War, that in the eighth year I would be expelled from the Church, that in the ninth year, with Tyrrell dead, von Hügel would remain alone, unbeaten, on the battlefield, determined to serve the Church in spite of herself through knowledge; "our archbishop" [Mignot] watching from afar, sadly and thoughtfully, the wrecking of our hopes. (Loisy 1930–31, I:578; translation in Ranchetti 1969, 35)

ENGLISH MODERNISM: A PLAN AND A VISION

> Von Hügel was not only a modernist, but an archmodernist to the extent that he was surely the pioneer and leader of modernism in England. . . . However, it also needs to be borne in mind that von Hügel was always very circumspect and level-headed. He never spoke before weighing his words and throughout the conflict he avoided the excesses of both left and right.
> —Maude Petre, in P.-L. Couchoud, *Congrès d'histoire du Christianisme: Jubilé Alfred Loisy*

THE BARON AND HIS PLAN

Baron Friedrich von Hügel was an important figure in English Catholicism at the turn of the century, and his modernism has been widely debated (see Loome 1979). As with every reform leader, there was more to von Hügel than his involvement in a reform movement. Some have minimized his commitment to the movement, either to cover up his participation in a condemned movement, or because much of his involvement was of a behind-the-scenes sort that is not immediately obvious. Bernard Holland's volume of von Hügel's *Selected Letters* (1927), for example, has no letters from von Hügel to Loisy, despite their voluminous correspondence.[23] There is no doubt that von Hügel was a modernist, as his diaries and letters convincingly demonstrate.

Vidler has suggested three reasons for affirming von Hügel's place in the movement. First, von Hügel was the "chief engineer" of the movement (Vidler 1970, 113) and coordinated the modernists' networks (see chap. 5). Second, von Hügel himself "held advanced modernist opinions as a biblical critic," was averse to scholastic theology, and distrusted papal authoritarianism (ibid., 126–127). Furthermore, he frequently championed controversial causes or views by taking a public stance on them (ibid., 118). Even von Hügel's magnum opus, *The Mystical Element*

of Religion as Studied in Saint Catherine of Genoa and Her Friends
(1908*b*), which was written during the modernist period, was an indirect
attempt to develop an historical criticism within the Catholic tradition.
He argued that carrying out research in the various sciences "of Astronomy and Geology, of Botany and Zoology, of Human Physiology
and Psychology, of Philosophy and History" according to their own
immanent principles and methods would lead to "ethical, spiritually helpful results" (Petre 1918, 77).

Von Hügel was a man of means, which gave him independence to
carry out his scholarly work. He was acquainted with many of the foremost scholars of the period, and maintained a wide variety of contacts
in academia and within the church. His intellectual bearing and his plan
for revitalizing the church were central to the development of the modernist movement. Although a devout Catholic, his interests and friends
ranged far and wide, and he had an ability to recognize and appreciate
scholarly excellence.

It was no accident that von Hügel was a champion of historical
methods. As he wrote to Professor Percy Gardner at Oxford, "my father
and all the foundations of my scholarship and knowledge, and a good
seven-tenths or more of my reading, are German" (1927, 110–111). One
could scarcely be raised on German scholarship in the latter half of the
nineteenth century and not be familiar with historical methods. Von
Hügel was personally acquainted with the outstanding ecclesiastical and
biblical scholars of the period. He corresponded with Ernst Troeltsch,
H. J. Holtzmann, S. R. Driver, Robertson Smith, Louis Duchesne, and
others, as well as with modernists in England, France, and Italy.

Moreover, von Hügel had, as Petre put it, "a German thoroughness
of plan" for the renewal of the church; at times, he seemed convinced
that he had the resources necessary to carry it out successfully. His hope
was that Loisy's exegesis, Blondel's apologetics, and Tyrrell's religious
pragmatism might be absorbed into the church's life, in much the same
way that Newman's doctrine of development had been incorporated (Ranchetti 1969, 56). "For you, always the truth, never simply orthodoxy,"
von Hügel had been advised by French priest Henri Huvelin (von Hügel
1927, 58 ff.), although that pursuit of "la verité" was not always easy
for von Hügel.

Although the baron later changed his attitude toward the modernist
movement, this occurred well after the movement per se was effectively
dead, when he simply acknowledged the futility of continued struggle.
Von Hügel distinguished between modernism as a generic term referring
to the need to reinterpret the faith in every age, and that specific usage
referring to the condemned movement. Whereas the work in the former
"never ceases for long," the other[24]

"Modernism" is a strictly circumscribed affair, one that is really over and done . . . beginning, no doubt, during the later years of Leo XIII, but ending with the death of Father T[yrrell] and with Loisy's alienation from the positive content that had been fought for—also from the suppression of *Rinnovamento* onwards.

In the final analysis, the baron was probably more effective in his supportive activities than in his original scholarship, at least during his modernist period. He was, nonetheless, a man of great learning who was widely read and knowledgeable about the latest developments in scholarship. He was held in high esteem personally and intellectually by some of the brightest scholars of the period.

Petre contended that his influence was pervasive and persistent, even if sometimes hidden.[25] Henri Bremond, who in his own circumspect way was closely associated with the modernists, wrote to von Hügel,

I really want you to realise how truly you are our *Peter* and we are living upon your thoughts and from your inspirations. I could easily draw the *courbe* of my intellectual and spiritual life and mark your influence at all the important ascensions (in Vidler 1970, 125).

Tyrrell was probably the closest to von Hügel of all the modernists. They saw each other frequently, and von Hügel had a profound influence on Tyrrell's life and work.

GEORGE TYRRELL'S MODERNIST VISION

L'Evangile et l'Eglise contained a modest program of perhaps necessary reforms; Tyrrell's work is a prophecy of revolution; both may rest together in the graveyard of heresies.
—Alfred Loisy, *Mémoires*

Despite differences in how they resolved their ambivalence in their respective lives, coupled with a lack of personal contact, Loisy and Tyrrell were inextricably bound together at the center of the modernist movement.[26] The strength of Tyrrell's religious beliefs may have enabled him to be bolder in his criticism of the church than the more cautious Loisy. Also significant were the differences between French and English Catholicism, differences in personality, and the fact that Tyrrell, unlike Loisy or von Hügel, was a convert to Catholicism.

Whereas Loisy was cautious and had, at least at first, some faith in the receptivity of his work by church authorities, Tyrrell was radically critical of the church hierarchy early in the history of the modernist movement. Even Tyrrell's critics believed that he was consistent and sincere. Tyrrell wrote to von Hügel claiming to be[27]

still young and inexperienced enough to marvel at the fatal blindness that makes
Rome devour her most serviceable children, not in exceptional deliria of purposed
fear but steadily and systematically so that honestly and unequivocally the Church
seems to be invariably on the wrong side.

The papal condemnation of modernism eradicated Loisy's involvement in the movement. Tyrrell maintained that the church was greater
than its leadership at any given moment in history, however, and "died
professing to defend Catholic principles against the Vatican heresies"
(Vidler 1934, 181). In 1908, Tyrrell claimed that the strength of

the present wave of revolt . . . is spent, and we now need a period of quiet to
gather force for a greater and further effort. In eliciting *Lamentabili* and *Pascendi*
and the mad decrees of the Biblical Commission the present struggle has set the
old system on a path of self-destruction from which there is no return. (Tyrrell
1920, 117–118)

An Anglican by birth and raised in a poor family, Tyrrell later converted to Catholicism and became a Jesuit and a scholastic theologian—a
fact which contains more than a little irony, since the Jesuits came to represent everything in Roman Catholicism to which he was opposed.[28] Tyrrell
was beset with difficulties early in his career, however, as he attempted
to hold opposing ideologies in tension (Schultenover 1981*b*, 48–49).
Throughout his career, his most important role was as a writer on spiritual
life. Yet his notion of that life was often at variance with official Roman
theology; it implied, as clearly as did Loisy's scientific historiography,
the necessity of far-reaching changes in the structure of the church. "I
feel my work is to hammer away at the great unwieldly carcass of the
Roman communion and wake it up from its medieval dreams," Tyrrell
wrote. Thus, he, like Loisy, was interested in "a synthesis of catholicism
and Science—not the supremacy of the latter" (Tyrrell [1908] 1920, 119).
Tyrrell wrote in a lucid, polemical style filled with analogies and
metaphors. After being impressed by A. D. White's work, *A History of
the Warfare of Science with Theology in Christendom* (1896–97), Tyrrell
told von Hügel:[29]

White's volumes (now finished) convince me that theology will pursue its
course of destruction until at last its own presuppositions and raison d'etre are
brought into the controversy. Alice took the Wonderland Court-trial seriously
until she remembered that after all her judges were but a pack of cards. Of late
it has all come home to me in that form. It is not their red robes but my own
judgment about them that gives the pack of Cardinals any title to my consideration. Like Elizabeth, it has frocked them and can unfrock them.

Situations which are defined as real are real in their consequences, yet social definitions and structures are human constructions and are therefore amenable to change. This is precisely the lesson that was learned from historiographic studies—namely, that the church was a human product, that it had changed through time and was susceptible to processes of adaptation.

It was Tyrrell's devotional book, *Nova et Vetera* (1897), that attracted the attention of von Hügel, who initiated the relationship between them. Von Hügel increased Tyrrell's awareness of the need for more precise thinking, producing a considerable impact on his intellectual career.[30] Whereas Loisy attempted to separate theology and history, leaving the theological implications of his work largely unexpressed, Tyrrell boldly addressed the relationship between the two. Under von Hügel's influence, he became interested in historical criticism and spent a great deal of time studying the critical scholars.

Tyrrell taught for a while shortly after entering the Jesuits, but ironically, it was his excessive (although unorthodox) scholasticism that led to his dismissal from the chair of philosophy at St. Mary's Hall in Stonyhurst.[31] He was sent to join a staff of Jesuit writers at Farm Street in London, where he prepared a number of articles for the Jesuit periodical, *The Month*. The early Tyrrell advocated a return to Thomas as a method, not as a compendium of doctrines, believing that Thomas provided an appropriate model if interpreted in a flexible manner, as Tyrrell believed Thomas had intended. In Thomas's work Tyrrell found hope for uniting the causes of liberty and authority (Schultenover 1981*b*, 37).

Tyrrell's dissatisfaction even with a flexible scholasticism grew, and he went through a period between 1897 and 1900 which Petre has labeled "mediating liberalism." He criticized scholasticism cautiously at first, in an article entitled "The Relation of Theology to Devotion" (see Tyrrell 1899). In a manner similar to Loisy's distinction between religious faith and the official theology of the church, Tyrrell argued that the major purpose of metaphysical or natural theology is not to give us any more comprehensible idea of God; rather, "it impresses upon us the necessary inadequacy of our human way of regarding Him" (1901, I:234). Theology, therefore, is merely a way of thinking about religion: "devotion and religion existed before theology, in the way that art existed before art-criticism" (ibid., I:252). Scholastic theology was not to be confused with the Catholic faith.

Jesuit authorities in England initially had no quarrel with the article, but it was quite the opposite in Rome. Tyrrell was required to write a "clarification" of his article—entitled "A Perverted Devotion"—which appeared in *The Month* in December 1899. His writing liberties were radically curtailed, and shortly thereafter he was relieved of his responsibilities as a leader of religious retreats. He then moved to a small Jesuit mission in Richmond (Yorkshire), where he quietly wrote articles that he published anonymously, a practice which later alienated some of his English supporters. Tyrrell also wrote to a future audience, convinced that "some day what is written in darkness will be brought to light."[32] In 1902 the authorities censored Tyrrell's *Oil and Wine* ([1902] 1907), and eventually the conflict with Jesuit authorities came to a head. Following his "Letter to a Professor," printed for private circulation early in 1904 and published in 1906 as *A Much-Abused Letter*, he was dismissed from the Society.

The controversial letter became one of Tyrrell's best-known works (Petre 1912, II:196). In it, he counseled a "professor of anthropology" to distinguish between official Catholicism and a "yet unformulated Catholicism" in the making, which would help meet the intellectual difficulties created by scientific historiography (Tyrrell 1906*a*).

Although von Hügel provided the most decisive intellectual influence on Tyrrell's thought,[33] and it was through Tyrrell that Loisy's work became important,[34] Tyrrell was also influenced by the pragmatist William James, Arthur James (later Lord) Balfour, and Matthew Arnold (especially Arnold's *Literature and Dogma*). The relationship between science and dogma was the theme that dominated much of his thought and work (see Root 1977). Efforts by scholastic theologians to dominate scientific research by extrascientific motives, Tyrrell wrote, had led to

the very embarrassing admission that, as a fact, science and religion are mutually hostile, that candor and freedom of enquiry are dangerous to faith. To thus have falsified one of the first principles of morality, which tells us that conscience and truth are inseparable allies; to have perverted conscientiousness into a cause of mental darkness rather than of light, is the deadliest fruit of the dogmatic fallacy. (Tyrrell 1907, 224–225)

Tyrrell was convinced of the Catholicity of his work, whatever the opinions of the current Roman authorities. Despite the position of the Catholic authorities, Tyrrell continued to believe, as he wrote in a letter in 1907, that "the compatibility of freedom and authority, of science and revelation, is surely a most essential and fundamental Catholic principle" (Tyrrell 1920, 133).

Tyrrell drew upon Loisy's work in his final and most comprehensive work, *Christianity at the Crossroads* ([1909] 1910). He first attacks "liberal Protestantism, with its bland faith and hope in the present order, its refusal to face the incurable tragedy of human life" (ibid., 95). Tyrrell objected to the view of Jesus as a great human being, developed by

Protestant theologians as a way of reinterpreting Christianity for modern skeptics. Most Catholic modernists found the compromise untenable, and devoted much of their effort toward developing a solution to the "Christological problem" which would maintain both the humanity and the divinity of Jesus.

In the second section of *Christianity at the Crossroads,* Tyrrell explored the implications of the scientific study of religion to demonstrate the viability of Catholicism as a universal religion. That Catholicism of the future, however, was not to be the Catholicism now "in the grip of the exploiter"—namely, the Vatican bureaucracy which was strangling the church—but rather "Catholicism as a living and lived religion" (ibid., 280). Tyrrell's vision was more comprehensive than Loisy's. He was more concerned with interpreting the implications of science than with its actual practice. Both Tyrrell and Loisy were in agreement on one thing, however: the necessity of substituting for the official theology one which took full account of the facts disclosed by historical criticism. Following Loisy's disillusionment with Catholicism, his excommunication from the church, and von Hügel's increased caution, Tyrrell became the central spokesperson for what was left of the modernist movement.[35]

PHILOSOPHICAL MODERNISM

Von Hügel considered himself a philosopher of religion and approached the modernist crisis with a broad knowledge of modern philosophy and its problems (see Heaney 1969, 150). He was personally acquainted with the neo-Hegelian Edward Caird in Britain, the neo-idealist Rudolf Eucken in Germany, as well as LeRoy, Laberthonnière, and Blondel in France. Although they were adversaries of scholastic philosophy, and tended to work on the problems they found by means of an historical-scientific approach, most of the modernists were informed by modern philosophy as well.

It was natural, then, that both von Hügel and Tyrrell followed with interest the work of what Vidler has termed "philosophical modernism." There is some debate about the validity of designating French philosophers Laberthonnière, LeRoy, and especially Blondel as modernists. All were concerned with modernist issues, however, and each made a contribution to a growing reaction against the scholastic hegemony in Catholic intellectual matters which was being fostered by the Holy See. Whether or not they were actually modernists (for no one accepted the papal definition of modernism) is not of concern here, but the way in which their work related to modernism is.

A religious philosopher on the faculty of the Collège Stanislas, Blondel (1861–1949) was scandalized by the rationalistic attitudes in the philosophical milieu at the Ecole Normale Supérieure, in which the possibility of the validity of supernatural truth was out of the question.[36] Yet he was equally critical of the scholastic establishment, and would accept neither the inevitability of the split between philosophy and Christianity in France nor the "extrinsicism" of scholastic philosophy. "Do they think," Blondel wrote, "that they can dispose of a Hegel or a Bergson with a few stupid remarks or scornful outbursts?" (in Lubac 1957–1965, I:70–71).

In his thesis at the Sorbonne, *L'Action: Essai d'une critique de la vie et d'une science de la pratique* (1893), Blondel developed an approach to philosophy designed to appeal to the philosophers of the Sorbonne, while not denying Catholic concerns for transcendent truth. He began, as his title indicates, with human action as a basis for his philosophy—that is, as "the point on which the powers of Nature, the light of the understanding, the strength of the will and even the benefits of grace converge" ([1893] 1970, 196).

Blondel developed a "method of immanence," a term which he adopted from his philosophical critics. Although he was fairly successful in satisfying many of his philosophical critics—the audience for whom his *Letter on Apologetics* (1896) was written—he sparked a controversy among the scholastic theologians, which illustrated the scholastics' isolation from their contemporary culture (Haight 1974, 638). Ironically, Blondel's attempts to develop a Catholic apologetic were more favorably received by nonreligious philosophers than they were by the scholastics. His work aroused such a storm that, plagued with self-doubt and rumors that people were pressing for his condemnation in Rome, he withdrew from public debate of the apologetic question.[37]

Lucien Laberthonnière, a young French Oratorian dissatisfied with scholasticism, read *L'Action* in 1894 and wrote to Blondel saying, "for my part, I don't even dare tell you all the values I see in your book, lest I appear given to exaggeration" (Blondel and Laberthonnière 1961, 66). Laberthonnière entered the debate in defense of Blondel's method with an influential article, "Le problem religieus," in the *Annales de philosophie crétienne* (1897), an important publication of which Laberthonnière became editor in 1905, while Blondel was the secret owner (Blondel and Valensin 1957, I:175–181). The *Annales,* a distinguished journal with a long history, became an organ for the dissemination of Blondel's method of immanence and of progressive Catholic work until its suppression by ecclesiastical authorities in 1913.[38] Debate over the apologetic question was a prelude to the modernist crisis and was addressed by a number of scholars, including Ollé-Laprune, Fonsegrive, Bremond, and others (Haight 1974, 642). Such efforts were often associated with movements of political liberalism and Catholic action. Laberthonnière's involvement with the French Catholic democratic student movement—the Sillon, for example—did not seem incongruent with his philosophical endeavors.

In the second phase of philosophical modernism, questions of apologetics and the biblical question of scientific criticism began to dovetail (ibid.). In his controversy with Loisy over historical and theological methods, Blondel complained that Loisy's limiting of Jesus's consciousness was a negation of Jesus's divinity. In his critique of Loisy, "Histoire et dogme" (1904), Blondel attempted to steer a course between two positions that he rejected—what he called Loisy's "historicism," and scholastic "extrinsicism."[39] Blondel wished to bring about a reform in Catholic thought by contrasting his alternative to more radical reforms, a technique used frequently by reformers who wish to appear moderate and thus ingratiate themselves with the power structure. Blondel's objection to extrinsicism is that faith is imposed upon the passive believer authoritatively from the outside, while historicism, operating purely on an empirical and positive level, distorts the religious or transcendental character of religious events (Haight 1974, 645–646; cf. Barmann 1972, 122).

Much confusion was created by the character of the controversies of this period. Whereas apologetic or theological questions can be theoretically distinct from historical questions, they are practically interrelated. Theology has an ahistorical tendency that was caricatured in nineteenth-century scholasticism. Loisy's historical work had theological implications that could hardly be avoided, just as the theology of any period is to some extent determined by the historical context in which it is formed. Even "Loisy himself was scandalized by his own conclusions," and he attempted to unite a history and doctrine that were seemingly irreconcilable (Haight 1974, 648). Blondel was shocked by Loisy's historical methods; he could not comprehend scientific scriptural exegesis. As a result, the historicism of which Blondel accused Loisy was, as Haight contends, a misinterpretation based upon a misunderstanding of the nature of Loisy's task.

It is ironic that while theology and history were being defined as more distinct than ever before in the history of Catholicism, with the adoption of ahistorical scholasticism as an official theology, the theologians and the historians collided. Unfortunately, their respective worlds and languages were so far removed that even someone as clearly anti-scholastic as Blondel could not appreciate the biblical historians' work.

The third question raised by philosophical modernism concerns the nature of dogma, which was dealt with primarily by LeRoy. There were many similarities between LeRoy's and Loisy's concepts, although they were developed independently and Loisy was skeptical of the worth of any philosophical endeavor (Loisy 1930–31, II:381, 447). LeRoy received his doctorate in 1898 in mathematics, turning to philosophy and later succeeding his mentor, Henri Bergson, in his chair of philosophy at the Collège de France and in the Academie Français. LeRoy's work on the nature of dogma was his most significant contribution to modernism, particularly two works—a 1905 article, "Qu'est-ce qu'un dogme?" and *Dogme et Critique* (1907). His philosophy was a reaction against a twofold enemy: scientism, in the sense of the argument that there is no real knowledge outside of the exact sciences; and idealism, which limits and determines reality by means of abstract, notional, or intellectualistic logic (Haight 1974, 652; Gillet 1964, 530–533).

A philosophical pragmatist,[40] LeRoy followed Blondel in stressing the primacy of action. The meaning of a truth is to be judged by its consequences and the services it renders—that is, "by the vivifying influence which it exercises over the whole body of knowledge" to which it is related (LeRoy 1907, 58). The importance of a dogma lies not in some sense of its innate authority (as the Roman hierarchy claimed) but in its function in establishing the boundaries of the faith for a community of people. "First of all—unless I am mistaken," LeRoy argues, "dogma has a negative sense. It excludes and condemns certain errors rather than determines truth in any positive way" (ibid., 201). Religious dogmas thus become guidelines for a belief system that is to be lived, rather than a coherent system of propositions to which one is to give unequivocal intellectual adherence:

> Christianity indeed—as it cannot too often be repeated—is not a scheme of speculative philosophy but a source and a rule of life, a discipline of moral and religious action—in short, a body of practical means for gaining salvation. Why then, should there by anything very surprising in saying that dogmas related primarily to conduct rather than to purely reflective knowledge? (LeRoy 1907, 206)

LeRoy's position was a restatement of an ancient understanding of the nature of dogma as a *via negativa*—an understanding almost entirely forgotten in the absolutist conflicts in which the church was embroiled at the time (Vidler 1965, 54). The Holy See's intervention in matters of theology resulted in the extension of dogmas to unprecedented spheres. LeRoy's view of dogma helped to establish a philosophical position from which one could accept Loisy's critical studies without a concomitant loss of faith. For LeRoy, dogmas were not absolute truths, but guidelines for action. LeRoy found Loisy's work helpful and wrote to him when Loisy was excommunicated, telling him how much he and others were indebted to Loisy for having fortified their faith.[41]

LeRoy's relationship with Blondel and Laberthonnière was an uneasy alliance, although LeRoy contributed frequently to the *Annales*. LeRoy also participated in a discussion group, the Société d'Etudes Religieuse, which was founded by Laberthonnière in January of 1905 and met at his residence. The group included a number of Blondel's close friends, although Blondel was not himself involved because he was not living in Paris. In April of 1906, Laberthonnière's *Essais de philosophie religieuse* and *Le Réalisme chrétien* were both placed on the *Index*. Some members of the Blondel circle held LeRoy—who was the least circumspect among them—responsible for the condemnation, claiming that his "recklessness" drew the attention of the authorities to Laberthonnière. In 1906, LeRoy published a long, controversial article on the notion of miracle that displeased Blondel immensely. Both Blondel and Laberthonnière began to distance themselves from him.

The philosophical modernists, particularly through LeRoy, were integrally related to the von Hügel–Loisy–Tyrrell end of the movement, and both English and Italian modernists drew upon their thought. Von Hügel corresponded with LeRoy, Laberthonnière, and Blondel, and Tyrrell recognized a number of affinities between his own work and LeRoy's.[42] One of LeRoy's more well-known statements is reminiscent of Tyrrell's vision of a new Catholicism: "The time of *partial heresies* has gone by. . . . We no longer deny one dogma rather than another. . . . It is the idea of dogma itself that raises opposition and objections" (in Petre 1918, 37).

Just as von Hügel played a pivotal role in linking together many of the different aspects of modernist thought, so LeRoy provided a link between the philosophical modernists and the "sociopolitical modernists," through his relationship to Marc Sangnier and the Sillon.

SANGNIER AND THE SILLON

The charismatic figure of Marc Sangnier, an engaging young man from a wealthy and distinguished French Catholic family, began to stir the interest of many a student at the Collège Stanislas during the 1890s. His forceful enthusiasm aroused hopes for reconciling his two loves, the French Republic and the Roman Catholic Church. The ranks of enthusiasts swelled; by the end of 1903, the association of French workers and students known as the Sillon ("The Furrow") had spread throughout

France, its most important groups being in Nancy, Epinal, Belfort, Bordeaux, Rouhaix, Lyon, Tours, Limoges, and Orléans. Meetings of the Sillon created a charge of intense intimacy, drawing 450 delegates in Belfort in May of 1903, and 2,000 in Paris the following February (Dansette 1961, II:274–275).

The Sillonists were characterized not by intellectual reformulations, but by a fervent dedication, as progressive Catholics, to active participation in the formation of democratic France. As one participant put it,

> We felt a great need to talk to one another about all these ardent desires that were burning in our hearts . . . to form and maintain ourselves a sort of common soul . . . to prepare ourselves for the great battles ahead by a sort of fraternal vigil of arms. . . . In this small room . . . mysteriously hidden underground . . . the crowd of us used to dash jostling one another, with this thrilling sensation of a great task to be undertaken. (in Caron 1966, 55–60)

Forming small study groups, opening reading rooms, and uniting students, middle-class, and working people, the Sillon stimulated the discussion of various social problems. This movement is important to Catholic modernism for at least three reasons. First, it demonstrated the large amount of ambivalence and discontent experienced by young Catholics toward the end of the nineteenth century. Second, the modernists themselves admired the Sillon and abhorred its eventual condemnation. LeRoy and Laberthonnière were directly involved with the movement, and Mignot attempted to rally support for it among the bishops. "I have been in close contact with a number of Sillonists," Mignot wrote to Loisy, "and I have always admired them for their simple faith, their generosity, their devotion, and their piety which is infinitely superior to that of the *Jeunesse Catholique.*"[43]

Finally, and most important, the growth and suppression of the Sillonist movement demonstrated that the issue of papal authority and the status of conservative members of the ecclesiastical hierarchy had become a major test of the orthodoxy of any Catholic group. Political democracy was considered dangerous because it was undermining the authority of the papacy and the episcopacy.

The Sillonists were drawn primarily to Sangnier's charismatic leadership, and the group never developed any formal structure. The movement gradually became politicized, however—a development which Vidler (1970, 202–205) attributes to five factors. First, the movement expanded and its members grew old enough to become involved in public affairs. Second, there were no existing political blocs that they could support. The movement arose at the time of the Dreyfus affair, when little middle ground existed in French politics; the right was conservative, the left anticlerical and intolerant. Third, the Sillonist conception of democracy became more intellectually precise and more viable for shaping a democratic political movement. Fourth, the Sillon's increasing involvement with the trade union movement led to more specific political goals. The Sillonists were in sympathy with socialism and looked forward to the end of the capitalist system, but were opposed to an overthrow by violent means. Fifth, agitation for specific issues led to the desire for a republican party.

Roman authorities were initially rather supportive of the movement; for the first time in decades, a widespread enthusiasm for the church was emerging among French youth. Following Pius X's succession to the papacy in 1903, the Sillonists turned to Rome for continued affirmation of their work, and they received it. Sangnier and a group of twenty were received by Pius X in 1903, and in the following year six hundred Sillonists made a pilgrimage to Rome. Sangnier's address was received warmly by the pope, who kissed the flag of the French Republic.

Many of the church's conservatives were aghast at the Sillon's success in courting the pope's favor, and began to undermine the movement. The Sillonists' democratic ideologies did not fit the church's model of authority. The most formidable opposition came from the integralist Action Française, a reactionary organization of opponents to all forms of modernism and democracy which was led by Charles Maurras.[44] Action Française members began to attack the Sillon and Sangnier in the Catholic press, claiming that the Sillonists were weakening the spirit of absolute submission to the church hierarchy and threatening the bases of power upon which the church was founded. Following the 1907 condemnation of modernism, the Catholic right began to attack the Sillon on doctrinal grounds, charging that Sangnier was "theologically unsound and did not believe in hell" (Vidler 1970, 212).

Following an article criticizing the Sillon in the official part of the *Osservatore Romano*, Mignot recognized the gravity of the situation. In January 1910 he tried to rally episcopal opinion in France that was favorable to the Sillon. Finally, the inevitable came, in a letter sent to the archbishops and bishops of France on 25 August 1910. As Loisy wrote in his *Mémoires,*

> Pope Pius X, who pursued all genres of modernism, condemned social modernism by striking against the Sillon. . . . Of all the inauspicious acts perpetrated under the reign of Pius X, the condemnation of the *Sillon* was the most odious. (Loisy 1930–31, III:194)

Sangnier immediately submitted to the pope's condemnation, and the Sillon ceased to exist. Consistent with his cautious behavior toward ecclesiastical authorities throughout the history of the movement, Sangnier had no intention of challenging the pope's decision. But while in France political modernism was rather clearly distinguished from doctrinal modernism, in Italy the causes were closely intertwined.

THE ITALIAN RESPONSE

> "But what manner of faith is yours!" he exclaimed excitedly, "if you talk of deserting the Church because you are displeased with certain antiquated doctrines of her rules, with certain decrees of the Roman congregations, with certain tendencies in the government by a Pontiff? What manner of sons are you who talk of denying your mother because her dress is not to your taste? Can a dress change the maternal bosom?"
>
> —Fogazzaro's Benedetto, in *Il Santo*

Baron von Hügel urged Loisy to maintain contact with his Italian friends; Loisy's writings were extremely popular in Italy, and von Hügel was convinced that his Italian supporters could provide support at the Vatican, help alleviate the scholar's sense of isolation, and serve as spiritual guides. Modernism in Italy was a widespread, populist movement. Through their connection with von Hügel—and because of their alienation from the Roman-dominated religious culture of Italy—the Italians incorporated aspects of modernist thought and philosophical pragmatism, thus providing more of a synthesis than an original movement of thought. There was much originality in their synthesis, however, and Italian modernism was a powerful, multifaceted movement.

Whereas in France modernism developed "in the silence of libraries and studies," in Italy it was inseparable from mass action and propaganda, and from a desire for emancipation from ecclesiastical authority (Poulat 1962, 18). In Italy, political and religious modernism were more closely related than in France. Some attempts took place to separate political modernism from the movement toward the reform of religious culture— which was represented by the young Italian priest Ernesto Buonaiuti, Salvatore Minocchi, and the prominent novelist and statesman Antonio Fogazzaro (cf. Poulat 1962, 14; Ranchetti 1969, 131–133)—but the two groups were periodically drawn together and usually maintained contact.

Ranchetti (1969) suggests that the Italian modernist movement consisted of three phases, beginning with a textual criticism phase, in which Loisy's writings were the dominant influence. Von Hügel and Minocchi brought a number of young Italian Catholics into historiographic studies.

After Loisy's censure in 1903, the movement entered a philosophical phase, which was centered primarily around the writings of Tyrrell, Buonaiuti, and LeRoy. Finally, there was a political phase in which, despite their heterogeneity, many of the modernists were drawn together around the journal *Il Rinnovamento*.

Murri and Buonaiuti were frequently at odds, however, which resulted in two parallel movements—the Christian Democracy of Murri, and the religious modernism of Buonaiuti. Buonaiuti's first article was a critique of Murri's sociopolitical modernism, in the form of an open letter to Murri published in *Cultura sociale* in 1901. In his journal, *Studi religiosi*, Minocchi began sensitizing Italian scholars to developments in historical scholarship, which he considered the new center of religious discussion.

ITALIAN HISTORICAL STUDIES

> We must start teaching at once, not within the seminaries, which were closed to us through the fear and envy of those same ignorant old men, made presumptuous by their following within the Church; but through the press.
> —Salvatore Minocchi, *Memoirs*

When Minocchi arrived in Rome to study at the end of the century, he found an undercurrent of new thought emerging. His experience was parallel to Loisy's migration from provincial France to Paris. In his memoirs, Minocchi wrote that students in Rome at the time were steeped in an examination of philosophy, theology, historical and biblical studies. Leo XIII had precipitated a revival of intellectual life in Rome, but for Minocchi and others, that new intellectual vigor did not have its intended effect. "Modernism had already begun," he wrote, and

we gradually found it hard to reconcile present-day scientific thought with what we were learning, or to achieve the age-old harmony between science and faith, when confined to the Procrustean bed of dogma, within the limitations of the theological ideas of the Father and the philosophy of Saint Thomas. (in Ranchetti 1969, 82–83)

A friend gave Minocchi the first issues of Loisy's *L'Enseignement biblique,* and at the Fribourg International Catholic Scientific Congress in 1897, Minocchi's hopes for a reform movement were kindled. Papers by Lagrange and von Hügel (the latter read by Giovanni Semeria)[45] were applauded enthusiastically by those in attendance and made a great impression on Minocchi.

Although he attempted to maintain a course of circumspect moderation, Minocchi's reviews—*Revista bibliografica italiana* (1896–1899) and
Studi religiosi (1901–1907)—introduced the work of Loisy, Houtin, Tyrrell, Harnack, and Blondel to Italian religious thinkers. For the young
Minocchi, the conflict between the Roman Church and the modern world
was a generational conflict; the older generation did not understand that
the world had changed or that the new generation could re-create Catholic
thought. Minocchi gathered around him young men who had similar
dreams, one of the most important of whom was Ernesto Buonaiuti,
whose 1904 articles in the *Studi religiosi* were on Herbert Spencer's work
from the religious point of view, and on the development of neo-Thomism
at the University of Louvain.

Like Minocchi, Buonaiuti had been caught up in the intellectual
rejuvenation of Leo XIII's papacy, only to have his hopes shattered.
"Long and painful were those periods of perplexity through which we
passed when honest scientific research first brought down about our ears
the artificial structure of the scholastic interpretation of Catholicism,"
he wrote (Buonaiuti 1908, 170).[46] Buonaiuti and his progressive Italian
colleagues nonetheless could not ignore scholasticism; on the contrary,
they had to come to grips with neo-Thomism and "find a new syntheses,"
which they tried to formulate and impart "to our brethren, to whom the
language of scholasticism has become permanently and incurably incom-
prehensible" (ibid., 171). Buonaiuti thus turned to the history of the
thought of Thomas Aquinas, who had himself been

distrusted at first by his colleagues and superiors on account of his Aristotelian
sympathies. . . . Saint Thomas was thus the true Modernist of his time, the man
who strove with marvelous perseverance and genius to harmonise his faith with
the thought of that day. And we are the true successors of the scholastics in all
that was valuable in their work—in their keen sense of the adaptability of the
Christian religion to the ever-changing forms of philosophy and general culture.
(Buonaiuti 1908, 168)

For Buonaiuti, the crisis in Catholicism went far beyond any generational differences perceived by Minocchi. His response was not to denounce modern thought, but to see in it the possibility for a renewal of
Catholic thought. The destruction of Thomistic theology and philosophy—and the inflexibility of the Roman hierarchy—were merely the "dis-
appearance of an idol that has hypnotized too many souls. . . . All the
skeptical and brutal philosophy of monism and immanentism has worked
for us" (Buonaiuti 1908, 214). Buonaiuti sought a living religion that
was freed from the rigidity of official Catholicism. A Catholic science of

historical criticism could facilitate the process of freeing "true Catholicism" from its Vatican prison.

In 1903, however, Loisy's works were placed on the *Index of Prohibited Books,* and the cautious Buonaiuti and his friends turned elsewhere for inspiration. Without rejecting historical criticism, Buonaiuti moved toward Tyrrell's work and discovered in pragmatism an alternative to scholasticism. Buonaiuti identified with Tyrrell's "Letter to a Professor," in which Tyrrell wrote that one must leave the church if faith was simply a matter of mental assent to official theology. In moving from Loisy toward Tyrrell, the Italians failed to note the extent to which Tyrrell's thought drew upon Loisy, but they found in Tyrrell and LeRoy hope for a new formulation that would enable them to overcome the "historicistic rationalism" of the censured Loisy, by speaking not of the relative but of the developmental character of truth, more along the lines of Newman's doctrine of development.[47]

LeRoy's 1905 essay on dogma provided a turning point for the philosophically trained Buonaiuti and the group gathered around his review, *Nova et vetera.* Speaking as a layperson, LeRoy took for granted the freedom of science in the formulation of ideas. The Italian modernists, like LeRoy and Tyrrell, saw in pragmatism a philosophical approach that provided an attractive alternative to scholasticism.

Buonaiuti did not accept pragmatism uncritically, however; he did not wish merely to jump from one philosophical straitjacket into another. He declared emphatically that the presupposition of modernism is not a philosophy at all, but the critical method itself, which has

of its own accord, forced us to a very tentative and uncertain formulation of various philosophical conclusions, or better still, to a clearer exposition of certain ways of thinking to which Catholic apology has never been wholly a stranger. This independence of our criticism in respect to our purely tentative philosophy is evident in many ways. (Buonaiuti 1908, 15–16)

FOGAZZARO'S SAINT AND THE LAY REFORM

The famous poet and statesman Antonio Fogazzaro (1842–1911) articulated the new ideas of the Italian reformers, bringing them to life in the characters of his novels. Fogazzaro was acutely aware of the rift between the two cultures of the scientific community and official Catholicism. In the midst of a controversy over lectures he had given on a religious interpretation of the theory of evolution, Fogazzaro responded to a critic in the *Civiltà cattolica,*[48]

Of necessity we mix more than you do with the enemies of Christ and of the Church. The proudest, most intelligent, and most famous of these today agree in proclaiming the ruin of our faith through a scientific hypothesis supported by the great majority of natural scientists.

Fogazzaro stood between the two cultures and was determined to retain the best from both of them. He was soundly criticized in the *Civiltà cattolica* and elsewhere for having the audacity as a layperson to speak out on matters that were the exclusive province of the clergy. It was the laity, however, which seemed to Fogazzaro most capable of wresting the Catholic faith from the Roman establishment.

The hero of Fogazzaro's *Il Santo* (*The Saint*) was a layman, Benedetto, a saint who set out to reform the church and struggled with the agony of that task. In the story of Benedetto and his followers, the modernist movement comes alive in an Italian setting. In *Il Santo*, Benedetto's reputation spreads throughout the countryside and he gathers followers wherever he goes, speaking of a religious revival that will recognize two aspects of the church—the hierarchy and the laity.

According to Benedetto, the distinction between official Catholicism and the Catholicism of the modernist vision is similar to the difference between the clergy and the laity; it is also analogous to the distinction between the conscious and subconscious parts of the mind. Official Catholicism has its place, and Benedetto speaks of it with respect, but it is only one aspect of the church and cannot completely dominate it. Benedetto makes a pilgrimage to Rome where, in an audience with the pope, he appeals to the pontiff to heal the four wounds of the church—the spirits of falsehood, clerical domination, avarice, and immobility (see Fogazzaro [1904] 1906, ix).

As Fogazzaro wrote, "Benedetto, the Saint, is a new character in fiction, a mingling of Saint Francis and Dr. Döllinger, a man of today in intelligence and medieval in faith" (ibid., viii). *Il Santo* was an immediate success among Catholic progressives—and an immediate object of attack by the antimodernists. Although the *Civiltà cattolica* did not deny the book's literary merits or ignore Fogazzaro's growing reputation, an anonymous reviewer expressed regrets "that such a gifted writer . . . should have betrayed our expectations." Furthermore, the reviewer charged, Fogazzaro was thoroughly mistaken in his thesis: "It is not the Church that needs reforming, but rather society, which fails to listen to the Church, denies God, disregards his laws, and plunges into the most corrupt materialism and the most dreadful anarchy" (in Ranchetti 1969, 157). This review is revealing in the concerns it expresses. The real fear is one of anarchy, and for the Roman hierarchy anarchy was, by definition, disobedience of the Holy Pontiff.

MURRI'S NATIONAL DEMOCRATIC LEAGUE

> Some remedy must be found, and quickly found, for the misery and wretchedness which press so heavily at this moment on the large majority of the very poor. . . . A small number of very rich men have been able to lay upon the masses of the poor a yoke little better than slavery itself. To remedy these evils the *Socialists,* working on the poor man's envy of the rich, endeavor to destroy private property. . . . But their proposals are so clearly futile for all practical purposes, that if they were carried out the working man himself would be among the first to suffer.
>
> —Leo XIII, *Rerum Novarum*

The Vatican was anxious to link the heretical movement to a political rebellion led by Romolo Murri (1870–1944). There were some important personal ties, as well as some significant affinities, between the two parallel movements.

When Murri was twenty-one years old, Leo XIII met the challenge of socialism with a counteroffensive against the conditions of workers in his encyclical, *Rerum Novarum.* The pope thus established a precedent for the development of the Catholic Action Movement which, under the direction of the pope, was to enable the church to provide leadership in the area of political reform. For a while it appeared that the Roman establishment would welcome the activity of young Catholic reformers like Murri. Such enthusiasm dried up quickly, however, and "Catholic socialism" was almost forgotten when Pius X issued the encyclical *Il fermo proposito* in June 1905. Addressing the bishops of Italy, the pope proposed that a Catholic action association be established "in order to combat anti-Christian civilizations with every just and legal means" available.

Murri was strongly opposed to the action, because Pius X wished to cultivate the church's alliance with conservative political forces, whereas Murri wished to ally himself with working-class movements. Murri was part of a growing international movement that was deliberately independent of papal political policies (see Fogarty 1957). Sangnier from France, Sonnenschein from Germany, Vercesi, Murri, and others met in Rome more than once to strategize and share ideas for political reform (see Bedeschi 1959, 84). Murri's first strategy was to claim to be the interpreter of Pius X's program, but later he declared the autonomy of his own movement. Pius X would not tolerate such audacity; in a letter to Cardinal Svampa of Bologna (1 March 1905) that was later made public, the pope declared,

The so-called autonomous Christian Democrats, through their wish for an ill-understood freedom, show that they have shaken off all discipline; they seek new and dangerous goals the Church cannot approve; they affect an authoritative manner in order to assert themselves, in order to judge and criticize everything. (in Ranchetti 1969, 154)

Despite his political progressiveness, Murri retained a theological conservatism. In a remark to Loisy, von Hügel described Murri as having "scholastic procedures beyond all hope, one of the least historical, least critical, least mystical, and least enquiring spirits" (Loisy 1930–31, II:561). After Loisy's *L'Evangile et l'Eglise* was put on the *Index* in 1903, Murri clearly differentiated his type of reform from Loisy's, maintaining (along with the scholar's critics) that "Loisy's book in answer to Harnack might, in the case of unwary Catholics, do more harm than Harnack himself" (Murri 1901–1904, III:183). By thus approving of Loisy's condemnation, Murri was trying to disassociate himself from heresy.

The ambiguity of Murri's relationship to the modernist movement continued, however. What united Murri's political reform and the Fogazzaro–Buonaiuti–von Hügel circle was their common opposition to papal absolutism. A few weeks after Murri was suspended from his priestly office (15 April 1907), von Hügel remarked that although "Murri's direct thinkings and temper of mind are far too absolute and theocratic for me, his opposition to the ever-increasing direct claims of the Pope and Bishops in Italy, in even simply political and social affairs, is, in its substance, at least, undeniably legitimate."[49] Although he quickly condemned modernism after *Pascendi* (Loisy 1930–31, II:561), Murri also participated, at least peripherally, in the group that formed around the important modernist review, *Il Rinnovamento,* founded in January of 1907.

IL RINNOVAMENTO

The publication of the first issue of *Il Rinnovamento* signaled the final phase of the modernist movement. If there was ever reason to believe in the creation of a unified, coordinated movement for reform in the church at the turn of the century, it was to be found in the group that gathered for a short time around this review. Contributing to the effort were all of the major forces of renewal involved in the modernist movement up to that point, brought together and coordinated by laity, in part because of the pressure being placed on the clergy. Von Hügel and Fogazzaro were the major inspiration for the new publication, and all three of its coeditors were laymen—Antonio Aiace Alfieri, Alessandro Casati, and Tommaso Gallarati Scotti.

Its pages included, first of all, Fogazzaro's Catholic spirituality and vision of a lay reform movement, a background factor that infused the group and the publication with its spirit. Second, there was a continued interest in criticism, maintained primarily by von Hügel and Stefano Jacini (see Ranchetti 1969, 182). By the time *Il Rinnovamento* was established, Loisy was already alienated from the hopes of the reformers, but was convinced by von Hügel to contribute (see Loisy 1930–31, III:42). Von Hügel himself also published Loisy's ideas in the journal, his major effort being a four-part article of more than 150 pages on Loisy's *Les Evangiles synoptiques*.

Il Rinnovamento's pages were also steeped in the philosophical pragmatism of Buonaiuti, writing under the pseudonym Paolo Baldini. Although Buonaiuti later clashed with the *Rinnovamento* group, he argued forcefully for a philosophical system that provided an alternative to scholasticism. Tyrrell's work also appeared in the journal, although only in translations of previously published articles, and not entirely with Tyrrell's approval. Despite Tyrrell's own radicalism, he became increasingly disturbed with the tenor of the Italian movement.

Part of the problem, from Tyrrell's point of view, was that the Italians were confusing religious reform with political reform and the Catholic Action Movement. "If it is only a question of social progress and educational reform," Tyrrell wrote to von Hügel, "the world can look after itself and I see no use in lugging religion into the business" (Petre 1912, II:350). Indeed, one strong influence in *Il Rinnovamento*'s pages was the political reform advocated by Murri and Gallarati Scotti, as well as "cultural news," which provided a critique of religious affairs and ideas in Europe (Ranchetti 1969, 182).

Although the *Rinnovamento* reformers were themselves primarily aristocrats, the new vision of Catholicism which they were forming was inspired both by the elite intellectuals and genteel culture of modern progressive thought on the one hand, and by the resurgence of a new form of Catholic populism on the other.

Il Rinnovamento was not to remain on the Italian ecclesiastical horizon for long, however; its tone and efforts to spread "heretical" ideas greatly distressed the Roman establishment, and on 4 May 1907, only five months after its first issue, Cardinal Steinhuber, the prefect of the Sacred Congregation of the Index, published a letter in the *Osservatore Romano* condemning the review. In it, he charged that *Il Rinnovamento* had "been founded with a view of fostering a most dangerous spirit of independence from the authority of the church and the supremacy of private judgment over that of the church herself and of erecting itself into a school to prepare an anti-Catholic renewal of minds" (in Barmann 1971, 183–185).

Although it continued publication for a time, *Il Rinnovamento* was finally repressed by the authorities in October of 1909. Von Hügel wrote to Petre that[50]

I must express . . . my deep piercing grief at the cessation thus of the only solidly scientific Catholic organ that remained to us, and of the *one* institution that, by its very existence, proved the possibility of a dignified, thoroughly Catholic limitation and thwarting of Curialist Absolutism. That, even in the midst of Fr. T[yrrell]'s going, the solid persistence of *Rinn.* had not, of course, directly consoled me in and for that irreparable loss, but still had left me feeling that a centre of work, a beacon-light remained, capable of eventual expansion. And now this too has gone!

Both Tyrrell and *Il Rinnovamento* were dead; with their passing, the modernist movement was essentially over. Efforts to resolve ambivalences by reforming the church had proved impossible. Before dealing systematically with the modernists' efforts to cultivate that movement—and with the hierarchy's tactics to thwart them—I will therefore examine the ambivalent context of the movement by looking at the spectrum of responses that developed among the modernist scholars.

4

Coping With Ambivalence

One can identify a spectrum of modernist responses to the ambivalence of their situations by beginning with Loisy, whose controversial career best exemplifies the modernists' dilemma. Ambivalence was particularly striking in Loisy's case because of his position and role in the movement, which gave him more visibility than many who faced similar uncertainties. It is helpful to compare Loisy's situation to those of others, ranging from the deliberate fraud perpetrated by the French priest Joseph Turmel—who lost his faith entirely but continued to function as a priest—to the American priests who resigned after the condemnation of modernism.

Between the two extremes are the cases of Mignot, Houtin, Petre, and many others. Mignot kept his carefully guarded modernist beliefs private, while publicly fostering an impression of orthodoxy as a bishop of the church. Houtin denounced Catholicism, continued to wear the priestly garb, and criticized those who attempted to stay within the church while rejecting official Catholic doctrines. Petre never hid her modernism from anyone, but contended that it was compatible with Catholicism, even after modernism had been condemned.

AMBIVALENCE IN ALFRED LOISY'S
MODERNIST CAREER

Alfred Loisy's life, career, and work created a storm that has not abated forty years after his death. His own friends and supporters developed complex and often contradictory viewpoints concerning Loisy. Subsequent historical accounts, including his own *Mémoires* (1930–31) and Houtin and Sartiaux's *Vie de Loisy* (1960), have failed to resolve what Vidler has called "the enigma of Abbé Loisy."[1]

A major issue is whether or not Loisy lost his faith early in his career and was an impostor by the time his *L'Evangile et l'Eglise* (1903) was published. Both defenders of Loisy's faith and his opponents can find substantiation for their positions in Loisy's own *Chose passées* (1913) and *Mémoires* (1930–31). Historians, friends, and opponents of Loisy have far too often attempted to resolve the enigma on psychological or theological grounds. Although the issue can never be finally resolved, some progress can be made by examining what is known about his career and faith in light of Merton and Barber's (1976) concept of sociological ambivalence. What emerges is not so much an individual phenomenon restricted to Loisy as a social phenomenon built into the structure of his status—and that of many others who were subject to the same ambivalence to varying degrees. That the ambivalence was more striking for Loisy was due as much to his position and role in the reform movement as to his personality and character.

First, ambivalence arose out of his status as both priest and critic, a matter that Bremond first elaborated upon—under the pseudonym Sylvain LeBlanc—in *Un clerc qui n'a pas trahi* (1931).[2] As a biblical critic, Loisy was subjected to the norms of objectivity, skepticism, and scientific inquiry; as a priest, he was subject to antiscientific demands made by the Roman establishment. Loisy continued to identify himself as both a priest and a scholar, as the tombstone inscription that he requested at his death in 1940 shows.[3] Bremond contended that Loisy did not allow either vocation to lead him to betray the other; they were parallel careers that were not opposed to one another, despite the conflicting demands that they sometimes presented.

Ambivalence was created for Loisy by the very nature of professional occupations—an ambivalence which was exacerbated by the historical conflicts in which it occurred. Loisy's professional life was a complex combination of shifting relationships between professionals and clients, in which at times one party was the professional and the other the client, whereas at other times the roles were reversed. As a priestly savant teaching at the Institut Catholique, Loisy had two sets of clients—his students, and the ecclesiastical organization as represented by the church hierarchy. Yet the ecclesiastical hierarchy (his bishops, the Roman congregations, and, ultimately, the pope) were also professionals who sometimes treated Loisy as though he were a client. Not only did they hire Loisy to train clergy for the church but they were themselves professionals on whom

Loisy was dependent for religious guidance. This complicated situation compounded the ambivalence normally present in professional–client relationships.

Another source of ambivalence came from the long-term nature of the relationship between a priest and the church, which involves the accumulation of ambivalence over time. The priestly vow is intended to be a lifelong commitment by both the priest and the institution. There were clear signs at the beginning of Loisy's career that his services would be unsatisfactory to the hierarchy. Loisy later questioned why he was not told to follow some other route, and given a parish or some other task, rather than being expected to continue in the difficult role of priestly savant. The church, however, had invested in Loisy's academic training, both in terms of financial resources spent on his schooling and in terms of expectations. The hierarchy was hesitant to break the "contract" that had been made. Similarly, although there were rumors as early as 1903 that Loisy's excommunication was imminent, it did not occur until five years later, and even then, only after last-minute appeals.[4]

Another source of ambivalence arises from the special competence of a professional, which tends to result in the accumulation of ambivalence among clients. Herein lies the crux of "l'affaire Loisy" from a sociological perspective. Each party in the conflict was making claims that contradicted the other side's claims. For Loisy, the question was who had the authority to interpret the scriptures, and on what basis. The ecclesiastical authorities claimed to have ultimate religious authority, whereas Loisy upheld the right of free scientific inquiry. In *Lamentabili* (1908), the Holy See defined its position on the controversy by upholding the right of the papal office to "determine the genuine sense of the Sacred Scriptures." Any attempt by Loisy and other scholars to claim authority in scientific studies of the Bible (which opposed official teachings of the church) was perceived as an intolerable challenge to papal authority.

Loisy nonetheless recognized the limitations of science, objecting to unlimited authority by either scientists or theologians:

> Theology and science . . . both have made the mistake of thinking that their power was unlimited. Science has its limits, because it can only apply to the knowable, and the knowable in experience is determined, is relative. Theology has its limits because it deals with the unknowable, which it must not reduce to the proportions of the already known. . . . Nothing copies more slavishly the spirit of certain scholastic theologians today than the spirit of popular rationalism. (Loisy [1913] 1968, 183–184)

Loisy's objection was not that the church would not permit absolute freedom but that it would permit him hardly any freedom whatsoever.

"Liberty is but a means, not an end," Loisy claimed, and the pursuit of truth is most successful "not through liberty alone, but through harmony between the authority which instructs and directs and the free activity which learns, which seeks, and which finds" ([1913] 1968, 188). According to Loisy, the church and the official theology "have not the remotest conception of" the possibility of freedom of criticism in scientific research into the subject of religion (ibid., 181). Such freedom of inquiry was essential to the norms of the professional scientist popular at the time. Loisy suggested that "if science had waited to ask permission of theology before going ahead, it would not have taken a step beyond the Fifteenth Century; and if it should choose today to show itself docile before the admonitions of the theologians, its development would be brought to a sudden standstill" (ibid., 180–181; cf. Loisy 1930–31, I:339 ff.).

The problem, however, was not simply one of choosing between theology and science, because some types of theology were just as anathema as science was. Rather, it was a question of what type of inquiry was associated with the interests of the hierarchy and which method became associated with the interests of the dissidents. As the conflict unfolded, questions of professional and institutional authority were raised again and again, under the guise of an objective debate concerning the merits of each approach. In one sense, what was at stake in the modernist crisis was the professional authority of the research scientists versus that of the ecclesiastical authorities and scholastic theologians. At that level, the clash was simply a conflict between persons of different status within the institution.

The modernist crisis went much deeper than that, however, because it was the explicit duty of the Catholic scholar-priest to submit not only to the authority of the ecclesiastical hierarchy but also to the principles of research science. Conflicting demands often result in expression of the contradiction of norms through "an oscillation of behaviors" (Merton and Barber 1976, 8). Thus it is not so much a weakness of an individual's character as it is a problem inherent in the situation that produces seemingly contradictory behaviors. An individual may, of course, prolong or mitigate such actions through sheer force of will against the situation as it is structured. This is precisely what Loisy attempted to do.

Members of the ecclesiastical hierarchy lacked the specialized knowledge required to develop scholarly interpretations of the scriptures. The pope was given authority in matters of faith and doctrine, yet he was not a biblical scholar, nor were the members of the Congregations of the Index who passed judgment on scholarly works. The encyclical *Providentissimus Deus* and the Biblical Commission provided a measure of official recognition of the problem, but did not solve it.[5] Loisy found the idea of the commission distasteful. For the hierarchy to ask for advice from members of the Biblical Commission was like getting a second opinion from a physician whom one knows in advance will agree with one's own diagnosis, rather than with the unpopular decision of another doctor. The commission provided a handpicked group of scholars who could be called upon to provide expert witness to protect orthodox Catholic positions from the scandalous conclusions of Loisy and other modernist scholars.

A problem also arises in evaluating a professional's motives in a situation in which the professional may gain from the continuation of a client's troubles. Biblical criticism raised the issue of the client's status. According to its critics, the church had a grave problem: traditional interpretations of scripture were simply no longer plausible in a scientific age, and some form of reinterpretation was essential. For the ecclesiastical hierarchy, the crisis required not a reinterpretation of scriptures, but a defense of orthodox interpretations.

The unwilling dependence of the church hierarchy on scholars such as Loisy tended to skew the hierarchy's "interpretation of even the most disinterested activities of the professional toward their being seen as self-interested" (ibid., 28). To entrust persons with the study and teaching of the scriptures was a risk that the church was forced to take. Neither the pope and his close advisors nor the bishops could personally teach seminarians and the laity attending Catholic universities. When professionals like Loisy demanded recognition of their independent, professional competence, members of the hierarchy were offended. As the conflicts escalated, each side increasingly defined the others' actions as self-interested.

A final source of sociological ambivalence in a professional–client relationship is the common problem of discrepant appraisals of role performance. Because of the expectation that "people occupying different positions in a social structure will tend to differ in their appraisals of the same social situations," one would expect to find that "different criteria of the effectiveness of professional work would be employed by professionals and their clients" (ibid.).

From the hierarchy's perspective, the effectiveness of a scholar was determined by the extent to which the scholar's work reinforced and supported the church's tradition. From the point of view of the scholar, however, the primary evaluative criterion for scholarly work was creative and accurate interpretation of the subject, as judged by the scholar's colleagues (regardless of the church's official position on the matter) and according to the emerging rules of scientific inquiry.

Loisy's response to the ambivalence of his situation was to reformulate the issues. As the conflict over his work evolved, his own crisis of faith emerged, and one of the mysteries of the entire modernist period is whether Loisy was indeed a fraud during the height of the modernist controversy. In Houtin and Sartiaux's *Vie de Loisy* (1960),[6] Loisy is charged with having duped his friends and followers when he was in fact merely an atheist in disguise. Houtin claimed that in a conversation with Loisy in February of 1907, Loisy confessed that twenty years earlier he had ceased to believe in a personal God, a future life, or the supernatural. "And so it is that this man," Houtin wrote,

> with whom I spoke on intimate terms so many times as a Christian and as a Catholic, this man who strove to keep me within the Church and even to make me accept the Index, had deceived me in the same way as he has deceived his numerous readers. All his negative conclusions inspire a healthy repulsion within me. He could have spared me from investigations, anxiety and tears if only he had been frank with me about the results of his research when I visited him five years ago, if only he had demonstrated to me immediately how certain basic Christian texts were without historical validity instead of leaving me to make inquiries for myself. (Houtin and Sartiaux 1960, 157–158)

There is evidence to suggest that there is some truth in Houtin's charges; there was an oscillation in Loisy's religious beliefs during the modernist crisis. There is also sufficient evidence to suggest that his actions and beliefs were not entirely fraudulent, either. They were not surprising, given his situation, nor do they necessarily imply Houtin's accusatory interpretation.

It is not my purpose to make any moral or theological judgments about Loisy's faith during the period, but to show how the interpretation put forth by Houtin was a simplistic and misleading evaluation of a situation that was complex, both psychologically and sociologically. The conclusion that Loisy was either totally faithful or totally fraudulent is unrealistic and unnecessary. It reflects a lack of understanding of the complexity of human motivations and actions, and it also reveals the different ways in which Loisy and Houtin responded to the ambivalence built into their similar social situations.

Houtin's interpretation was a product of a polarized milieu in which people were pressured to formulate absolutist definitions of the situation—that is, to choose between the results of scientific research and the pronouncements of the church. Loisy refused to develop a simplistic resolution of the ambivalence he faced. He wished to remain in the church while maintaining a belief in the efficacy of scientific criticism, even at the expense of particular doctrines of the church. This amounted to the almost impossible task of defining a Catholicism that permitted, rather than prohibited, doubts—a definition ruled out by the defensive papal hierarchy. Loisy's situation becomes even clearer when contrasted with that of Turmel and Houtin, two French priests who constructed different solutions to their crises.

TURMEL AND HOUTIN

Loisy, Houtin, and Turmel all had similar experiences leading up to their crises of faith. They came from relatively poor families in the provinces and were dependent upon the church for their spiritual life as well as for educational and career opportunities, which resulted in a love–hate relationship with the institution.

Like Loisy, Turmel's study of the scriptures led him to conclusions that contradicted the official teachings of the church (e.g., the Mosaic authorship of the Pentateuch). He became increasingly convinced that the church's teachings were not only misleading but also deceptive. According to his own account, in 1886 Turmel became aware that his faith in Catholicism was lost. He gave up saying his breviary offices[7] and praying in private but, convinced that he had no alternative profession open to him, he decided to remain in the priesthood. Because the church had deceived him, Turmel concluded that he could justifiably deceive the church: "Having decided to remain in the Church, I did not have to make any change in my manner of life. Nothing was modified, except that henceforth I had two more hours a day for study which had previously been taken up with pious exercises" (Turmel 1935, 48).

Turmel clashed with church authorities in 1892 and was deprived of his position as a professor of dogmatic theology at the diocesan seminary at Rennes. He was appointed chaplain to the Little Sisters of the Poor in Rennes and continued his studies. Turmel said mass and heard confessions but never preached or taught catechism, and he became "one of the most erudite patristic scholars of the time" (Vidler 1970, 58). Despite the fact that some of his works were denounced to the Holy Office, he was requested by the Jesuits of the Institut Catholique in Paris to write a study, *History of Positive Theology* (1904). At the same time, he published more controversial works under several pseudonyms.

Two articles on the virgin birth and the doctrine of the Trinity, published in Loisy's *Revue d'histoire et de littérature religieuses* under the pseudonyms Herzog and Dupin, were violently attacked. The controversy led to the condemnation of the review in 1907. In the articles, Turmel had inadvisedly used material that he had previously published under his own name; Louis Saltet, a professor at the Catholic Institute

of Toulouse, discovered the overlap and denounced him. Turmel wrote
to Monsignor Dubourg, the archbishop of Rennes, claiming unequivocally
that he was neither Herzog nor Dupin nor did he know anything about
them. He solemnly stated that he disapproved of all conclusions that did
not conform to orthodoxy. As a Catholic priest, he declared, "I profess
all that the Roman Church professes, and reject all that it rejects" (Houtin
1913, 400).[8] When the editorial secretary of the review, Paul Lejay, died
suddenly in 1920, a postcard from Turmel, writen to Lejay in 1907, was
found, indicating that Turmel was in fact both Dupin and Herzog (see
Rivière [1913] 1929, 500–501). Following this unmasking, and despite
his submission to the archbishop of Rennes, Turmel was excommunicated
and declared to be *vitandus* (shunned).[9] Even then, he continued to live
as a priest and wrote to Loisy, saying,[10]

> The blow with which Rome reckons to have crushed me can make no change
> in my manner of life which, for many years, has been that of a hermit who goes
> out only once a week to the library (and hitherto each morning to say
> mass). . . . Rome is causing horrible suffering to the simple souls of my entourage.
> That is what is embittering my life and is going to embitter it for many long
> months. At my age one does not move house or even renew one's linen. I am
> keeping my house with its modest garden, I continue to wear the soutane, I
> remain Abbé Turmel. (I even say mass on Sundays to reassure my housekeeper
> who otherwise would become crazed.)

Turmel dealt with the ambivalence of his situation by perpetrating
a fraud. He continued to function as a priest but gave up his dogmatic
beliefs. A word of caution must be added, however: despite his deceptions,
the conclusion of some historians that he was a nonbeliever might be too
simplistic. As in the case of Loisy, Turmel's alleged loss of faith is an
extremely complicated issue, related to the sharp conflicts of the period.
It was not uncommon for people to lose their faith in orthodox Catholic
teachings and yet continue to participate in the rituals and life of the
church. The official Catholicism of the period was an "all or nothing"
proposition. If Turmel had lost his faith completely, it is difficult to
explain his continued attachment to the rituals of the church and his
wearing of priestly garb.

For Sartiaux, Houtin, and many opponents of modernism, Turmel
was the example par excellence of the impossibility of maintaining an
adherence both to Catholicism and to scientific scholarship. Houtin may
have relished debunking Turmel because it further justified his own actions. Vidler, who has always written with historical circumspection but
with sympathy for the movement, has refused even to describe Turmel
as a modernist, "since at no time did he hope or work for a modernizing
of Catholicism or believe in its possibility." Vidler is inclined to agree

with Jean Steinmann that Turmel's case "must be diagnosed as one of a 'sort of morbid schizophrenia'" (Vidler 1970, 61; cf. Steinmann 1962). If it was schizophrenia, it must be attributed not only to psychological difficulties but also the conflicting demands of the role of scholar-priest.

ALBERT HOUTIN

Houtin's response to a similar ambivalence in his social situation was different from both Turmel's and Loisy's. Born into a poor rural family in 1867, Houtin, like Loisy and Turmel, was raised as an orthodox Catholic and received his early education from the local priest. He was ordained at the age of twenty-four and became a historian on the faculty of the diocesan seminary at Angers, where he had been a student.

Houtin never served a parish or preached a sermon. Under the influence of works by Duchesne and others, he learned historical criticism, and was troubled by problems with the historicity of the French bishops, notably Saint René, a patron of the diocese of Angers. According to legend, Saint René had been restored to life after having been dead for seven years (Houtin 1901). After questioning the legend in print, Houtin was promptly forced to resign his teaching post; he retired to Paris, where he lived with his parents and turned his attention to "la question biblique."

The bishop of Angers let Houtin have a *celebret* (permission to say Mass) after his resignation from the seminary, but it was not renewed after March 1903, and his work *La question biblique chez les Catholiques au XIXe siècle* (1902) was put on the *Index* in 1903. Houtin subsequently had no ecclesiastical status but continued to wear his soutane "as the old uniform of idealism" (Houtin 1927, 433). Loisy contended that Houtin did so to avoid grieving his mother, rather than for spiritual reasons.[11]

Houtin responded to the ambivalence in his own role as a scholar-priest by developing a passion for detecting fraud in other priests. He came to see deception in all spheres of life; at one point, he wrote that

personal interest dictates to most men what they dare to call their "convictions" not only in matters of religion but in every sphere of thought. Just as some people require honours and wealth by zealously but insincerely defending the religions in which they were born, so other people exploit to their profit the ideas of the State and of the Fatherland, about which they are as skeptical as ecclesiastics are about religious institutions. (Houtin 1927, 79)

I will leave it to psychologists and historians to comment on the extent to which Houtin was exhibiting a tendency to project onto others his own skepticism and duplicity; he was, despite his continued wearing of the soutane, more honest about his skepticism and lack of belief in orthodox Catholicism than was Turmel. What is sociologically significant is the strain placed upon Houtin by the ambivalence of his role as scholar-priest, and his response to his situation—namely, his denunciation of others in a similar situation. His work was a source of considerable embarrassment to those who felt it possible to remain in the church and continue their scientific research.[12]

HOUTIN'S CASE AGAINST LOISY

Loisy's alleged duplicity must be seen in the context of Houtin's charges against him. According to Houtin, Loisy never failed to "defend his client," implying that it was only to protect his professional status that Loisy kept his skepticism to himself.

The picture that Houtin and Sartiaux painted of Loisy was a negative one indeed, and not totally without basis, although I am convinced, with Vidler, that their charges "grossly exaggerated Loisy's faults" (Vidler 1970, 32). One of the most difficult passages for defenders of Loisy is one which he wrote in his journal in 1886 and which he later reproduced in his autobiographic *Choses passées* ([1913] 1968, 101):

> For several months past, I have not been able to arouse in myself the slightest religious feeling. Since my second year in the seminary, habits of piety have been steadily counteracted in me by the dread of submitting to illusion. Perhaps that fear has been a weakness, but it no longer has a bearing, having totally lost its object. . . . I have hardly a thing to look forward to. I am determined to work and to serve the Church, which created, and to which pertains, the education of the human race. Without breaking with her tradition, and on condition of retaining its spirit in preference to its letter, she remains an essential institution, and the most divine on earth. . . . The interior conflict that I have undergone for ten years past, and which has only ceased in these recent months, has greatly exhausted me. I shall never recover my youthful resiliency of spirit. Well for me if only a little strength is left! All the freedom I have to think my own thoughts does not compensate for the restraints on my freedom of action imposed by my position.

This juxtaposition of the freedom of Loisy's inner thoughts with the restraints imposed by his position highlights his sociological ambivalence at least as much as it reveals his deceptions. It is only when one takes out of context such remarks as "for several months past, I have not been able to arouse in myself the slightest religious feeling" that Houtin's charges have any validity. What is more striking, especially in his private correspondence and notes, is the extent to which Loisy held both extremely strong religious beliefs and grave doubts about orthodox Catholicism. Given the mental gymnastics required to accommodate both the official Catholicism of the period and the findings of the biblical sciences (however exaggerated they, too, might have been at that time), it is not so astonishing to find an individual vacillating between belief and doubt. In a sense, it was not Loisy so much as it was the Vatican who claimed that Loisy no longer believed in the Catholic faith.

Three further observations which Vidler makes help to substantiate that position. First, it is important to note both the context in which Loisy wrote the frank piece of pessimism just quoted and what happened to him in subsequent years. The entry was written in 1885–86 during a period of deep depression about his faith, based on his belief "that a transformation of Catholicism was impossible." Afterward, his teaching duties at the Institut Catholique, his chaplaincy at Neuilly, and his friendship with von Hügel "made me hope afresh and attempt a reconciliation."[13]

Second, it is helpful to note a distinction between dogmatic and mystical faith which Bremond made in defense of Loisy. Bremond contended that by 1904, Loisy

no longer had faith, if one means by faith adherence of the mind to revealed dogmas. But he still has faith, if one means by that a . . . mystical adherence of the whole being to the invisible realities of which he still believes the Catholic Church is the principle and indispensable guardian. He loves the Church. There is no love which does not imply faith, and how much more real and living a faith than that which the theologians define. . . . From the confused block of his original beliefs, all the dogmatic element has disappeared; all the mystical element remains, though it is being more and more shaken. (Bremond 1931, 45)

Bremond was emphasizing a point that Houtin and Sartiaux missed, but that was at the core of much of the modernists' writings—the distinction between Catholicism as a religion and scholastic theology. For Bremond, as for von Hügel, what needed to be recovered in Catholicism was the "mystical element of religion,"[14] which appears throughout Bremond's writings.[15] From his point of view, Loisy's work was valuable because the scholar was using scientific methods to recover the mystical element of Catholicism, freeing it from the official theology of the church.

There are also indications that Loisy maintained his religious feelings long after the modernist period; they may have become even stronger than at the height of the controversies.[16] Louis Canet, Loisy's literary executor and the most intimate of his followers, reported that Loisy prayed and spent time every morning in meditation (Petre 1944, 100). One of the most convincing accounts of Loisy's religious convictions was written by the French diplomat Raymond de Boyer de Sainte Suzanne,[17] who as a young man became acquainted with Loisy, and later wrote that

Loisy sincerely and profoundly considered himself a Christian for a long time, faithful in spirit and in truth to Christianity, since he believed in the living presence of the spirit in the world, because he thought that the soul of religion was charity (which he later referred to as self-sacrificing love) and because the whole time he remained in the Church, he never for one moment doubted that this fundamental truth was perceived and put into practice by Christ, the early Christians, the innumerable mystics who succeeded one another without interruption in the bosom of Christianity. The cause of evil is not to be found in a drying up of the indescribable, mystical outburst born of Christianity, but in the eroding effect of dogma. (Boyer de Sainte Suzanne 1968, 157)

Three incidents suggest that Loisy did not lose his faith. First, Loisy was present at a conference in Pontigny a few years before his death. Having been declared *vitandus,* Loisy could not enter the Abbey for the mass on Sunday.[18] Canet reportedly discovered him outside with tears in his eyes (Petre 1944, 56). Second, among Loisy's books now in the Sorbonne is a telling remark which he made in the margin of an article by Louis de Lacger, who wrote, "while M. Loisy's Catholic friends regarded him as a defender both of the Gospel and of the Church against the anaemic evangelicalism of liberal protestantism, the author in his heart of hearts had long ago rejected the Gospel." Loisy had refuted Lacger's contention with the simple note, "Ah! c'est faux."[19]

Finally, two years before his death, Loisy wrote to Boyer de Sainte Suzanne that he walked and wrote painfully, but could still work and that he waited for relief "like my ancestor Job" (Boyer 1968, 214). Then, several days before his death, he spoke again of Job; Boyer attaches significance to Loisy's conscious identification with Job, because it speaks of someone who suffers a great deal, but maintains "an unconditional loyalty to God" (ibid., 152).

There are, then, legitimate interpretations of Loisy's life and work which are quite different from those offered by Houtin and Sartiaux. After reviewing the charges made against Loisy, Vidler concluded "that Loisy's account of himself has not been seriously discredited." Vidler regarded "Monsignor Mignot, Henry Bremond and Miss Petre as much better judges of his character than Houtin, Sartiaux and their followers" (1970, 55).[20] Moreover, one cannot fully accept any critical judgment made by Houtin, who had a "fondness for alleging that clerics were more or less infidels in disguise" (ibid., 32), and who caricatured the positions of a number of people, including John Ireland, archbishop of Saint Paul; John Spalding, bishop of Peoria; Lilley; and Tyrrell (see Houtin 1927, 187).

Merton and Barber's (1976) concept of sociological ambivalence suggests that it is necessary to accept neither Houtin and Sartiaux's interpretation of Loisy's modernist career nor an unequivocal defense of his sincerity. Rather, what Loisy actually experienced may well have been a socially imposed ambivalence—literally a situation in which the valence of his relationship to Catholicism was both positive and negative at the same time.

Loisy was not alone in his ambivalence, by any means, but he was one of the more extreme cases, both because of his personal response to that ambivalence and because of the hierarchy's labeling him as an insurgent. The intellectual development of other figures in the movement (such as von Hügel, Tyrrell, LeRoy, and Buonaiuti) provides similar cases, if not all as strikingly ambivalent as the enigma of Abbé Loisy.

MONSIGNOR MIGNOT

After Loisy, Monsignor Eûdoxe-Irénée Mignot (1842–1918) was the most important of the French modernists, but his modernism remained largely a private affair. The archbishop of Albi was in touch with, and faithfully supportive of, a number of modernist figures, notably Loisy and von Hügel. Loisy's *Mémoires* are full of admiration for Mignot,[21] who provided necessary encouragement for Loisy at times when the latter was disenchanted with the possibility of reform. In 1896, for example, Mignot wrote to Loisy, saying,[22]

> You will allow me not to believe in your philosophy or your pessimism. As I have already told you, you have an important role to play in the study of biblical questions in France, a great trail to blaze. The most important thing at present is for you to get over your cold, which has interrupted your studies, and to present us with your Pentateuch.

Like many other modernists, Mignot was raised in the provinces, where he was the son of a village schoolmaster. Mignot was exposed to progressive influences upon his arrival in Paris to study. Although not a professional scholar, Mignot was widely read and was convinced of the need for critical studies, writing to Loisy that[23]

> I should like to write . . . a history of the religion of Israel which would show that the revelation of God did not fall down in one piece from heaven to earth; that the Bible is not a gramophone on which the word of God is recorded; that men played a large part in the development of the divine thought; that it was only at quite a late stage that the idea of God was disengaged from the darkness of polytheism. . . . I should like to show how the history of Israel logically leads on to Christianity without at the same time explaining it like the theologians as a mechanical fulfillment, so to speak, of the prophecies.

As a bishop, Mignot was confronted by conflicting demands similar to those faced by Loisy, Houtin, and Turmel. Mignot felt that as a leader in the church it was necessary to keep abreast of developments in ecclesiastical and biblical scholarship. In 1903 he wrote to von Hügel that in several years their ideas would be those of the church, and that they must continue to study history rather than assuming that "all questions were resolved by Saint Thomas."[24]

On the other hand, Mignot felt that it was impossible for a bishop to express publicly his opinions concerning biblical scholarship without creating a scandal, which he wished to avoid at any price.[25] His belief in the development of critical science thus contradicted his duties as a bishop. He found his fellow bishops incompetent in matters of biblical criticism and felt that many were "hostile to what they view as dangerous novelties, as are most of the Consultants of the Index and of the Holy Office."[26]

Mignot became actively involved in supporting members of the emerging modernist networks. He was in frequent correspondence with Loisy and von Hügel, providing support, encouragement, and information about developments in Rome and elsewhere in the hierarchy, and suggesting strategies for reform. Mignot often offered advice of moderation, but he did so to further what he perceived as the common cause, rather than to thwart what he thought was a dangerous movement.

When Loisy submitted the manuscript of L'Evangile et l'Eglise to Mignot, the archbishop responded with enthusiasm, recommending that he proceed with publication. "I do not think that they would be able to condemn you for it," he wrote, "and on the contrary, that publication will place you in the first rank of Christian critics."[27] Although Mignot did not agree with everything that Loisy wrote (see Vidler 1970, 99; Houtin 1920–1924, III:282), he remained firm in his support, even after Loisy's excommunication. It is obvious from his letters to Loisy and von Hügel that Mignot considered them to be involved in a common cause. He was working in his own subtle way to open doors for Loisy and others to continue their work for reform.

Mignon remained circumspect, however, in his writings and public statements, giving little evidence of his support of the modernists, and this gap between his public statements and his private efforts led to charges of duplicity. The eminent scholar Marie-Joseph Lagrange wrote a long letter in 1932 to Saint-Cyr-au-Mont-d'Or (Rhone) implying that Mignot's actions were even more deplorable than von Hügel's:

Aside from Duchesne, von Hügel and Batiffol's positions were clear since both wrote in confidence in the same spirit that they proclaimed in public. Loisy's stinging reproaches which were levelled against Batiffol were based—twice if I'm not mistaken—on that old joke about the old fogeys in the Synoptic Gospels. He really doesn't have any serious allegations to make if he referred twice to that nonsense. Von Hügel was a disciple of Loisy both in public and in private; but in the end he saw the light. God willing, may you find in M. Mignot's papers a single expression of regret for his obstinate defense of Loisy! His problem is that his published works are irreproachable and have been very useful as far as I can judge, while his letters to Loisy have been deplorable added to the fact that the latter was malicious enough to publish them. (in Bécamel 1969, 274)

Mignot's attempts to fulfill contradictory demands by maintaining a publicly orthodox stance while working quietly behind the scenes for a "heretical" movement resulted in yet another scandal. Mignot never received any attacks like the denunciations of Loisy and the charges of deception against a number of priests, but there are telling parallels between their attempts to maintain different stances in public and in private.

Because of the stifling intellectual atmosphere of the time, many scholars followed the same line as Mignot. Bremond was one of the most significant—although he was clearly sympathetic with the modernists, he avoided making his modernist proclivities public as long as possible. There is no question about his modernist position, however, nor about the fact that he was on intimate terms with several of the modernists.[28] He wrote to Loisy at the end of 1907, for example, suggesting that Tyrrell's *Through Scylla and Charybdis* and Loisy's own "livres rouges" would be "the sum of official teaching in twenty years" (in Bernard–Maitre 1968, 21). What is somewhat surprising is that the modernists not only did not prod Bremond into a public stance on their controversies, but appeared to want to protect him.[29]

MAUDE PETRE

[Modernism] can find a home in neither . . . a Church by which it is rejected [nor in] . . . a world by which it is slighted . . . because it believes in both. It is, in fact, one of two things. It is either the last explosive movement of vitality in institutions doomed to proximate extinction, at least in so far as they can be considered of world-wide importance, or it is the beginning of a new condition of things, in which the Church shall be subservient to the religious and spiritual needs of humanity.
—Maude Petre, *Modernism*

If anyone in the modernist movement was apparently consistent throughout in her behavior, both publicly and privately, it was Maude Petre, who remained a modernist to her dying day, long after the movement had been condemned. Yet her situation too was fraught with ambivalence, from the very beginning of her career. Long after Loisy had left the movement, Tyrrell had died, and von Hügel's modernism had grown cold, Petre carried on the work of the movement. She published Tyrrell's works posthumously and wrote a series of books and articles about the movement's failures and fruits. A vital figure in the modernist movement, Petre had a warmth and lively intelligence that facilitated her intimacy with a number of its major figures.

Born into an aristocratic English family in 1862, Petre was the granddaughter of the Earl of Wicklow on her mother's side, and of Lord Petre, on her father's; Lord Petre was a descendant of Sir William Petre, who served as Under Secretary of State in the reigns of Henry VIII, Edward VI, and Mary. From both sides of her family, she inherited a spirit of independence and a devout but unorthodox Catholic faith—qualities which she retained throughout her life. Her mother, Petre wrote in her autobiography, was "what we now call a feminist," and was a supporter of such causes as stronger laws against "brutal drunken husbands who had ill-treated their wives" (1937a, 11). The ninth Lord Petre deliberately ignored Pope Clement XII's ban against Freemasonry to become the Grand Master of the English fraternity in 1772.

At the age of twenty-one, Petre made a pilgrimage to Rome on the advice of her Jesuit confessor, who was concerned about her problems with Catholic dogma. His prescription for her doubts was a course of study in the philosophy of Thomas Aquinas. Her aunt explained to enquiring friends that "Maude had gone to Rome to study for the priesthood" (Walker 1944, ix).

Petre entered the sisterhood of the "Daughters of Mary," where she promoted orphanages, settlements among the poor, and the instruction of converts. She was soon made superior of the English and Irish province of the order. In that position of authority, she was faced with contradictory normative demands. She had acquired a considerable amount of skepticism, and she developed an unorthodox approach to Catholic dogmas and the authority structure of the church. After a distinguished ten-year period of service as head of the order, she felt it necessary to relinquish her position because of her opposition to the "harsh military conception of obedience and authority enforced by the Vatican in the name of Pius X" (ibid., x).

Although she could not "close my eyes to the latest developments of science," she never lost her Catholic faith. Her faith was one that was "only too conscious of its own inadequacy and insecurity, and which has yet weathered the storms of a lifetime, and hopes to hold on until the veil is rent, and the substance of things hoped for becomes the substance of things realized and beheld" (Petre 1937a, xxxv). She felt, however, that the church was endangered by the exaggerated notions of papal authority prevalent at the turn of the century. An insightful observer of the modernist crisis, Petre argued that the problem of authority in the church was "the root problem of the whole modernist controversy." The notions of papal authority and the extreme respect paid to the person and office of the pope constituted a form of idolatry and an abuse both of the office and of the church. "To over-estimate the dignity of his [the pope's] person is to lower the dignity of the church," she contended:

> The authority of the Pope has been strained to the point of destroying its own sanction, for subordinate authority has been set at naught in its interest, which means that the element of self-will has been allowed to prevail in high places, and we know that self-will is destructive authority. (Petre 1918, 142)

For Petre, the issue of authority in the church was a very complex one: more problematical than dissidence at the lower levels of the church was the self-interested abuse of authority at very high levels of the church. The papal office is supposed to "represent authority in its purest and most disinterested form," but the ideal has been perverted. Ironically, she notes, "the growing claims of official authority have been . . . unchecked in their development in the Catholic Church, while in all other forms of society they have been opposed by the counter-claims of the people" (Petre 1918, 145).

Although Petre's position might have been prejudiced by a turn-of-the-century optimism and a belief in democracy and science, there is a great deal of sociological validity in her observation. Other forms of authoritative rule also grew up in reaction against democratization (e.g., the Napoleonic empires), and at the time of her writing the church certainly was one of the most important and enduring of authoritarian political structures.

For Petre, the works of Tyrrell, von Hügel, and Loisy provided some resolution of the conflicts created by the sociological ambivalence of her situation. Her role in the movement has been underrated by most commentaries because she was more an historian and reporter than an original thinker, so that her numerous works are frequently vehicles for the thought of Loisy, von Hügel, Tyrrell, and others, more than for her own ideas. It is likely that the nature of her role in the movement is related to her being a woman at a time when women were confined to secondary roles in virtually all settings.

Despite the secondary nature of much of her work, Petre's activity was crucial not only during the movement itself, but also in terms of recording it for history. It is possible that without Petre's efforts, Tyrrell would have been buried with little notice. As his literary executor and biographer, she made his life and work available to a much wider audience than would otherwise have been the case. Her affection and respect for Tyrrell and his work became a dominant interest in her intellectual life, and his death was a turning point.

Petre attempted to resolve the sociological ambivalence created by her situation first by resigning from her position within the church, and then by throwing herself into a supportive role in the modernist movement. Although her ability to stay in the church could be attributed to her personality (for she was a strong and aggressive woman), it was in large part a function of her social situation. For one thing, she was living and working in England, where religious tolerance was much more prevalent, both within the Roman Church and outside of it, than it was in France or Italy. In Britain, where they were a minority, Roman Catholics were more tolerant of a wide spectrum of views than in France and Italy, where Catholicism was the dominant religion. Nor was anticlericalism as strong in England as it was in France and Italy, since anticlerical movements developed primarily in countries where Catholicism was dominant and thus a major political force that threatened progressive movements (see Chadwick 1975).

Second, Petre resigned from her official position within the church early in the controversy, thereby reducing much of the ambivalence and conflict that she encountered as a church official. Those facing the most violent conflicts were scholar-priests (such as Loisy, Houtin, and Turmel) who were subject to strong contradictory norms.

Third, it is of no little consequence that Petre[30] was from a wealthy and influential old Catholic family in England. Her professional, social, and personal contacts in the English hierarchy provided her with considerable protection from the inquisitors, which was not available to people like Loisy and others from modest families.

Finally, it is possible that Petre was not considered a threat because she was a woman and therefore not to be taken seriously. If that is true, the rationale proved to be incorrect, because her influence was considerable. Petre's association with von Hügel, Tyrrell, Bremond, Lilley, and others—as well as her reading of works by Loisy and Fogazzaro, and of von Hügel's vast scholarly collections from Germany, France, and Italy—provided a resolution of some of the ambivalence she faced.

Others had similar experiences, finding themselves in highly ambivalent situations and often feeling isolated from their fellow Catholics. A number of scholars began to be drawn together, first around the work of such progressive scholars, and later as a means of protecting themselves from the Roman establishment's attempts to suppress critical thought and scholarship within the church. It was out of these developments that a modernist network began to form.

5
A Movement Emerges

A number of scholars were gradually drawn together by common interests in scientific research, by their repugnance at Vatican attempts to suppress intellectual inquiry, and in some cases, by their simultaneous suppression by church authorities. As with all social movements, the social structure of the modernist movement begins to fade when examined in detail, but an examination of the modernists' papers clearly reveals the broad outline of a loose network of Catholics working to reform the Roman Church toward the end of the nineteenth century.

Loisy and Tyrrell were not organizers of reform movements; they were writers and scholars absorbed in their work. It was Baron von Hügel who took upon himself the responsibility of attempting to create a movement out of the disparate attempts to resolve the ambivalences that faced Catholic scholars at the time. Few people had social networks as extensive as those of von Hügel,[1] who was in close contact with the leadership of the church and with a wide range of people from varying backgrounds and creeds. More than a decade after the "end" of the modernist movement, Soderblom noted that the von Hügels' home still formed a "pilgrim's resort" for searching "and religiously thinking personalities from various countries and communions."[2]

Von Hügel's commitment to the Roman Church was unshakable, but his interpretations of Catholicism were extremely "broad"—a term he used frequently as a compliment in referring to people whose viewpoints he appreciated.[3] Troeltsch referred to him as the "patriarch and soul of the multifaceted community of pious, yet progressive [religious] circles" (Troeltsch 1922–1925, II:45–67; cf. Rollmann 1978, 52).

The baron had a vision of how the modernist project was to proceed—a vision with which his colleagues did not always agree. As Petre suggests, von Hügel

was indefatigable in the service of a friend so long as that friend was serving the cause in which he believed; and though he never wholly abandoned anyone, nor renounced the claims of old friendship, he quickly cooled when his friends took an independent line which he deemed injurious to their common cause. . . . For he had a German thoroughness of plan, and each of us was expected to take his part towards the fulfillment of that plan. But many, in that time of religious crisis in which he and his leading friends first came together, had no such defined plan; they were pushing their way through unknown forests of the mind. (Petre 1944, 30–31)

Von Hügel tried to create cohesion within a group that resisted organization, and he was unable to avoid some of the difficulties involved in mobilizing a movement of intellectuals. Time after time, von Hügel came into conflict with his friends and colleagues. He clashed with Blondel over Loisy's work, for example, virtually eradicating the relationship. After writing a letter to Tyrrell concerning Tyrrell's excommunication, von Hügel noted in his diary, "I fear that this letter somehow changed his tone towards me."[4] "Von Hügel had a place for each one in his scheme," Petre complained, comparing him to a chess player. He "was apt to sacrifice the man to the scheme. He planned his every action and prepared everything beforehand" (Petre 1937b, 6).

Without the baron's efforts, it is doubtful that a Catholic modernist movement would have developed; there would have been pockets of activity along similar lines, but they would have remained isolated. It was clearly von Hügel who shaped the direction in which the nascent movement developed. His intellectual powers, resources, and contacts made him someone to whom the progressive scholars turned when they could receive support from few others so competent and influential. Petre said that she could admit that von Hügel was not a modernist only if there was no such thing as a modernist. "If von Hügel did not have a part in it, who did?" she asked (ibid., 9).

THE VON HÜGEL CONNECTION

Von Hügel's letters and diaries in the St. Andrews University Library reveal, as do Loisy's *Mémoires* and the von Hügel–Tyrrell correspondence in the British Library, that the baron was in contact with more members of the modernist movement than was anyone else. Most modernists tended to move in nationally oriented circles (Loisy in France, Tyrrell in England, Buonaiuti in Italy), but von Hügel maintained contacts across national boundaries.

VON HUGEL'S NETWORK BUILDING

Von Hügel used five strategies to cultivate his networks, most of them related to his wealth and position of influence. First of all, he was a man of letters with sufficient leisure and motivation for maintaining a voluminous correspondence. Consequently he was able to obtain information and to influence events more than the other reformers, with the possible exception of Mignot. Second, he wrote and solicited book reviews and articles at strategic times. When a new book was published by Loisy or Tyrrell, he went to great lengths to see to it that it was reviewed, by writing or sending books to potential reviewers, and so forth.

Third, he was an amiable and aggressive conversationalist who entertained frequently and visited people throughout Europe as the von Hügels visited people back and forth between London and their winter home in Italy. Fourth, he distributed large quantities of modernist books, pamphlets, journals, and manuscripts to interested and influential people. Finally, von Hügel offered, and in some cases provided, financial support for individuals and projects that he considered important.

A MAN OF LETTERS

Von Hügel's flair for drawing people into the modernist enterprise was one of the most significant activities in the formation of the movement. The scrupulously intentional von Hügel wrote long, involved discussions of important scholarly issues. His first letter to Lilley provides a good example of his style and strategies for soliciting potential supporters. Lilley, the Anglican Vicar of Saint Mary's, Paddington Green, had just written two articles[5] that showed an appreciation for Loisy and his work. Enclosing a letter of introduction from Henry Scott Holland, precentor of Saint Paul's Cathedral, von Hügel introduced himself and explained his reason for writing, adding words of praise for Loisy:[6]

> You can, then easily imagine with what pleasure I read your papers, I think what specifically struck and indeed delighted me in them, was the way in which you appeared conscious throughout of the first-class quality of his mind, and of all he has got to teach anyone and everybody.

Just two days later, von Hügel received a long letter from Lilley in reply,[7] and the following month von Hügel invited Lilley to dine as his guest at a meeting of the Synthetic Society.[8] His letters were not mere social pleasantries; the baron always had a purpose in mind, and he used his correspondence to promote the movement. In his first letter to Lilley, von Hügel suggested that he might "venture to send you a copy of a book by my close friend, the Reverend George Tyrrell, a truly deep and brilliant Irishman, and a Jesuit as liberal as his close friend Père Bremond, the Frenchman."[9] In his second letter, von Hügel suggested that Lilley might be interested in forthcoming works by Laberthonnière and Petre, hoping that he would "be able and willing to give them both a warm and sympathetic welcome in the 'Guardian.'"[10] Lilley received no less than forty-nine letters from von Hügel over a seven-year period following that first letter.[11] Von Hügel introduced Lilley to Loisy, Tyrrell, and Petre, and Lilley's papers reveal an extensive correspondence with all three of them.[12]

Since many of the modernists were separated by extreme distances, correspondence became the chief means of communication, and these letters comprise a rather detailed record of the key figures in the movement. Von Hügel's letters in the St. Andrews University Library reveal an extensive correspondence,[13] which served at least three functions. The most obvious purpose was to disseminate information and to make contacts among similarly minded individuals. Introductory letters often included proposals of a meeting, if the person lived within proximity of his home or on the route of one of his many journeys. Because the baron was hard of hearing, some of his most important contributions to the movement came by way of his correspondence, in which he analyzed problems, provided detailed comments on manuscripts, and so on.

A second purpose of von Hügel's letter writing was its supportive function. He wrote to encourage people by praising their ideas, providing constructive criticism, and helping them to overcome their ubiquitous isolation. In 1907, for example, von Hügel wrote to Petre:[14]

> Our group is having to bear such a long strain, that it is no wonder we are all more or less broken down; yet our cause is so great and inspiring, and the war is likely to last still so long a time, that we simply do all we can to keep and get not only passably well, but with a surplusage of nerve and vitality,—things which, depend upon it, will be wanted to the last shred.

Von Hügel's support was not uncritical. His accolades were generous but not indiscriminate. Had they been, their value would have been diminished. Part of the impact of von Hügel's letters came from his ability to provide the kind of support required by intellectual production—an enthusiastic expression of support that was so convincing as to allow for criticism. A letter written to Tyrrell 1 October 1907 is instructive of von Hügel's style. Following two searing articles by Tyrrell in the London *Times,* von Hügel wrote that two things about them were certain. First, he wrote that their substance was "deep and true and great, and that there was and is a crying need for such expositions either now or soon." However, von Hügel added that the articles were also "very hot, vehement and sarcastic. I hope very much that this heat, which in some places, is so apt, and in all is so understandable, may not . . . deflect otherwise likely and winnable minds from the substantial content and real, final aim of your papers." The baron quickly added that he would not even have mentioned his "secondary criticism" if it had not been for a letter from Alfieri "in which his love and admiration for, and care for your influence and for its continuous extension shine out most touchingly." Some of the Italian modernists, Alfieri reported, had "been somewhat seriously pained and upset by the personal tone,—the tone toward the Pope" of a letter that Tyrrell had written to an Italian journal (von Hügel 1927, 141–142).

Von Hügel's criticisms were not always appreciated; they were sometimes perceived as being motivated not by academic or intellectual so much as by political considerations. He was a diplomat with his friends, but also with his adversaries, and his role within the movement included frequent calls for moderation. He was, furthermore, not hesitant to make strong suggestions for courses of action.[15]

A third function of von Hügel's letters was to engage in intellectual debate, and at times refutation, as in his exchange with Blondel following the latter's critique of Loisy's *L'Evangile et l'Eglise* (see Blondel 1904). The baron had hoped to find a convergence between Blondel's philosophy of action and Loisy's exegesis, but Blondel had criticized Loisy publicly. Because friendships among intellectuals often require some degree of intellectual assent, von Hügel and Blondel's relationship was severely strained.[16] Such difficulties were even more ominous because of escalating opposition by the Roman authorities. Blondel was anxious to distance himself from suspect persons or ideas. The baron published an article in *La Quinzaine* on 1 June 1904, defending Loisy against Blondel's charges of "historicism," and Blondel's friend the Abbé Wehrlé responded with an attack on von Hügel. Following the publication of Wehrlé's article, von Hügel complained that he saw[17]

in the most strenuously rhetorical, most implacably heresy-hunting paragraphs, not only the inspiration but the actual writing of my close friend Maurice Blondel; and that I cannot avoid admitting to myself that, even though he is sincere in his opinions, his present distinctly feverish and over-emphatic insistence upon them, cannot be altogether dissociated from the storm clouds visible on the ecclesiastical heavens.

A final way in which von Hügel used his correspondence was to solicit support from others for various modernist scholars. In addition to urging open-minded individuals to read the modernists' publications, he wrote letters of introduction and explanation, including letters to persons in the Catholic hierarchy. His diaries record, for example, that von Hügel wrote an "important letter of congratulation in favor of Loisy to Cardinal Merry del Val" in November 1903, in the midst of the controversy surrounding Loisy's *L'Evangile et l'Eglise*. Apparently the cardinal was not inclined to receive von Hügel's support for Loisy with enthusiasm, however. Von Hügel entered an underlined note in his diary on 18 November that he had received a *"short, entirely evasive, possibly snubby note from Cardinal Merry del Val"* (emphasis in the original). The baron was not easily daunted, however, and wrote the following day to Cardinal Rampolla, "for Loisy," including congratulations on the cardinal's selection as president of the Biblical Commission.[18] He was sometimes successful in soliciting support in the Roman hierarchy. In a letter to Tyrrell on 4 December 1899, for example, von Hügel discussed a letter he had written on Loisy's behalf to Cardinal Mathieu, "who is open-minded at all events on historical points (he volunteered to Loisy to at any time fight his battles for him at Rome, where, as you know, he is resident French Cardinal)" (von Hügel 1927, 8).

Despite von Hügel's identification with the modernists, his opinions were respectfully entertained by the hierarchy. He also provided an important source of information about developments in Rome. When Tyrrell was experiencing difficulties with his Jesuit superiors in 1900, the Baron wrote to his new friend that "since Newman's death, there has been no English-speaking Catholic whose work appeals to me, and pierces, I think, to the very centre of questions to a degree at all really comparable to yours. And your trouble has, hence, been most really *my* trouble also."[19]

REFORM BY REVIEWING

As soon as von Hügel received copies of Loisy's *L'Evangile et l'Eglise*, on 19 November 1902, he began soliciting reviews for it in English journals.[20] He wrote to Gardner, for example, informing him that he had sent him copies of Loisy's work, although he feared that Gardner's Protestant readers would not be entirely pleased with his conclusions. "Still," von Hügel wrote, "I do not suppose that, say, the *Hibbert Journal* was founded to give a fair hearing to views only in proportion to their comfortableness" (1927, 112). Gardner agreed to review the book and read it "with the greatest interest and much appreciation,"[21] but was less positive in his review than von Hügel had hoped.

Von Hügel also wrote letters of support to individuals who published positive remarks about Loisy, such as Dom Cuthbert Butler (later the abbot of Downside) and Father W. H. Kent of Manning's clerical foundation at Bayswater.[22] Von Hügel's diaries and letters, especially from 1903 to 1908, reveal an intense lobbying effort. He recognized the importance of a network of support for reform. During this period, von Hügel was tirelessly writing letters and articles and reviews in English, French, and Italian. For example, he wrote a review of LeRoy's work in the *Hibbert Journal*; solicited an article by LeRoy for *Il Rinnovamento*; wrote an article on Loisy for the *Encyclopedia Britannica*; and suggested to Mignot in which journals he hoped Mignot might write favorable articles.[23]

DISTRIBUTING MODERNIST WRITINGS

Much of von Hügel's energy—and not an insignificant amount of his money—was spent in distributing modernist writings, both published and unpublished. Particularly crucial was the dissemination of works which were most sensitive, or which could only be privately distributed. A few months after the publication of *L'Evangile et l'Eglise,* Tyrrell published a work, under the pseudonym Hilaire Bourdon, entitled *The Church and the Future* (1903), with "a French title along with the English one, to veil as far as possible the true authorship." The work was a synthesis of Tyrrell's thought and created quite a stir, as von Hügel had predicted. Von Hügel saw to its careful distribution, drawing up a list of people to whom he thought it should be sent "both on account of their gainedness or gainableness to such ideas; of their importance; and of their loyalty and discretion."[24]

Von Hügel's diaries and letters are full of references to his sending multiple copies of various books and articles as gifts or as loans, and he was instrumental in guiding the reading of many people. His most ambitious distribution project was with *Il Rinnovamento*.[25] His promotion of this review was highly successful in involving some individuals in the nascent movement; selling a newspaper or review such as *Il Rinnovamento* offered a way for sympathizers to become involved in a concrete manner. A Mrs. Cancellor[26] was an active and enthusiastic supporter whom the baron recruited, as were the publisher William J. Williams of Williams and Norgate and von Hügel's contacts in Cambridge and Oxford who promoted the journal.[27]

Although poor health often restricted his travels, von Hügel's wealth facilitated them, and his regular family trips to warmer winter climates often turned into modernist campaign trips. He also received an endless

stream of visitors and was forever organizing or joining societies or meetings that furthered his intellectual and religious interests.

CONVERSATIONS AND INTERVIEWS

One of the baron's favorite activities was the traditional "walking conversation." He would frequently invite Tyrrell, Petre, Lilley, or some other
friend to come to tea, lunch, or dinner, and to go for a walk on the
Hampstead Heath or, after his move in 1903, in the Kensington Gardens.
Such walks, even when accompanied only by his dog Taufel, were not
merely for exercise; they were primarily a time for reflection and conversation. Von Hügel apparently had acquired a combination of the manners
of European and English gentry, which gave him an air of self-confidence
and a flair for conversation; he was a master of the social graces, although
his increasing deafness caused him a great deal of difficulty and often
resulted in monologues.[28]

At Loisy's urging, von Hügel called on Mignot, whose episcopal
residence was near Saint-Raphael, where the von Hügel family was spend-
ing the winter of 1893–94. Loisy suggested that the day was "memorable
in the history of Catholic modernism; I would be strongly inclined to see
it as one of the dates which might be given as its beginning."[29]

The following winter the baron visited Loisy at Neuilly, just after
the latter's expulsion from the Institut Catholique. When he arrived in
Rome, von Hügel obtained an interview with the papal secretary of state,
Cardinal Rampolla, to discuss both the validity of Anglican orders and
biblical studies. The baron boldly defended critical scholarship, arguing
that *Providentissimus Deus* had had adverse effects on Catholicism in
England among intelligent people (Barmann 1972, 55 ff.). He argued
that Loisy was helpful in bringing undergraduates into the Roman Church,
especially at Cambridge, and pointed out that Loisy was well known and
highly respected in English university and academic circles.[30]

Wherever he went, the baron sought out friends who concurred
about the need for intellectual reform in the church. His association with
the Italian modernists was initiated in the 1890s, when Genocchi hosted
meetings at the Casa dei Missionari in Rome. There von Hügel met with
French scholars Duchesne and Vigouroux, American bishops Spalding
and O'Connell, and Italian scholars Semeria, Ghignoni, don Brizio, Casciola, Minocchi, and Fogazzaro. As Minocchi explains,

> The philosophy of the Jesuits, Billot's theology, Thomism itself, were all
> abused there; and equally so were Father Cornely's "pseudo-critical" attitude
> and even more so the Abbé Vigoroux's views on the Bible. We discussed the

neo-Catholic theology of Ollé-Laprune and of Blondel with interest, and in particular that of Laberthonnière. But above all we approved of Loisy's work. . . . We laughed and sneered at the Roman court but no more than we did at the Jesuits. The recent pontifical letter [8 September 1899] to the French clergy in favour of the "pore text" of Thomism and the condemnation of what was called Americanism were likewise branded. . . . But besides, it was clear and well known in the Vatican that Genocchi wished or urged or allowed *much that was true* to be said informally among Catholics. The only thing was it must not be written or expressed in public. The Roman Church always behaved like this, Duchesne explained to us: indifferent to logical speculations and very careful of the way things were going and the religious feeling of the people. (in Ranchetti 1969, 87–88)

In France as well as Italy, von Hügel undertook a whirlwind round of visits in search of support for his cause.[31] On 14 April 1907, Chevalier took von Hügel to a meeting organized by Abbé Portal of about forty young men (thirty of whom were clergymen), where the baron spoke on "The 'New Theology' and Religion in England." Von Hügel's record of his French visit demonstrates the existence of a rather varied group of people interested in modernist issues—a group which reached far beyond the names and faces normally present in accounts of the movement, since most did not play visible roles in its leadership. That a predominantly clerical group would go to hear a layman speak on theology was remarkable.

In England, the baron moved among several circles of aristocratic and highly educated people, and had close friends in the academic community. He belonged to numerous groups, including the Cambridge Philological Society, the Hellenic Society, the Numismatic Society, the Synthetic Society, and the London Society for the Study of Religion, using them as forums for modernist ideas.

Von Hügel's relationship with the Italians who published *Il Rinnovamento* was of primary importance. He attended a crucial gathering of that group in Molveno, shortly after *Lamentabili* had been issued condemning modernist propositions. This gathering came as close to being a "movement strategy meeting" as any gathering throughout the period, but it was too late to have any real effect on the movement's future; little future remained. Explicitly modernist meetings were not held on any broad scale until the eve of the movement's condemnation, providing further evidence that what explicit modernist organization did exist was inadvertently elicited by the Vatican's effort to suppress modernist scholarship. It was primarily because of the suppression that the modernists were thrown together to form a common defense and a supportive network as insurgents labeled by Vatican officials.

Von Hügel's account of the meeting in his diary (16–19 August 1907) is like something out of the pages of a Fogazzaro novel. It demonstrates the leadership role that he played in the movement and his advocacy of scientific criticism. He was the major link between the Italian modernists and those elsewhere, and was a moderator who urged "careful charity and magnanimity towards" their opponents.

He also pushed the group in a religious direction; he began two of the three mornings of the meeting by going to a nearby church, and he spoke to the group of the necessity of a "deep, self-renouncing Christian life." Finally, von Hügel's "little parting speech" reveals his strategies for the movement. Von Hügel resisted the development of any formal organization or closed system. In a letter to Loisy about the meeting, von Hügel said that he had[32]

"requested all to pray and to struggle," each doing his duty, "to the full and with strength . . . to suppress any differences between himself and his companions in the battle during this time of severe crisis." Our movement's unity is in its "general orientation," notwithstanding the divergences among our ideas on specific points. . . . Let us be wary of advocating "a closed system, of adhering to just any theory in place of hard work, a full life and noble, fruitful suffering!"

FINANCING THE MOVEMENT

Another important activity of the Baron's was his generous financial support of various people and projects. Von Hügel gave substantial amounts of money to *Il Rinnovamento* and solicited funds for it from a number of his friends, particularly Lilley and Newsom (see Barmann 1972, 208). Although his influence would probably have been considerable at any rate, the fact that he was a major financial backer of the review placed him in a position of considerable influence in its decision-making processes.

He also offered support to Loisy and Tyrrell when their careers in the church were in jeopardy and their financial situation uncertain. When Loisy became ill in 1899, von Hügel offered him a pension of 200 francs a year, although Loisy felt it unnecessary and declined.[33] Von Hügel offered Tyrrell the option of living near his family and taking his lunches and dinners with them, which he did.[34] There were other instances of von Hügel's help, such as his willingness to find a publisher and if necessary to pay for the translation of one of Tyrrell's works into Italian.[35] The closeness of their relationship is indicated by a comment in von Hügel's diary on 8 July 1907: "Dined alone with Tyrrell and Miss Lance." Tyrrell became a part of the von Hügel family.

The cost to von Hügel of reprints and postage alone must have been considerable, since he frequently mailed manuscripts, reprints, and books, as well as hundreds of letters. There are indications of other small donations to modernist causes: money to help in the publication of Buonaiuti's *Nova et Vetera,* for example, and legal fees for a young English priest who sought legal advice when he was dismissed from his position in 1908 for remarks made in a discussion with a fellow priest during the period of Vatican suppression of modernism.[36]

At no point did von Hügel attempt to institutionalize the movement by creating a formal organization; the ecclesiastical authorities would immediately have perceived such a structure as a threat to Vatican hegemony. Rather, the baron quietly supported various people and projects here and there, providing a network that facilitated the work of various scholars, particularly in Britain, France, Italy, and Germany.[37]

VON HÜGEL'S INTERNATIONAL CORRESPONDENTS

GREAT BRITAIN

Emile Poulat, a noted expert on French modernism, has claimed that the modernists scarcely exercised any influence in Britain (1962, 18). Although not as significant as the French movement, more modernism existed among the British than Poulat acknowledges. Von Hügel's diaries document a great deal of modernist activity, although much of it, as Poulat points out, was with Anglicans, among whom Loisy had a number of followers (ibid.).

The most important of von Hügel's modernist friends in Britain were Tyrrell and Petre.[38] Other correspondents who were not as obviously modernist, either because their positions were not always public or because they had ambivalent opinions about modernism, have slid into the background or disappeared altogether from the record. Some efforts to collect information about their involvement with the movement have been made by Vidler (1970) and Barmann (1972). Although one must be cautious about assuming that because von Hügel corresponded or ate with someone, his guest was automatically "implicated" in the modernist affair, there were few around von Hügel from about 1903 until 1908 who were not caught up in the modernist storm. Relationships with unsympathetic individuals cooled as the baron poured his energies into the movement.

Several of von Hügel's correspondents were non-Catholics, but many British Catholics were actively involved in reading and supporting his modernist friends. One of the baron's strategies was to convince Catholic authorities that Loisy and Tyrrell were indispensable to Catholicism because of the impact they made among prominent scholars and educated people in Britain, Catholic and non-Catholic alike.

Because the intellectual community in Britain was overwhelmingly non-Catholic, it was important to cultivate the latter's support, particularly among scholarly circles in London, Oxford, and Cambridge, where the baron found intellectual stimulation. As a result of his efforts, the works of Loisy and Tyrrell were widely known and respected in Britain. Lilley was the most active Anglican in the movement, and he maintained close contact with von Hügel, as the frequency of their correspondence demonstrates.[39] Other important Anglican sympathizers included the scholarly Anglican curate G. C. Rawlinson, who visited with Loisy, Mignot, Laberthonnière, and LeRoy.[40]

A letter to the Reverend Canon Newsom, the warden of King's College London Hostel (and later master of Selwyn College, Cambridge), helps to clarify the baron's position on the relationship between modernism and his Anglican friends. On 7 September 1909 he wrote to Newsom about Tyrrell, suggesting

that "Modernism" is in no sense an exclusively R. C. trouble; that the problems which haunted T[yrrell] had helped to break his like are besetting every form of traditional, institutional Christianity; [they are] ... thoroughly common to Canon Sanday and Pope Pius X, Bishop Gore and Cardinal Merry del Val. ... As our friend Lilley has said so well, "The pressing divisions are no more *vertical,* denominational,—they are *horizontal,* interdenominational." (von Hügel 1927, 167)

Von Hügel nonetheless had a strong sense of Catholic identity, a point he made clear to Loisy in a comment on Fawkes, who had said that "liberal Catholicism is in no sense the antagonist or rival of liberal Protestantism" (Fawkes 1913, 277). "Fawkes is a good and intelligent man," von Hügel wrote to Loisy, "but I often ask myself just where his Catholicism lies. I find devilishly little of it here" (Loisy 1930–31, II:425).

Not all of the baron's correspondents were necessarily modernists, but he drew many of them into the affairs of the movement because of their positions with journals and publishing houses—notably Wilfrid Ward, editor of the *Dublin Review,* and William J. Williams of Williams and Norgate.[41] Another important category of modernist sympathizer was a group of progressive women who gathered around von Hügel. Unfortunately, they have been ignored in much of the modernist literature, both because of their secondary role in the movement and because it is difficult to find information about them.

Several of von Hügel's friends, including Adeline Chapman, Mrs. Cancellor, and Ida Taylor, were actively involved in promoting the modernist cause, pushing *Il Rinnovamento,* reading modernist works, and visiting frequently with von Hügel himself.[42] Other frequent visitors in the von Hügel household were drawn into the movement: von Hügel's cousin Elizabeth Sharp, Juliet and Mildred Mansel, and Eveline Lance. Lance ("Evie") appears frequently in the diaries as a houseguest with whom the baron had long conversations about modernism. Von Hügel gave these friends copies of various articles and loaned them books. Kitty Clutton, a good friend of Tyrrell and a sister-in-law of Petre's sister, was also in frequent contact with von Hügel as well as with other modernists. She lived in Richmond and often associated with Tyrrell, Petre, Ward, Caird, and others.[43]

Mary Ward, Matthew Arnold's niece, wrote two novels about the issues of modernism and was a frequent dinner guest at the von Hügels' along with her husband, Humphrey Ward, an Oxford Fellow and later the art critic for the London *Times*. She maintained a lively interest in Loisy and Tyrrell, and following her extremely popular *Robert Elsmere* ([1888] 1967), she wrote a Catholic counterpart to that Protestant novel, *The Case of Richard Meynell* (1911). The former work, an international bestseller, was about an Anglican clergyman who lost his belief in traditional Christianity.

Another individual whose participation in the baron's modernist efforts has been underrated[44] is journalist Robert Dell, a graduate of University College, Oxford, who was converted to Catholicism in 1897. Dell was described by the *Times* as "one of the most familiar figures in international journalism in Paris and Geneva during the last thirty years" (Vidler 1970, 167). He was in Paris during the final crisis of the movement, and corresponded frequently with von Hügel[45] as well as with Lilley and Houtin. Dell was not known for his moderation, and more than once his aggressive espousal of modernism was criticized by von Hügel.[46]

The baron had a substantial impact on the learned world of England. A final word on von Hügel's activities in England is offered by Tyrrell's musing in a letter to Lilley, in which he said that "von Hügel and Bremond together are very amusing. Bremond and I have decided that the Baron is God. The attribute of omniscience is beyond repute, and the others must be entailed."[47]

FRANCE

Baron von Hügel's modernist activities were not confined to England. Through his relationships with Loisy and later with Mignot, LeRoy, Chevalier, and others, he maintained an active interest in French Catholicism. Loisy's correspondence was most important; it was at the core of the entire movement and was initiated by von Hügel in 1893.[48] The frequency of their correspondence varied, but remained intense throughout the modernist period, as the letters in the Loisy papers at the Bibliothèque Nationale in Paris indicate (see appendix B). The most intense periods of correspondence were 1903–04, following the condemnation of *L'Evangile et l'Eglise,* and again in 1907–08, after the condemnation of modernism.

After Loisy, von Hügel's most important French correspondent was Mignot.[49] The baron maintained a correspondence with Mignot for some years, although its frequency dropped off quickly after the condemnation of the movement. The von Hügel–Mignot letters contain discussions about how to avoid one crisis or another, and information both about what was occurring in Rome and elsewhere and about substantive considerations. The focus of many letters was "our excellent Loisy"[50] and strategies concerning support for him and others.[51] As the movement progressed, the baron's relationship with LeRoy became very important. Whereas Blondel had found LeRoy rather rash, LeRoy's letters to von Hügel reveal a somewhat different approach. For example, he followed a "von Hügelian" line of caution in response to the Vatican's condemnation of modernism:[52]

> This, then, is how we should deal with M. Loisy. Play for time by doing nothing; that, I believe, is the best course of action. What would be the use of getting into a fight and provoking most drastic steps? Our true strength lies in work coupled in an imperturbable manner with a Christian life: let us stick to that.

The strategy which LeRoy was suggesting was that followed by his close friend and colleague, Pierre Teilhard de Chardin, who was forbidden to publish during his lifetime, but who continued to write for posthumous publication and had a large impact on the Second Vatican Council long after his death (see Lindbeck 1970).

Other important French correspondents of the baron included Charles Denis, a priest in the diocese of Beauvais who bought the *Annales de philosophie chrétienne* in 1895, leaving it to Blondel upon his death in 1905 (Poulat 1962, 345). Denis and von Hügel developed a rather extensive correspondence the year before Denis's death. The famous *Lettres Romaines* were published in the *Annales,* and shortly thereafter Denis's Lenten sermons were placed on the *Index of Prohibited Books.* Another progressive editor, George Fonsegrive of *La Quinzaine,* who corresponded with von Hügel, was the subject of considerable controversy as well (see Loisy 1930–31, II:97, 570–572). Their correspondence subsided somewhat after *La Quinzaine* was forced to cease publication in 1907.

Two less well-known French modernists developed extensive links with von Hügel: Jacques Chevalier, who spent a good deal of time in England,[53] and Jacques Zeiller. Chevalier, a young professor of philosophy at the University of Grenoble, is mentioned only briefly by Vidler (1970, 184–185) as an associate of the modernists and a friend of Lilley and Young, with whom Chevalier corresponded. In his *Mémoires*, Loisy mentioned the "excellent young men," including Jacques Chevalier, who in 1907 began to worry about the distance that Loisy had apparently traveled from Catholic orthodoxy.

This is not to say that Chevalier was no longer a modernist; at the time, he was carrying on an extensive correspondence with von Hügel (twenty-three letters in 1907 alone—more than any other French modernist except Loisy). Chevalier's cooling reception of Loisy's work was due less to lack of sympathy than to prudence as the ecclesiastical axe began to fall. Chevalier made his sympathies clear in a letter to Young in 1907:[54]

> We shall never defeat violence by violent means, but by observing the holy decrees of Christian charity and silence: time is on the side of truth; we lose nothing, but win everything by waiting. Let us only hope that the authorities, alert to the ever-increasing signs of menace, touched by our patience, and yet fully aware and guided by our unshakeable assurance and the Holy Spirit, will not lead kindred spirits to rebellion and not push the crisis to any extreme.

Zeiller was apparently a lay scholar on the faculty of the Catholic University of Fribourg (Poulat 1962, 275). Although he is not discussed in the standard studies of modernism,[55] he developed a frequent correspondence with von Hügel toward the end of the modernist period, and in his *Mémoires*, Loisy mentioned Zeiller as someone who shared von Hügel's ideas and who was accustomed to his manner (Loisy 1930–31, III:364).

The baron wrote and spoke fluently in French, so he had little difficulty in maintaining relationships with a wide variety of French scholars, becoming an important leader in French modernism. Despite their conflicts, Loisy wrote to von Hügel on 25 November 1901, saying "you are the true Father of the Church, the true Augustine" (Petre 1944, 40).

ITALY

Von Hügel was born in Florence and spent a great deal of time in Italy with his family. Furthermore, Rome was the center of the Catholic world and it was beneficial to the modernist movement to maintain sources of information and support there. More important, a number of persons in

Italy shared the baron's concern for reform in the church. Letters to and from the Italians recorded in von Hügel's diaries show that he maintained regular contact with Alfieri, Semeria, Scotti, Gallavresi, and Fogazzaro, among others (see appendix A). As his hopes for Loisy and Tyrrell dimmed—and particularly as Loisy became disillusioned—von Hügel turned increasingly to Italy, where a group of intelligent, energetic followers of Loisy, Tyrrell, and von Hügel organized a modernist journal with his help.

Much of the responsibility for *Il Rinnovamento* fell to von Hügel, to whom the younger editors turned for intellectual and financial assistance, as well as for spiritual and moral support. Many collaborators for *Il Rinnovamento*, particularly outside of Italy, were solicited by von Hügel or through his assistance and advice.[56]

Among the Italian modernists, von Hügel's most frequent correspondence was with Alfieri (one of the three coeditors of the review); much of it was related to the policies of the journal. The extensiveness of this correspondence, initiated after *Il Rinnovamento* was conceived, indicates more that Alfieri was the baron's prime contact with the review than that he was the baron's most important Italian contact. Von Hügel writes more enthusiastically about Semeria, to whom he did not write as frequently. Alfieri usually appears in Loisy's *Mémoires* in connection with the two other editors of the review, Casati and Scotti, rather than because of his own particular contributions. But Alfieri's extensive correspondence with von Hügel suggests that he played a more central role in the movement than most chroniclers have suggested.[57] Alfieri's role was not entirely administrative, either; von Hügel reported in his diaries, for example, that in 1907 Alfieri arrived at his hotel in Levico, Italy, and stayed for two full days, keeping von Hügel "fully employed with talks on one's life-subjects," including an extensive reading and discussion of *Lamentabili*.[58] Despite some dissension in the ranks, von Hügel had confidence in Alfieri's direction of *Il Rinnovamento* and defended him in a conflict with Casati over who was to take major administrative responsibilities.[59]

Semeria, considered by his adversaries to be the leader of Italian modernism, was a second major Italian correspondent of von Hügel's. He traveled with Minocchi to Russia to visit Tolstoy, and was one of the first of the Italian modernists to develop a relationship with von Hügel.[60] In 1905 Semeria visited London and, at von Hügel's invitation, addressed the London Society for the Study of Religion.[61] Semeria had a winning personality and was widely admired and respected among the Italian modernists. The Italian Barnabite was also much encouraged by von Hügel, who respected his opinions and valued his friendship; it was often to Semeria that the baron turned for advice.[62]

Count Scotti, one of the three coeditors of *Il Rinnovamento,* was another of von Hügel's Italian colleagues. A friend and biographer of Fogazzaro and a founder of *Il Rinnovamento,* Scotti remained a source of encouragement for von Hügel until the final demise of the review. He was proclaimed honorary president of the First National Congress of the *Lega democratica nazionale* and tried to unite the political and doctrinal wings of the movement.[63]

Perhaps the most distinguished of von Hügel's Italian correspondents was Fogazzaro, whose role in the movement became increasingly significant as modernism approached its final days. The two men exhibited a great deal of mutual respect and admiration. Following the condemnations in the *Pascendi,* von Hügel wrote to Ward about the fact that Rome was concentrating its condemnations on Loisy, Tyrrell, and Fogazzaro. "The latter three," von Hügel wrote,[64]

have done far too much for the Church's most difficult interests, the official spokesmen of the Church have, for the present, proved themselves far too competent and just in these deep waters, for it to be right that we should do anything towards producing such a concentration.

Fogazzaro and von Hügel had much in common besides their intellectual and religious affinities. Fogazzaro cultivated links among likeminded Italian Catholics and, like von Hügel, played a particularly crucial role in linking clergy and laity. He also added a certain stature to the movement and cultivated his contacts within important circles.

Giovanni Genocchi, of the Congregation of the Sacred Heart, also maintained a cordial relationship with the baron, although as a member of the Vatican's Biblical Commission, he found himself in the ambivalent position of being under frequent attack by modernists and antimodernists alike. His sympathy for the modernists is evident, however, and for many of them, he was a friend and confidant (see Turvasi 1979; Ranchetti 1969, 32). Genocchi was committed to historical criticism and many of the principles of modernism; he had an "esprit liberal" and was in frequent trouble with antimodernist forces. Loisy judged him to have a rather good head in criticism, but felt he was perhaps too political (Poulat 1962, 356). Among the modernists, Genocchi played a moderating role and provided information about the ongoing situation in Rome.[65] His correspondence with the baron began to decline toward the later, more troubled period. On the Biblical Commission, Genocchi was helpless in mitigating the effect of antimodernist forces.

Another young scholar in the Milan group was Gallavresi, whose correspondence with von Hügel was frequent, but who remained uneasy about some of the implications of the baron's and Loisy's ideas (see Loisy 1930–31, II:62). Similarly, the Benedictine scholar Germane Morin was sympathetic with von Hügel's efforts, but became disaffected when things heated up in Rome.[66] Brizio Casciola was a scholar-priest associated with *Il Rinnovamento* whom von Hügel described as "a saint: utterly and purposely out of all touch with the official world; and as open as the day, as Loisy or Duchesne or Blondel, an admirer of the best of Wellhausen and Holtzmann" (in Barmann 1972, 62).

Other notable modernist figures in Italy had surprisingly infrequent correspondence with von Hügel. The *Il Rinnovamento* coeditor Casati, for example, had very little contact by mail with the baron (according to von Hügel's diaries), and von Hügel records receiving only three letters from Murri, all of them in 1904. Nor did Buonaiuti and von Hügel meet until July 1907, when Crespi brought Buonaiuti to the baron's home.[67] Buonaiuti wrote very highly of von Hügel in his description of the gathering of Italian modernists at Molveno in 1907 (Buonaiuti [1945] 1969).

In Italy, as in England, there was a group of women who were active in the movement, but who do not appear in the standard historical accounts—notably Concetta Ginntini, and Contessa Lillian Priuli-Bon (from Verona).[68] One can assume from the baron's correspondence—and from Fogazzaro's novel, *Il Santo*—that there were Italian women involved in the modernists' efforts, although it is difficult to discern the nature of their role.

GERMANY

Von Hügel claimed to be German in terms of both familial and intellectual ancestry (1927, 110–111), and he read German scholarship frequently.[69] Those German scholars with whom he had the most contact included Eucken, Holtzmann, Rothmanner, Sauer, Troeltsch, and Vaihinger (see appendix A). Modernism in Germany was quite different from modernism in other European countries. It emerged at a time of university liberalism and reform Catholicism (see Poulat 1962, 17), but there was no Catholic modernist movement in Germany, as there was in France, Italy, and England. The baron's relationship with the Germans was a source of information and inspiration, rather than a potential ground for modernist reform. Scientific historiography was developed primarily in Germany, and was the source of much of von Hügel's scholarly orientation.

The baron's closest colleagues in Germany were the Protestant scholars Eucken and Troeltsch. There are ninety-three letters from Eucken among the von Hügel papers in the St. Andrews Library (surpassed in number only by the Loisy and Tyrrell correspondence), which provides one indication of the personal and intellectual importance of the relationship. Von Hügel also developed a close relationship with Troeltsch, who influenced Tyrrell, Loisy (see Loisy 1930–31), Buonaiuti ([1945] 1969), and, of course, the baron himself. Von Hügel often recalled his relationship with Eucken and Troeltsch when dealing with Protestant colleagues in England who were skeptical about Loisy's Catholicism.

Troeltsch was very interested in both Loisy and Tyrrell; he read their work appreciatively, and wrote to von Hügel that they were all involved in the same struggle (see von Hügel 1927, 151). Von Hügel was, in turn, enthusiastic about Troeltsch's work and urged his friends to read it.[70] He used his influence at Oxford toward Troeltsch's receiving an honorary degree there (ibid., 145), and felt an important personal kinship with the German scholar.[71]

Troeltsch and von Hügel were drawn to each other by a common belief in the importance of historical scholarship. "He has the most sensitive consciousness of the complexity and relativity of all history and its evidences," von Hügel wrote to Tyrrell, "[which he combines with] a truly touching spiritual and personally devotional sense."[72] Troeltsch saw himself and von Hügel as facing similar trials in their encounters with church officials, and claimed that the two of them were a species endangered by ecclesiastical officials (see Rollmann 1978, 48). Following a year of correspondence, the pair met when von Hügel went to Heidelberg in 1902.[73] Although they were never to meet again (due to war and illness), they had a lengthy and significant correspondence until Troeltsch's death in 1923.

Another German scholar with whom von Hügel had considerable contact was the eminent Strassburg New Testament scholar, Heinrich J. Holtzmann.[74] Although his most important scholarly work preceded the period during which the two corresponded (1901–1910), Holtzmann came to von Hügel's attention when he reviewed books by Minocchi and Semeria. Von Hügel relied heavily upon Holtzmann's New Testament scholarship, as can be seen in his 1894 articles in the *Dublin Review*, which called for a liberal interpretation of Leo XIII's encyclical, *Providentissimus Deus* (1893).

Holtzmann found a number of affinities with the modernists, although the Roman hierarchy's suppression of their scholarship reinforced his own Protestantism. He was more than happy to oblige von Hügel and his friends by writing reviews and pressing for a positive reception of their work among German scholars. Despite some difficulties with their Catholicism, Holtzmann admired the scholarship of Loisy, Semeria, Minocchi, and Tyrrell.[75] What he liked about the modernists, in addition to the quality of their scholarship, was their effort to obtain greater freedom of inquiry and their demand for "the utilization of modern scientific progress, especially of modern philosophy instead of scholasticism" (Holtzmann 1903, 169–170; Rollmann 1979, 140).

Although peripheral to the political strategies of the modernist movement, von Hügel's German friends provided important intellectual input and support for the movement's participants, especially von Hügel himself. Much of what excited von Hügel about Loisy's work, it seems to me, is that it used the critical methods employed by German scholars, but without their Protestant underpinnings and theological implications.

VON HÜGEL'S MODERNIST NETWORK

In sum, the modernist movement was a group of relatively isolated scholars exploring different aspects of forbidden conceptual territory, their efforts constantly thwarted by the authorities of the church. What is remarkable is not that von Hügel was able to do so little, but that he accomplished so much. The problem of organizing a reform movement among intellectuals was best expressed by the fictional character Abbé Mariner in Fogazzaro's *Il Santo* ([1904] 1906, 134):

> Associations may be useful in helping to raise salaries, they may promote industries and commerce; but science and truth, never. Reforms will surely be brought about some day, because ideas are stronger than men, and are always pressing forward; but by arraying them in armour, and marching them forward in companies, you expose them to a terrible fire, which will check their progress for a long time to come.

In the heat of battle, ideas become associated with the interests of the warring factions, and hence become distorted. The modernists did not act through mass mobilization and enthusiastic mobs (although there was a hint of that from time to time in Italy), but quietly, in libraries and studies, in letters, articles, and books.

REFORM ACTIVITIES: CORRESPONDING AND PUBLISHING

As a reform movement among scholars, the work of the modernist movement consisted primarily of writing and publishing, of private exchanges of thoughts and ideas, and of the publication of articles and books.

PUBLISHING

Although it was a social movement, modernist activities were somewhat individualistic, as are any intellectual activities. There is a limit to the degree to which one person can be involved in the creation of another's intellectual production, and the final product is largely that of the individual scholar. Yet even the solitary scholar is engaged in a highly social activity in the privacy of his or her study, by drawing upon an intellectual tradition and writing for an anticipated audience. The scholar's perception of who that audience is and how it will respond to the final product has a formative influence on the product's creation.

The issue of the audience for whom works were written was very important in the modernist controversy. The problem of audience segregation (Goffmann 1959) becomes acute when, as the term "published" implies, the ideas in a book or journal article are made public—that is, become available to any literate person with the means and interest to acquire them. Church officials believed that the publication of Loisy, Tyrrell, and others would create a scandal throughout the church. They advised Loisy to write in Latin, but Loisy claimed that his audience was limited to scholars, who would not be disturbed by his books. French Catholicism had, in his opinion, been too afraid of scandalizing scholars. "To each his own clientele," Loisy wrote. "Good, honest simple folk people don't read it" (1903a; xxxii).

There is a sense in which the church authorities were correct: however, the publication of Loisy's books did disseminate his ideas beyond the small circle of scholars who were engaged in biblical criticism, and often fostered a simplistic impression that overlooked the subtle aspects of his work. There was an enthusiastic audience of young clergymen and seminarians who were likely to pass on some of Loisy's ideas to their parishioners in simplified form. And his ideas were discussed among many who had not read anything he had written, as Loisy himself charged.[76] This threat was even more genuine with Tyrrell and Fogazzaro, both of whom wrote in a more popular vein.

In 1892, early in the movement's history, Loisy founded the *Enseignement biblique* to publish a summary of his lectures at the Institut Catholique. There was immediate resistance from Duchesne, who, according to Loisy, "horrified Monsignor d'Hulst by remonstrating with him as to the possible outcome of such an enterprise, since it was sure to arouse a protest from the Dominicans of the *Revue biblique,* assisted by Abbé Vigouroux" ([1913] 1968, 116–117). Loisy claimed that Duchesne's fear was exaggerated, "as my little periodical was too insignificant to rival any other," but the authorities agreed with Duchesne, and it was eventually an article in the *Enseignement biblique* that led to Loisy's dismissal from the Institut. Whereas it was suspect to discuss such issues in the privacy of the classroom, it was even worse to do so in public, because this undermined the authority of the church and precipitated rumors far beyond the scholarly community.

Loisy also collaborated with the *Revue critique,* edited by Abbé Arthur Chuquet (Loisy [1913] 1968, 167; 1930–31, I:201), and wrote under a pseudonym for the *Revue du clergé français* (Loisy [1913] 1968, 173 ff.). In 1896, Loisy established the *Revue d'histoire et de littérature religieuses* with the help of two friends who were professors at the Institut Catholique, several laymen, and Mignot (Loisy 1930–31, I:395).

The *Annales de philosophie chrétienne* became an important forum for modernist issues, despite conflicts among its owner, Maurice Blondel, its editor, Laberthonnière, and the frequent modernist contributor, LeRoy. It was in the *Annales* that the mysterious "Lettres Romaines," written by an anonymous Italian modernist,[77] were published. The letters, which praised and defended Loisy's scholarly efforts, were sent to von Hügel by Semeria (see Barmann 1972, 196–197) and were published in the first few months of 1904. Other journals—notably *La Quinzaine* and *Demain*[78]—also became sympathetic organs for the airing of modernist ideas.

The most important review from Italy, *Il Rinnovamento,* has already been discussed in some detail. A number of other Italian reviews provided a forum for modernist issues and an institutional focus for people with similar interests. Minocchi's editorship of the *Revista bibliografica italiana* (1896–1899) and his *Studi religiosi* (1901–1907) helped organize young Italian clerical scholars and disseminated works by Loisy, Houtin, Harnack, Tyrrell, Buonaiuti, and Blondel.[79]

Murri founded *Vita nova* shortly after his ordination in 1892 (the first issue did not appear, however, until February 1895). In 1898 he produced the first issue of the prominent clerical review, *Cultura sociale,* which had 4,000 subscribers shortly after its appearance (Ranchetti 1969, 101). Murri also founded *Revisita di Cultura,* which was suspended for some time and then reappeared in 1909. Other journals related to modernism in Italy included *Vita religiosa*[80] and the Florentine *Rassegna nazionale,* which published an Italian translation of von Hügel's *Pilot* article on Loisy.

In addition to journal articles, the books that the modernists published were central for the movement. The various publishers who assisted the modernists in publishing their work played a key role—notably Picard and Nourry in France, and Longmann's and Williams & Norgate in

England. Von Hügel always urged Tyrrell to sign his articles (Petre 1937*b*, 147), but several modernists—including Tyrrell and Loisy—published under pseudonyms, thus creating some conflicts within the movement. Moreover, as the church became increasingly intolerant of the modernists' publications, much of their activity was driven underground.

CORRESPONDENCE

It was difficult for Catholics to do scholarly work outside of the scholastic framework without the support and constructive criticism of others who understood what they were doing. The modernists' correspondence provided that support; later, as conflicts with church authorities escalated, such correspondence was crucial for exchanging information about developments in various circles of the church, discussing strategies, and so on.

In addition to the records of correspondence in von Hügel's diaries, there are three other major sources of information about the correspondence among the modernists, all of which demonstrate the conscious existence of a reform movement: the Loisy and Houtin Papers in the Bibliothèque nationale, Paris; the Lilley and Ward Papers in the St. Andrews University Library; and the von Hügel–Tyrrell letters and Petre Papers in the British Library.

Loisy's Correspondence

Loisy's two most important correspondents during the modernist period were von Hügel and Mignot.[81] Mignot played an extremely important role in Loisy's career for three reasons: he was a bishop of the church and supported Loisy's work within the church hierarchy; he was a Frenchman in sympathy with some of the more characteristically French aspects of Loisy's scholarship; and he was an extremely supportive friend and colleague. On occasion, as with the publication of *L'Evangile et l'Eglise,* Loisy consulted Mignot rather than von Hügel for advice.

After von Hügel and Mignot, Albert Houtin wrote most frequently to Loisy during the modernist period.[82] Despite the hostile outcome of their relationship (each felt that he had been deceived in the friendship), the two men carried on a remarkably frequent correspondence, particularly after 1908.[83] Houtin, a chronicler of scholarly life among Catholics of the time, was in touch with a wide variety of people. He provided Loisy with information about activities in the intellectual community and in the church, although Loisy later became suspicious of his interpretations.

After Houtin and Marquise Arconati-Visconti (with whom Loisy did not correspond until after his own participation in the modernist movement had ended),[84] Jewish scholar and archeologist Salomon Reinach is the next most frequent correspondent, with a total of forty-three letters to Loisy between 1900 and 1908. A number of Loisy's adversaries insisted upon pointing to this relationship as clear evidence that modernism was a plot by the Jews and Masons to destroy the Catholic Church, just as they maintained that Loisy's relationship with Sabatier somehow proved that modernism was a Protestant plot. Such interpretations reflect the conspiratorial attitude into which many conservative Catholics were pressed by their definition of the situation as one in which various forces of modernity were uniting against Catholicism.[85] Reinach, a professor at the Collège de France and a supporter of Loisy's candidacy for a chair there, was an historian of religion and archeologist who maintained an interest in all religious affairs. After the condemnation of the movement, Reinach wrote, "not since the Council of Trent has the scientific study of the scriptures been so severely impeded" (Houtin 1913, 212).

Dr. Emile Joseph Dillon, a scholarly journalist and for some time the Russian correspondent for the *Daily Telegraph,* played an important role in Loisy's career as well, and was a frequent correspondent.[86] Dillon was Loisy's agent for an English translation of *L'Evangile et l'Eglise* (Loisy 1930–31, II:248); he was also the author of a bitingly critical, anonymous article in the *Contemporary Review* (Dillon 1894; Barmann 1972, 42) entitled "The Papal Encyclical and the Bible."

Loisy's other correspondents included Sabatier and Fawkes, both of whom featured prominently in the movement. Sabatier's interest in Catholicism was stimulated by his research on Saint Francis of Assisi, which established his reputation among Catholic and Protestant scholars alike. Louis Havet, president of the fourth section of the Ecole des Hautes Etudes and professor at the Collège de France, was the initiator of Loisy's candidacy at the college and an important correspondent, as was the scholar-priest Paul Lejay.[87]

Hippolyte Renaudin (1853–1916) was curé of Saint-Alpin de Chalons from 1903 until he was appointed archpriest of Sezanne in 1912 (Poulat 1960, 396). Monsignor LaCroix, bishop of Tarantaise during the modernist crisis, was a scholarly bishop with several parallels to Mignot. He founded the *Revue du clergé française* in 1893, and after the encyclical *Pascendi* (1907) resigned his episcopate and was named director of studies at the Section of Religious Sciences of the Ecole Pratique des Hautes Etudes.

Bremond and Loisy also maintained a regular correspondence and a warm friendship. Bremond was a quiet defender of Loisy only because he wished to protect his relationship with the church and with the society of Jesus, of which he was a member until 1904. He claimed to have "too little faith to be a modernist" (ibid., 335), but was much admired by Tyrrell, von Hügel, and Petre, as well as by Loisy.[88]

From 1897 until 1910, Loisy maintained a regular correspondence with Hyacinthe Loyson (1827–1912), a Catholic priest who separated from the church after the First Vatican Council. Although he remained a religious person and was in contact with many progressive religious figures, Loyson moved toward an antidogmatic ecumenism, expressed in his statement that "the greatest religion is that which worships, without either speaking of or to God" (ibid., 376).

Loisy also wrote to Joseph Turmel (1859–1943) throughout the period, as well as to Franz Cumont, the prolific Belgian historian of religion who was a professor at the University of Gand from 1892–1910. Cumont was a collaborator with Loisy in the *Revue d'histoire et de littérature religieuses*. Although Loisy maintained contact with the Italian modernists, the only one with whom he corresponded regularly was Genocchi, the modernists' friend on the Biblical Commission.

One of the most surprising facts about Loisy's correspondence is the dearth of direct contact with Tyrrell. Although each was constantly informed about one another by von Hügel and each read the other's works, the two men at the core of the modernist movement never met. Loisy received (or at least saved) only fifteen letters from Tyrrell, all written between 1902 and 1908.[89] Despite the lack of intimate contact, a familiarity and mutual respect is quite evident in the letters.[90]

Finally, Loisy claimed that Ernest Babut was "the most active of my collaborators and . . . one of my most dear friends. . . . He had in him the makings of a great scholar. He was gifted with extraordinary perception and at times a refined subtlety; but he understood with clarity and with justice and in depth" (Loisy 1930–31, III:283). Loisy's papers, however, contain only thirty-eight letters from Babut.[91]

Two patterns emerge from Loisy's correspondence. First, despite a preponderance of French correspondents, Loisy's letter writing was wide-ranging and international in character. He was frequently in contact with people outside of France, and hence participated in an international scholarly community despite his lack of travel. Second, and more important, Loisy's correspondence was with scholars—many of them scholar-priests who were facing the same ambivalences in their social situation as Loisy himself, and who wrote to tell him how important his work was to their own faith and work.

With the exceptions of Mignot and LaCroix, officials in the church were virtually out of contact with Loisy. The president of the Biblical

Commission, Cardinal Rampolla, wrote only one letter to the major biblical scholar of the period (if the collection of Loisy's correspondence contains all of his correspondence). Between 1900 and 1908, there are only eight letters from Loisy's own bishop, Cardinal Richard. Of the eight, five are within a three-month period (25 December 1902 through 11 March 1904) during which the cardinal was trying to suppress Loisy's *L'Evangile et l'Eglise*. The correspondence suggests that Loisy was defining his interests not on the basis of what church authorities thought about his work, but primarily in terms of what the scholarly community felt about it.

Cardinal Richard and Loisy were living in two different cultures, although they were members of the same church and lived in the same city during much of the modernist crisis. The strain between them can be seen in a passage that Loisy wrote about the period following Richard's condemnation of his work in 1903:

> Cardinal Richard never suspected that the things he said were for me a veritable torture. I was unable to control all the movement of impatience or of indignation that his tone and attitude aroused. I respected this old man, who was worthy of respect; but he did not himself impose it upon me, and I do not know if there is anyone in the world to whom I have expressed myself with more utter freedom, I may almost say with more brutal frankness. It was repugnant to me to multiply these nerve-racking sessions which revealed the Church to me with all its disguises thrown off, and showed, as well, how vain was my purpose to remain in it. (Loisy [1913] 1968, 257)

The relationship between Richard and Loisy personifies and exemplifies—perhaps more than any other during the period—the radical ambivalence of relations between the ecclesiastical hierarchy and the modernist scholars. Mutual repugnance and mutual respect existed along with mutual misunderstanding; neither side could fathom the definitions of the situation which the other side maintained, so it was almost impossible for the two groups to communicate. For Loisy, Richard symbolized all that he hated about the church: it was Richard who looked over his shoulder as he worked and who denied him freedom of inquiry as a scholar. For the cardinal, Loisy was the symbol of all that he feared in the modern world, in that Loisy was a scholar who insisted upon publishing research that clearly contradicted established doctrines, even though he was a priest sworn to serve the church.

The Lilley Correspondence

Anglican Canon Alfred Leslie Lilley (1860–1940) was actively involved in the movement because of his scholarly proclivities, his interest in modernist issues, and his friendship with von Hügel and Tyrrell. Lilley's correspondence in the archives of the St. Andrews University Library includes letters from key figures in the movement and hundreds of references to Loisy, Tyrrell, and others.

The number of letters a given individual wrote to Lilley can be taken as a rough indicator of the strength of the bond between that individual and Lilley.[92] Similarly, the number of references to an individual in a given letter to Lilley provides some indication of that person's position in the modernist networks with which Lilley was associated (i.e., primarily the English branch of the movement; see appendix C). Beyond the circle of Tyrrell, von Hügel, and Petre, there is a significant drop in the amount of correspondence.[93]

SOCIAL NETWORKS AND ORGANIZATIONAL FAILURES

Most investigations of modernism have avoided the problem of who to include in and who to exclude from the movement by examining particular individuals who were clearly modernists, such as Loisy, Tyrrell, and Petre. Beyond such seminal figures, the boundaries become fuzzy and the conflicts sharper.[94]

Nevertheless, there was a self-conscious movement that was created to reform the Roman Catholic Church, however unclear and disorganized that movement may have been. Specific efforts to maintain contact—through correspondence, exchanging articles and books, and personal visits—provide sufficient evidence of such a movement, and the correspondence just examined provides a rough sketch of its contours. People involved in the modernist movement knew who was and who was not a member. But despite their shared concerns and the self-consciousness of the group (which was caricatured in the Vatican's pronouncements), there was never any formal organization. This was so for a number of reasons.

First of all—despite an apparently widespread following, with estimates varying from 1,500 to 20,000 "members" (Houtin 1913, 269–272)—modernism was primarily a movement of scholars, and the subtleties of scholarship are not amenable to mass movements or formal organizations. It is clear from the correspondence of the movement's participants that most of those in direct contact with Loisy and von Hügel were scholars involved in specialized research and in teaching at universities.

It was always difficult to come to agreement, and in a highly politicized climate, many intellectual conflicts took on the nature of political or personal attacks. Alliances and conflicts often formed around intellectual affinities and differences, and it was virtually impossible for anyone to provide unifying leadership. Loisy was in many ways the most obvious candidate because of the centrality of his scholarship, but he was not interested in organizing a movement and probably did not have the skills and temperament to do so. Von Hügel was more interested in such an organization, but could not count upon the adherence of the others to his plans. Loisy and Tyrrell both explicitly rejected his advice and leadership at key points, and sometimes resented his interference.

The sharp break between von Hügel and both Blondel and Ward—plus the more subtle differences among von Hügel, Tyrrell, and Loisy—rendered a well-organized movement virtually impossible. To these difficulties must be added the hostile environment and institutional barriers that impeded the activities of the modernists. Moreover, there was no common philosophical position (Loisy 1930–31, II:565 ff.) or overall agreement on issues or methodologies, partly because of the nature of the intellectual task and the process of debate that surrounded the modernists' scholarly activity. As Loisy himself conjectured in retrospect, "with less pure intellectuality and more religious enthusiasm, [the movement] might have been a stronger force" ([1913] 1968, 310).

Second, these differences were exacerbated by geographical distances, as well as by linguistic and cultural differences. Despite von Hügel's coordinating activities and the multilingual skills among the modernists, there were formidable boundaries to communication and understanding. For example, Loisy's correspondence shows a strong national orientation, despite his international following. Different national contexts contributed to different definitions of the situation, and von Hügel's attempts to unite French, Italian, and British sympathizers had only meager success. Loisy's poor health, apparent lack of interest in travel, and possible nationalism did not assist the process of bringing together the various national factions of the movement.

A third contributing factor was a set of personality traits that militated against the formation of a movement. According to Petre, Loisy, "though not vindictive, was keenly resentful of direct opposition, unforgiving, and apt to brood over slights and offences"—characteristics that he exhibited with his adversaries and friends alike. Similar problems were created by von Hügel's tendency to cool quickly "when his friends took an independent line which he deemed injurious to their common cause" (Petre 1944, 30). Just as the modernists were unwilling to mold their research to the institutional demands of the church, so they tended to look askance at any attempts to institutionalize reform itself.

Behind all of the personality difficulties, geographical distances, and intellectual isolation—and underlying all of the movement's problems—were efforts by ecclesiastical authorities to destroy modernism. Almost as harmful to the movement as particular actions directed against its participants was the generally restrictive ambience in which the modernists existed. The church was strongly polarized, and it was the struggle within the church itself that did much to destroy hopes for a viable modernist movement. The frequent conflict—and the definitions it precipitated—created the greatest of difficulties for the modernists. The Catholic modernists were committed to remaining within the church, yet the Vatican refused to allow them to do so without renouncing some of their most cherished beliefs and some of the norms of "scientific scholarship."

The effects of clashes with church authorities were complex and multifaceted. The Vatican's suppression of modernist scholarship was what first motivated scholars to develop a reform movement. That same suppression, however, set limits on the extent to which such a movement could be organized, for a number of reasons. First, it was virtually impossible for persons opposed to the movement's general aims to understand or appreciate anything written or said by the modernists. The work of Loisy, Tyrrell, Fogazzaro, and others fell outside of the official definitions of Catholicism at the time, and were therefore automatically perceived by many as dangerous to Catholicism. In the same way, anything produced by the Vatican was viewed with immense suspicion by modernist scholars, making an objective response virtually impossible.

Their relationships with the Catholic hierarchy made life difficult for the modernists. Because of the constant attacks, there was dissension within the modernist ranks concerning both movement strategies and the intellectual content of the work itself, particularly the more controversial conclusions of scientific investigations. The modernists were constantly charging one another with misunderstanding their work, which resulted in radical breaks within the movement—notably between Blondel and the others. Blondel's attitude toward the authorities was one of such caution that even von Hügel seemed to act with abandon in comparison. Although Blondel created quite a stir with his own writings, he attempted formulations that were deliberately different from those of the modernists—"nothing merely transitory, ephemeral, or 'modern,'" he wrote, "no polemics or allusions to present conditions."[95] The Blondel–Loisy controversy was fueled by charges and countercharges of ignorance about each man's respective area of expertise: "Loisy, who reproaches his adversaries for being ignorant of exegesis, is accused by them of being ignorant of theology" (Poulat 1962, 615).

There were also serious charges of excessive radicalism within the ranks of the most committed modernists. The relationship between Tyrrell and the editors of *Il Rinnovamento* provides a clear example: there were times when the Italian modernists were disturbed by Tyrrell's radicalism, while Tyrrell complained to von Hügel that the Italians were getting carried away, lamenting "that Modernism is corrupting rapidly into a popular revolt."[96]

Von Hügel counseled patience as a fundamental strategy. In writing to Houtin, he suggested that "patience and heroic courage" would, in the end, "disarm the opposition."[97] Then, in the following month, Tyrrell wrote to Petre that he was "so glad that a few like Brizio realize the radical nature of the coming revolution. Laberthonnière, Bremond, and von Hügel certainly do not."[98]

Like their oscillations between belief and disbelief, such charges and countercharges among the closest collaboraters were expressions of the sociological ambivalence that impinged upon the life and work of the modernists. They were forever walking a tightrope between the demands of scholarship and those of the church. The constant pressure applied by church authorities, and the ever-present danger of censure and excommunication, created tensions among the modernists that destroyed any hope of overcoming other barriers to reform. In the final analysis, it was first and foremost the opposition by officials of the church that destroyed the modernists' attempts to organize a movement. By the end of the first decade of the twentieth century, the modernists were too weak—and the authorities were too strong—for the survival of a movement for modernist reform within the Roman Church.

6

Institutional Control of Modernist Dissidents

> When it is a question of a belief which is dear to us, we do not and cannot, permit a contrary belief to rear its head with impunity. . . . We inveigh against it, we work against it, we will to do something to it, and the sentiments so evolved cannot fail to translate themselves into actions. We run away from it, we hold it at a distance, we banish it from our society, etc.
>
> —Emile Durkheim, *The Division of Labor in Society*

> The short-sighted fear of scandal has been, and is, the curse of the church.
>
> —George Tyrrell, in Maude Petre,
> *Autobiography and Life of George Tyrrell*

Members of the Roman hierarchy responded to the crisis of modernism with a massive mobilization of the institution's defenses against an alleged international conspiracy, which was a caricature of the real movement. To their adversaries, the Catholic modernists came to represent all that was wrong with the modern world. Modernism was characterized as a deliberate conspiracy to destroy the church.

An ethos or spirit of antimodernism so captured the imaginations of many highly placed leaders of the church that a widespread "vigilance campaign" was instituted, creating a "reign of terror" within the church that lasted for a number of years and affected Catholic intellectual life for decades. By identifying dissidents (and potential dissidents) and labeling them as heretics, the ecclesiastical elite attempted to restore order within the church in a time of crisis.

THE LABELING OF HERETICS

Recent sociological studies of social movements have examined the social control of dissidents as a "process of labelling and treating dissenters as deviants."[1] As Wilson suggests, "control agents do not regard all political protest as deviant; some is ignored as irrelevant" (1970, 470). The task here is to discern why the modernist scholars were labeled as "deviant insiders" and subjected to a series of institutional controls.

The suppression of modernism was, in part, a response to the perceived dangers posed to the Catholic faith and to the church by the modernists' scholarship. It was also the result of the bureaucratic paranoia and absolutist tendencies that frequently emerge when elites are attacked by insurgents. Any explanation must take into account both the specific historical circumstances surrounding the controversy and the general characteristics of dissidence and of institutional responses to it. My analysis has suggested that both the causes and the consequences of dissidence are relative—namely, that they involve not only the intellectual content of a given protest but also the dialectical relationship between the critic and the criticized, the insurgents and the elites.

I have contended that ideas and interests are dialectically related. The way in which beliefs and ideas are formulated and articulated is influenced not only by the actual content or "truth" contained in them but also by the interests of the groups that adhere to them. Definitions of religious beliefs, worldviews, and political orientations are chosen both because they "make sense" to people and because they correspond to the interests and life-styles of those who choose them. Both the modernists and the ecclesiastical hierarchy defined Catholicism and science in ways that served their respective interests, and then gave to their definitions an aura of objective truth and universality.

Wilson points out that when studying social protest, it is important to acknowledge that "the relationship between social control agents and protesters is very much one of mutual perception" (ibid.), so that one must examine the interaction between the two groups and the definitions that each side has of the other. Responses to heterodoxy within an institution are a function both of the "social distance" between dissidents and the institution's leadership and of the "ideational distance"—that is, the degree of divergence between the beliefs of the elites and those of the dissidents. In chapter 1, I suggested two propositions about the relativity of dissidence. First, criticism from within a social organization may be more intellectually offensive than external criticism. The modernists did not merely repeat the standard criticisms of the anticlericals and non-believers, but claimed to be Catholic defenders of the faith, even though the Vatican itself identified them with external critics. Ideational distance is thus crucial in the dynamic situation that evolves whenever a "heresy" is perceived.

Second, mechanisms of control are activated by elites only when the social distance between elites and insurgents reaches—but does not exceed—a critical level. The relationship between ideational distance and social distance on the one hand, and suppressive activities by elites on the other, is curvilinear. If the ideational or social distance is either too high or too low, the critique can be ignored, but at a critical point between the two extremes, the dissidents are defined as dangerous. Immediate sanctions against deviant insiders are then available (and often effective), and such individuals can be used as "scapegoats" when linked to external enemies. By identifying modernists as deviant insiders, the papal hierarchy could define Catholicism on the basis of a common enemy. Thus the Roman leadership and the Catholic press cultivated a spirit of antimodernism that pervaded the church.

The labeling process is crucial because, as Coser notes, "provoking the enemy by proclaiming his 'dangerous intentions' may have the effect of a 'self-fulfilling prophecy': the 'enemy' will 'respond' and in this way actually become as dangerous to the group as it accused him of being in the first place" (Coser 1956, 105–106). Recent analyses of social control processes have specified the mechanisms by which such an effect is produced. The process of labeling and repressing dissenters can increase the likelihood of insurgency by limiting the potential partisans' options for fulfilling social roles other than the role of movement member (Gerlach and Hine 1970, 183). Repression may lead insurgents to increase their commitment to the cause as a way of justifying the investment already made (Wilson 1977, 474). It may convince activists that their efforts are truly threatening and that their cause is, therefore, important. It can create martyrs who become needed symbols around which others rally (G. Marx 1979, 118). Finally, repression can foster radicalization of the repressed group (Wilson 1977, 476; G. Marx 1979, 18). In sum, labeling and repressing a group can inadvertently provide crucial resources to an incipient movement and ultimately facilitate insurgency.

MECHANISMS OF CONTROL

The campaign against modernism was neither modest nor simple. Much of it was shrouded in secrecy, and is preserved only in documents either destroyed or not yet available. We can therefore do little more than piece together a tentative picture of the campaign from the public actions taken by the Vatican and other church officials; from the documents and information forwarded, either directly or indirectly, to the modernists (which are therefore sometimes biased); and from a collection of documents discovered during World War I, which reveals a secret international organization supported by the pope which was established to carry out the campaign against the modernists.[2] With those caveats, I will first examine the nature of the antimodernist spirit that pervaded the ecclesiastical hierarchy at the turn of the century, discussing it as an example of heresy-hunting activities. Second, I will outline some of the informal and quasi-official activities of various members of the church, which were designed to thwart the efforts of the modernists. Because these actions are full of innuendo, they are extremely difficult to interpret, and since much of the available information comes from the modernists themselves, it must be viewed with some reservation. Nonetheless, the available sources do reveal the general character of the antimodernist campaign. Third, I will analyze the official acts of the church against modernism—the *Index of Prohibited Books,* papal pronouncements, excommunications, the "committees of vigilance," and the antimodernist oath. Official antimodernist activity, although subject to interpretation, is more easily examined empirically because evidence is available in published source materials, archival letters to the modernists from the officials in question, and so on. Finally, I will discuss the quasi-official antimodernist movement of "integral Catholicism," especially the Sapinière and the Action Française.

HERESY AND THE SPIRIT OF ANTIMODERNISM

From the point of view of the scholastic orthodoxy of the time, the antimodernists were not wrong in condemning the modernists as heretics. Loisy, Tyrrell, von Hügel, and many others did not equivocate in their rejection of the Neo-Thomist definition of Catholicism. But the authorities were misleading in their picture of a monolithic conspiracy of heresy—despite the elements of truth in their argument—as is the case in any successful stereotype or caricature. At the crux of the controversy was the issue of papal authority and the exclusive right of the Vatican hierarchy to establish the boundaries of religious truth.

Douglas (1975, 56) suggests that "all boundaries which are used in ordering the social experience are treated as dangerous and polluting." Mechanisms designed to identify and punish heretics are thus used to identify social and ideological boundaries. Douglas also postulates that the way in which a society or social group handles its aberrant forms will parallel its relationships with outsiders. If boundary-crossing is welcome, a theology of mediation will be developed and success in exchange will be expected, but if there is a fear of exchange with strangers, there will be a pronounced odium for the hybrid.

Under continual attack, the Vatican grew to suspect anything related to the secular world. Because the modernists were in the church and refused to follow the directives of the papacy, they were considered dangerous to the stability of the institution and to the faith itself. Sabatier's analogy between the modernist crisis and the crisis in France following the French Revolution is instructive. "In 1793," he wrote, "there were many who thought that the end of the kingship was the end of France, the end of national unity." Similarly, he suggested, there "are many who imagine that the defeat of Pius X will be the end of all things—the end of faith, the end of unity, the end of all religion—that it will inaugurate the reign of fierce, materialistic anarchy" (Sabatier 1908, 102). In responding to that crisis, the Roman hierarchy cultivated a spirit of antimodernism that swept through the church.

The first of three characteristics of antimodernism identified by Petre is a "devotional attitude to the Papacy which is akin to personal idolatry" (1918, 189). The extent of that devotion to the pope is exhibited by a 1904 French pamphlet entitled "De la Devotion au Pape,"[3] which argues that

it is as impossible to be a good Christian without devotion to the Pope as without devotion to the Eucharist. If, therefore, we truly love the Pope, nothing will be dearer to us than the Pope's will; and even when obedience to the Pope means sacrifices, we shall never hesitate to follow any direction whatsoever emanating from Rome. Every objection will be silenced, every reasoning will go for nothing, every hesitation will yield before this unanswerable argument: "God wills and commands it because the Pope wills and commands it."

A second characteristic of antimodernism, according to Petre, is "that of timidity and fear. A priest is more afraid of being called a modernist than of being accused of negligence in his sacerdotal obligations and duties" (Petre 1918, 194). Most of the clergy lived in constant fear of being charged with infidelity. Finally, antimodernism fostered a spirit of suspicion and a keenness for the denunciation of others, much as the

Inquisition had cultivated a widespread sense of suspicion. Petre argued that one element of antimodernism's strength is "that its victims dare not complain, for to complain would be to render themselves liable to the suspicion of . . . having lapsed into modernism. . . . So bishops, and even Cardinals, suffer, in great part silently" (ibid., 196).

The institutional control of modernism was an all-consuming campaign that gradually required the energy of major segments of the ecclesiastical organization. Initially, a quasi-official picture of modernism emerged through efforts by individuals who were concerned about the orthodoxy of the writings by Loisy, Tyrrell, and others. Cardinal Richard, for example, wishing to guard the faith in his area of jurisdiction (Paris), sought help from Rome in condemning Loisy's *L'Evangile et l'Eglise*. Gradually the level of conflict escalated until even the pope's authority was called into question. The controversies shifted from a specific focus on Loisy's writings to an emphasis on the authority of the papal hierarchy and Loisy's lack of submission to it. Long before Rome took any official action against the modernists, an informal campaign against them was well under way.

INFORMAL CONTROL OF MODERNISM

It was not necessary that all modernism be the result of a conspiracy; individuals responding to similar ambivalences within an emerging tradition of historical criticism came to similar, independent conclusions. Nor was antimodernism poured from a single mold or directed uniformly from the Vatican. But what the antimodernists had that the modernists lacked was centralized leadership and the legitimacy and resources of the Roman establishment. The broad outline (if not the detail) of the campaign against modernism was formulated at the Vatican as part of an overall plan.

This is not to say that the Holy See directly initiated or carried out all aspects of the antimodernist campaign, nor is it to imply that there was always unanimity within the hierarchy. Some well-placed persons in the ecclesiastical hierarchy favored aspects of the modernists' efforts, and different factions sought to have their positions prevail in Rome. The pressure to present a unified front to a hostile world was so strong, however, that the Vatican's decisions were widely supported. Most of the debate was carried out privately and remains largely secret. Only pieces of the debate can be inferred, but a few clear segments of antimodernist sentiment can be isolated as influential, if not decisive, in bringing about the demise of modernism.

The Jesuits who were organized around the review *Civiltà cattolica,* published in Rome, provided the core of the neo-Thomist movement and of the antimodernist campaign, especially in its early stages. One might argue that they engaged in what Freud calls a "reaction formation"— namely, turning an impulse into its opposite. Faced by ambivalences from the scholarly community that were similar to those encountered by the modernists, the Jesuits responded by repressing all doubts and vigorously defending the status quo. As suggested in chapter 2, their unqualified opposition to everything "modern" was part of a well-organized drive to defend the church from the modern world by means of a Thomist revival.

The work of Loisy, Tyrrell, Fogazzaro, Buonaiuti, and the others did not fit into this plan. The *Civiltà cattolica* Jesuits were thus concerned both about the intellectual content of the modernists' work and about their relationship to the church authorities. As early as 15 and 31 October 1893, the review criticized Fogazzaro, charging that his lectures on evolution were inappropriate and that "Catholic laymen should not usurp the function of the priesthood."

All modern systems and methods of intellectual inquiry were considered intrinsically unsatisfactory. The Jesuits defined the conflict with modernism as a "war of two worlds"[4] and were very clear as to which "world" was in the right. They opposed modernist ideas not only from an intellectual and religious point of view but also because their own privileged position in the ecclesiastical hierarchy was threatened by any group with rising popularity. Ironically, however, the Jesuits themselves eventually came into conflict with Monsignor Benigni, organizer of the Sapinière (a major center of antimodernist activity discussed in more detail later in this chapter).

Another powerful center of antimodernist activity was found in the French episcopacy, particularly with the archbishop of Paris. Most of the episcopacy's activities were part of the official antimodernist campaign (discussed in the next section). Even those French bishops who were tolerant of modernism were under pressure to move against the modernists.

Two traditional daily Catholic papers in Paris, *L'Univers* and *La Verité française,* served as a major forum for attacks on Loisy's *L'Evangile et l'Eglise* and other modernist works. Abbé Hippolyte Gayraud (1856– 1911), a clerical member of the House of Deputies and a former Dominican professor of scholastic philosophy at the Institut Catholique at Toulouse, initiated the attacks on Loisy in the 24 October 1903 issue of *L'Univers.*[5] Gayraud claimed that he was not "hostile towards research nor to the methodology used by the critics, but I find that the whole business has gone too far and I fear that the effect of the criticisms is to make work which is both necessary and legitimate suspect." He went on to draw a sharp contrast between Loisy and other critics on the one hand, and Augustine, Thomas, and Bossuet on the other. Tyrrell coined a term, "Gayraud-Catholicism," to characterize the type of Catholicism which he felt could not survive in the modern world.[6]

Following Gayraud's articles came a series of essays by Abbé Maignen in *La Verité française,* an intransigent Catholic daily that broke off from *L'Univers.*[7] Maignen charged that *L'Evangile et l'Eglise* constituted a renewal of the past heresies of Arianism and Nestorianism, as well as "renanism" no longer in disguise. His articles touched off responses from Abbé Naudet, in *La Justice sociale* (19 December 1903), and from Georges Fonsegrive, editor of *La Quinzaine.* Fonsegrive compared Loisy's critics to vultures waiting outside a house who "already cry with pleasure while waiting for the cadavre" (1903, 441–453; Poulat 1962, 202).

Although a number of other antimodernist centers existed, such as the Dominicans of the *Revue biblique,*[8] there is one which is particularly worthy of discussion—the Society of Saint Sulpice and its superior general, Henri Icard (1805–1893), who undertook a series of initiatives against Loisy. The Paris house of the order was near the Institut Catholique, and a number of Institut students were at the order. According to Loisy, Icard was inflexible on matters of doctrine, giving him such standing with Cardinal Richard "that in any conflict between Saint Sulpice and the Catholic Institute he was certain to have the archbishopric on his side" (Loisy [1913] 1968, 113–114).

Another important journal in Paris, *Etudes,* attacked modernist ideas consistently from the 1880s on, long before there was any modernist movement. Their campaign is summarized by *Etudes* editor Joseph Brucker in "*Les Etudes* contre le modernisme de 1888 à 1907" (Brucker 1914), in which he defends the journal against charges that it had been "soft on modernism."[9] He outlines a consistent plan in the journal to fight against the ideas of Americanism, the "neo-Christian movement," Laberthonnière,[10] LeRoy, Sabatier, evolutionism, Loisy, d'Hulst, Hegelianism, rationalism, Fogazzaro, Tyrrell, Duchesne, and to some extent even Newman. Brucker repeatedly emphasizes that the *Etudes* signaled the errors of those ideas far in advance of any official condemnations, although its editors tried at all times to remain courteous, arguing that "in combatting error, the most important task is not to strike *strongly,* but to strike *justly*" (ibid., 23).

Through publications in the popular Catholic press and scholarly journals—and through behind-the-scenes charges and innuendos—several groups labeled the Loisy–von Hügel–Tyrrell network as an enemy of the church. By campaigning against the modernists and their ideas, those concerned about the crisis were able to do something in defense of the church. Little could be done to silence the anticlericals outside of the church, but Loisy and the others were within the jurisdiction of the ecclesiastical authorities. They could be reprimanded and, if necessary, silenced. As the controversy escalated, what had begun as an unofficial, fragmented campaign developed into a full-scale attack.

OFFICIAL ANTIMODERNISM

Institutional control mechanisms in the Roman Catholic Church are somewhat unique and very complex, having been constructed layer by layer over centuries of conflict. Pontifical government of the Roman Church is carried out by the Roman Curia, which functions as a cabinet and as a set of administrative offices, all of which are under the jurisdiction of the pope, as prescribed in the canons of the church. The most important offices of the Curia are called congregations, of which the most significant in the antimodernist campaign was the Congregation of the Holy Office, successor to the Congregation of the Index in 1917. The Holy Office was formed in 1542 as the successor of the Universal Roman Inquisition, established by Pope Gregory IX in 1229 for the suppression of heresy.

Four broad mechanisms of control were available to the hierarchy for the suppression of modernism. First, articles and books that were deemed heretical or dangerous could be placed on the *Index of Prohibited Books*. Second, the career of an individual Catholic priest could be manipulated, directly or indirectly, to force compliance with the Vatican's wishes. There is a hierarchy of controls related to the suspect individual's position in the institution. Clergy were subject to more sanctions than were laity, and members of religious orders were subject to more than were diocesan (or "secular") priests.

Third, the heretical ideas of an individual or group of individuals could be condemned by a decree of an ecclesiastical body or by an encyclical from the pope. In such an event, as with the placement of a book on the *Index*, the author could be forced to make a public retraction of all errors in the work and even to agree with the language of the condemnation—a requirement which more than one modernist scholar found particularly distasteful. Fourth, behind all the other measures lay the Vatican's ultimate weapon—namely, excommunication, which denies an individual "communion" with the church and its members. Those thus condemned are not allowed to attend or administer mass, to receive or give the sacraments, and members of the church in good stead are not to communicate with them. The Roman hierarchy employed all four types of control mechanisms in the escalating campaign against modernism, beginning with the *Index of Prohibited Books*.

THE *INDEX OF PROHIBITED BOOKS*

Few of the modernists—and even some who deliberately disassociated themselves from the modernists (e.g., Duchesne)—escaped having works placed on the *Index of Prohibited Books* (see appendix D). The sheer existence of the *Index* discouraged modernist publications. There were continual denunciations and rumors of condemnations in Rome, which created restraints for scholars in their work. Members of the Biblical Commission and of the Congregation of the Index must have comprised a segment of the audience for which the modernists were consciously writing. It is not clear exactly how the process worked,[11] since most of the behind-the-scenes lobbying occurred in secret, but there are indications that antimodernist forces actively advocated the condemnation of particular authors.

Bishops could also renounce works within their own diocese, so that such actions were often initiated at the local level. Loisy's *L'Evangile et l'Eglise,* for example, was first condemned by Cardinal Richard, and later by the authorities in Rome. There is some reason to believe that Leo XIII took some limited measures to protect scholarly freedom (see Baudrillart 1912–1914, 456), but there were frequent denunciations from France and Italy to the Congregation of the Index or to the Holy Office. It was not a frequent custom in England, however, where the atmosphere in the minority Catholic Church was more liberal than in France and Italy.

The routine denunciation of heretics, like all rituals, relieves anxiety. Such proclamations provided ritual occasions at which members of the church could respond to the church's difficulties and demonstrate their loyalty to the ecclesiastical authorities. Yet there was, naturally, considerable controversy surrounding the procedures of the *Index*. As Cardinal Merry del Val explained, in his defense of the *Index* in a letter to Ward,[12]

infallibility has not been claimed for the Roman Congregations, great as their authority is. . . . So, that I fail to understand your allusion to the Inquisition. What I am afraid the Holy Office or any other Roman Congregation does not trouble much about when formulating its decisions, is whether its finding will or will not be *acceptable* to the *average English* or *French* or *any other mind,* for that is hardly the safe standpoint to take in matters of this kind.

Loisy had five books placed on the *Index of Prohibited Books* on 16 December 1903. He wrote to Richard the following month, proclaiming "I receive with respect the judgment of the Sacred Congregation, and I myself condemn whatever may be found in my writings that is reprehensible." Unable to submit himself fully to the ritual of denouncing his own works, however, Loisy felt impelled to add that his adherence to the sentence of the Sacred Congregation is purely disciplinary in character. I reserve the right of my own conscience, and I do not intend, in inclining myself before the judgment rendered by the Sacred Congregation of the Holy Office, either to abandon or to retract the opinions which I have uttered in my capacity of historian and of critical exegete. (Loisy [1913] 1968, 250–251)

Merry del Val reportedly said that the letter did not have "even the tone of a humble and sincere submission." A subsequent letter from Merry del Val, read to Loisy by Richard, demanded an instantaneous retraction, without reserve, of the five condemned works. The alternative was excommunication (Loisy [1913] 1968, 250–253). Loisy thus wrote an additional letter to Merry del Val in which he was somewhat more submissive, but still claimed that he

should have been remiss in the obligation of sincerity if I had not made express reservation of my opinions as a historian and a critical exegete. It did not enter my mind that anyone could expect of me the pure and simple retraction of a whole body of ideas, forming the substance of my work, trenching upon various orders of knowledge over whch the magistracy of the Church has no direct control. (Loisy [1913] 1968, 255)

A "pure and simple retraction" is exactly what the authorities expected. Loisy's letter of "submission" was, on the contrary, a direct challenge to ecclesiastical authority.

Finally, at the insistence of friends, Loisy wrote directly to the pope to set the record straight concerning his personal position in the affair.[13] The letter was not an unconditional submission, and the pontiff could not possibly have interpreted it as sincere. Responding through Cardinal Richard, Pius X said that although the letter was addressed to his heart, it was not written from the heart, since it failed to contain the required act of obedience.

A final brief message was sent to the cardinal from Loisy; it was met with silence. The expected excommunication did not come, however, and there was a temporary lull in the hierarchy's attempts to silence Loisy. Although not successful in bringing about the desired effect immediately, the authorities' efforts did make a considerable impact on Loisy's career. He resigned from his teaching post and retired to a small cottage in Garnay. On 9 April 1904, he wrote in his journal that "the search for truth is not a trade by which a man can support himself; for a priest it is a supreme peril" ([1913] 1968, 272). In 1906, Loisy's *indult* and *celebret* expired and were not renewed, indicating to Loisy that he was being quietly put out of the way.

CAREER MANIPULATION

One effective measure for controlling the behavior of dissident clergy is to manipulate their careers, both to mitigate the direct effects of their writing or teaching upon the Catholic population and to serve as warning. A priest or member of a religious order could be removed from a teaching post, forbidden to publish, transferred to a remote post, or indirectly sanctioned, as when Loisy's students were barred from ordination by Cardinal Richard and the superior general of Saint Sulpice (Petre 1937*b*, 78).

Tyrrell, for example, moved from one sanction to another. When he developed a maverick form of scholasticism as an instructor at a Jesuit seminary, he was dismissed from his chair. When his articles were found controversial by the Jesuits in Rome, his writing activities were severely restricted. Later, he was relieved of his responsibility as a retreat leader and dismissed from the Society of Jesus. Loisy's controversial writings led first to prohibiting Saint Sulpice students from attending his classes, and then to his dismissal from the Institut Catholique and transfer to a girls' school outside of Paris. He was later forced to give up a teaching position at the Sorbonne, and was under constant pressure to refrain from publication.

Countless other progressive clergy were punished in varying degrees for their writings or public stances; nonscholastic theologians lost important university posts, critical scholars were eased out of Catholic institutes and replaced with more traditional scholars, and all clergy were later forced to sign antimodernist oaths. The crucial difference between clergy and lay modernists becomes clear at this point. Whereas members of the clergy were, in the final analysis, under the control of the hierarchy, the laity could be persuaded only by moral and religious means—that is, by calling upon their duty as Catholics to obey church authorities, and by relying upon threats of condemnation and excommunication.

THE HIERARCHY'S STRATEGY

A retrospective examination of the official decrees of the church from the mid-nineteenth century makes one wonder why anyone would mount a modernist or scientific reform movement within the Roman Church just a few decades later. From *Aeterni Patris,* which announced Leo XIII's revival of scholasticism, through the condemnation of Americanism in *Providentissimus Deus,* the encyclicals of Pius X, and the final official condemnation of modernism, the hierarchy took a consistent position on all the issues with which the modernists were concerned.

Pius X declared his position on modernism in his first encyclical,[14] *E supremi apostolatus cathedra,* of 4 October 1903, which spoke of "the insidious suggestions of a new, mistaken science that is not infused with Christ, and, with disguised and cunning arguments, seeks to let in the errors of rationalism and semi-rationalism." The encyclical clarified the pope's position on the authority of the ecclesiastical hierarchy and his attitude toward laity who dared to teach the clergy (probably an allusion to Fogazzaro, among others). The letter, which was addressed to the bishops, called upon them to enforce the notion of their own authority and that of the hierarchy in general. The laity, with the clergy, must work to restore humanity "not using its own judgment and ideas, but always directed and ordered by the Bishops; for no one, apart from you, whom the Holy spirit has appointed to rule the Church of God, is to teach, order, or preside over the Church."

The pope's second and third encyclicals, *Ad diem illum* (2 February 1904) and *Lucunda sane accidit* (12 March 1904), attacked the decline of faith and the heresies of the time. The former contended that "the point of departure of the enemies of religion" was that they "regard as mere fables original sin and the evils that were its consequence." By virtue of their false ideas, Christianity, through "Rationalism and Materialism," is

> torn up by the roots and destroyed, and there remains to Christian wisdom the glory of having to guard and protect the truth. It is moreover a vice common to the enemies of the faith of our time especially that they repudiate and proclaim the necessity of repudiating all respect and obedience for the authority of the church, and even of any human power. (Pius X [1904*a*] 1967, 331–334)

George Tyrrell

Supported by the *Civiltà cattolica*'s characterizations, the hierarchy began taking action against various modernist scholars. Tyrrell, for example, was increasingly subjected to censure by his Jesuit superiors. He claimed not to be personally afraid of censure, pointing out that "our Lord and His Apostles . . . were excommunicated for refusing to be silent," and that, as Saint Augustine testified, "no man (not even . . . Saint Ignatius) has ever served the Church largely without incurring the displeasure and censure of the officials."[15] Nonetheless, constant pressures from his Jesuit superiors impeded his work. Toward the end of his relationship with the Society of Jesus, Tyrrell informed his superiors of his dissatisfaction with the order:

> It has not been merely the steady opposition offered to my own writings, but far more the whole action of the Society in recent years in relation to progressive Catholicism, the patronage it has accorded to the school represented by the *Civiltà Cattolica*, *La Verité*, *La Croix*, and to writers like Abbé Maignen, Bishop Turinaz, Père Fontaine; its intrigues connected with bogus-Americanism, with the Washington University, above all with the case of Abbé Loisy, that have

convinced me of my mistake. I must now admit that the Society's instinctive opposition to my work is true to the actual spirit of the Order as it now exists. . . . Not progress, as formerly, but reaction and intransigence is the cause for which the Society now exists and works. (in Petre 1912, II:234)

Later in the same letter, Tyrrell claimed that the Jesuit order contained the "counter-extravagance of Protestantism: on this side, liberty misinterpreted as the contempt of authority; on that, authority misinterpreted as the contempt of liberty." Furthermore, "in buttressing authority, it has crushed liberty and established Absolutism" (Petre 1912, II:497).

Just as Father Tyrrell's life was filled with controversy, so were his death and burial in 1909, which showed the extent to which the church felt it must go to stamp out the modernist rebellion. Even though he was given the final rites at the time of his death, Tyrrell was refused a Catholic burial and had to be interred in the Storrington parish cemetery, which is available for persons of any creed. A handful of friends attended the quiet graveside service, and Bremond spoke a few words. Three days later, the bishop of Southwark wired to the prior of Storrington: "Do not allow Bremond to say Mass" (ibid., II:446). "It is the first time a priest is punished for what he has done by a death bed," Bremond wrote to Lilley, informing him that Cardinal Merry del Val had suspended him *a divinis.*[16] As Petre pointed out,

according to what has usually been taught, the Church regards the last act as the decisive one; the outlaw, the libertine, the tyrant, the apostate, are all her own children, whatever may have been their past, if they die with her seal upon their brow. (Petre 1912, II:436)

For Tyrrell, however, insurgency was the unforgivable sin.

Il Rinnovamento

> I sent you the *Rinnovamento* in case the modernism has not been quite bumped out of you, which I hope it has. I wish I knew a pill for that troublesome disease.
> —George Tyrrell to Maude Petre, 12 January 1908

The campaign against modernism was also directed at the group of young Italians who published *Il Rinnovamento*. Ranchetti claims that Semeria's letters to Minocchi reveal "a general fear of persecution, shown in repeated calls for prudence and secrecy" (1969, 179). In 1907 the Sacred Congregation of the Index finally decided to suppress publication of the review. On 29 April, Cardinal Andrea Steinhuber, prefect of the Index, wrote to Cardinal Ferrari, archbishop of Milan, where *Il Rin-*

novamento was published, expressing his disgust at seeing a "review clearly in conflict with Catholic teaching and the Catholic spirit." His objections concerned not only doctrinal disputes but also the revolt against ecclesiastical authority: "And while such men deal so haughtily with the most difficult theological matters and the most important of the Church's affairs," Cardinal Steinhuber wrote,

the editors boast that it is a *lay, non-confessional* review and distinguishes between official and non-official Catholicism, between the dogmas of the Church as truths to be believed, and the immanence of religion in individuals. In short, there is no doubt at all that the object of the review is to cultivate a very dangerous spirit of independence from the Church's teaching, to encourage private judgment at the expense of the Church's own judgment, and to set itself up to prepare an anti-Catholic renewal of the spirit. (in Ranchetti 1969, 197)

Alfieri, Casati, and Scotti replied three days after the contents of Steinhuber's letter were sent to them on 10 May:[17]

We, the undersigned, editors of the monthly *Rinnovamento,* reaffirming the full submission of Catholics to the ecclesiastical authorities, express profound distress that intentions which have always been foreign to it and conflict with our sincere love for the Church have been attributed to our work, and deny as fully and explicitly as possible the charge that in it we are trying to assume the role of teacher in the Church.

Their letter was not, however, the required submission without qualification. "But we do not believe we should stop publishing our review," the response continued, "since this would imply that we recognize the right of the Congregation of the Index to force the laity to cease scientific-religious, political and social studies, which should be and should appear independent."

Von Hügel approved of their response, arguing that a full submission would merely have played into the hands of the church's enemies, providing "fresh proof that Catholics can have no liberty of research and speculation, however careful they may be."[18] Because they were not clergymen, the suppression of the editors of *Il Rinnovamento* required informal and indirect action. On 6 November, Cardinal Ferrari forbade priests to buy or even to read the review, under pain of suspension *a divinis* ipso facto.

DECREES OF CONDEMNATION

The decree *Lamentabili,* issued 2 July 1907, announced a long-expected new "syllabus of errors" condemning sixty-five propositions concerning "sacred disciplines, the interpretation of the Sacred Scripture, the principal mysteries of the faith." The decree, issued by the "Holy Roman and Universal Inquisition," contended that it was

to be greatly deplored that among Catholics also not a few writers are to be found who, crossing the boundaries fixed by the Fathers and by the Church herself, seek out, in the plea of higher intelligence and in the name of historical considerations, that progress of dogmas which is in reality the corruption of the same. (Pius X 1908*a*, 217)

Many of the propositions were paraphrased from Loisy's writings,[19] and emphasized the magisterium and the integral truth of the gospels. Von Hügel urged Ward to stress three positions toward *Lamentabili* in his *Dublin Review*: (1) "a careful limitation of it to its real proportions and significance;" (2) an indication of the excessiveness (and therefore acceptability) of what he calls the "caricature" propositions in the document (as opposed to the more solid ones); and (3) "a careful, clear, sober but unshrinking exposition of the danger *to the Church,* to its inherent logic" of the "pressing of the *principle* of the other set of propositions."[20] But von Hügel was disappointed in Ward's moderate editorial position, and later wrote that he was "considering what to do about my subscription."[21]

On 8 September 1907, *Pascendi* was issued, containing an extensive systematization of the alleged "doctrines of the modernists." The encyclical contained a program for an antimodernist campaign, including the declaration that "anyone who is in any way found to be imbued with modernism is to be excluded without compunction" from offices throughout the church (Pius X [1908*b*] 1981, 93). The document first condemned scientific historiography and a number of specific implications growing out of that methodology: religious knowledge is compatible with some types of science and incompatible with others. Second, the Vatican's pronouncements drew boundaries between religious and scientific knowledge on the basis of subject matter: questions of scriptural interpretation are not to be subject to rules of scientific investigation, but only to the guidelines and decisions established by church officials.

Furthermore, Pius X appealed to his papal obligation to guard "with the greatest vigilance the deposit of the faith delivered to the saints, rejecting the profane novelties of words and oppositions of knowledge falsely so called." Modernism was simply another in a series of heresies that had surfaced through the ages, "for, owing to the efforts of the enemy of the human race, there have never been lacking 'men speaking perverse things' (Acts xx, 30), 'vain talkers and seducers' (Titus i, 10)" (ibid., 72).

Moreover, modernism represented a new threat to the church. "It must . . . be confessed," the encyclical read, "that the number of the enemies of the cross of Christ has in these last days increased exceedingly, who are striving, by acts entirely new and full of subtlety, to destroy the vital energy of the Church" (ibid., 72). The new heresy was dangerous because it was associated with anticlericalism, it employed the new method of scientific thought, and it challenged the Vatican's authority. Thus all the ingredients were present for a major campaign against heresy. There was a new set of ideas that fell outside of the scholastic framework within which official Catholicism had been cast; those ideas were expressed largely in the traditional language of orthodox Catholicism, yet they were allegedly linked to a massive external assault on the church. Finally, the principal creators of the heresy were deviant insiders within the jurisdiction of the hierarchy, but not so closely related as to be able to thwart a campaign against them. As the pope put it,

> That We make no delay in this matter is rendered necessary especially by the fact that the partisans of error are to be sought not only among the Church's open enemies; they lie hid, a thing to be deeply deplored and feared, in her very bosom and heart, and are the more mischievous, the less conspicuously they appear. We allude, Venerable Brethren, to many who belong to the Catholic laity, nay, and this is far more lamentable, to the ranks of the priesthood itself, who, feigning a love for the Church, lacking the firm protection of philosophy and theology, nay more, thoroughly imbued with the poisonous doctrines taught by the enemies of the Church, and lost to all sense of modesty, vaunt themselves as reformers of the Church; and, forming more boldly into line of attack, assail all that is most sacred in the work of Christ, not sparing even the person of the Divine Redeemer, whom, with sacreligious daring, they reduce to a simple, mere man.

The document is replete with images that explain why the modernists and their works are so repugnant. Three themes appear repeatedly. First, the modernists "lay the axe not to the branches and shoots, but to the very root, that is, to the faith and its deepest fibres" (ibid., 72). The scriptures are the infallible word of God, interpreted by an infallible tradition—that is, they are tenets incompatible with the methods of scientific historiography.

Second, "the danger is present almost in the very veins and heart of the Church, whose injury is the more certain from the very fact that their knowledge of her is more intimate" (ibid., 72)—that is to say, the insurgents are deviant insiders. The hierarchy charged that the modernists were imposters, and poor ones at that, for they are "men who are badly disguised."

A third theme is the modernists' failure to remain obedient to the authority of the church hierarchy, and "this almost destroys all hope of cure."

Their very doctrines have given such a bent to their minds, that they disdain all authority and brook no restraint; and relying upon a false conscience, they attempt to ascribe to a love of truth that which is in reality the result of pride and obstinacy. (Pius X [1908*b*] 1981, 72)

The encyclical identified two causes of modernism: curiosity and pride. Even "curiosity by itself, if not prudently regulated, suffices to account for all errors," and the true believer should suppress excessive curiosity by submitting any questions to church authorities. "But it is pride which exercises an incomparably greater sway over the soul to blind it and plunge it into error, and pride sits in Modernism as in its own house" (ibid., 90).

The independence of the scholarly community was more than a passing irritant to the Holy See. The danger lies in "*agnostic, immanentist,* and *evolutionist* criticism," and in the school organized around that methodology. The critics had formed a close alliance "independent of all differences of nationality or religion," characterized by a "boundless effrontery."

Let one of them but open his mouth and the others applaud him in chorus, proclaiming that science has made another step forward; let an outsider but hint at a desire to inspect the new discovery with his own eyes and they are on him in a body; deny it—and you are an ignoramus; is no praise too warm for you. In this way they win over any who, did they but realise what they are doing, would shrink back with horror. The impudence and domineering of some, and the thoughtlessness and imprudence of others, have combined to generate a pestilence in the air which penetrates everywhere and spreads the contagion. (ibid., 86)

Finally, the document provided an ingenious synthesis of various fragments of allegedly modernist thought, using the methods of scholastic philosophy:[22]

The Modernists (as they are commonly and rightly called) employ a very clear artifice, namely, to present their doctrines without order and systematic arrangement into one whole, scattered and disjointed one from another so as to appear to be in doubt and uncertainty, while they are in reality firm and steadfast. (ibid., 72)

The encyclical explained that modernism had an agnostic philosophical foundation, deformed religious history and erroneously spoke of an evolution of dogma, emphasized individual religious experiences, and subordinated faith to science. Furthermore, the modernists allegedly held that "as faith is to be subordinated to science, as far as phenomenal elements are concerned, so too in temporal matters the Church must be subject to the State" (ibid., 81). This comment was an apparent allusion to anticlerical conflicts and the French law of separation of church and state, which was passed just months before the condemnation was issued.

The *Pascendi* also emphasized the immensity of the modernist threat: "And now with Our eyes fixed upon the whole system, no one will be surprised that We should define it to be the synthesis of all heresies. . . . We have already intimated, their system means the destruction not of the Catholic religion alone, but of all religion" (ibid., 89). The modernists had turned their backs upon the Catholic tradition with works "exuding novelty in every page. . . . For them the scholarship of a writer is in direct proportion to the recklessness of his attacks on antiquity, and of his efforts to undermine tradition and the ecclesiastical magisterium" (ibid., 92).

Remedies for Modernism

A series of steps were proposed to remedy the crisis: "In the first place, with regard to studies, We will and strictly ordain that scholastic philosophy be made the basis of the sacred sciences" (ibid., 92). The natural sciences could be studied, but so only within explicit boundaries, and not to the neglect of "the more severe and lofty studies" (ibid., 93). Second, educational institutions within the church were to be expunged of all who adhere to the modernist errors:

Anyone who in any way is found to be imbued with Modernism is to be excluded without compunction from these offices, and those who already occupy them are to be withdrawn. The same policy is to be adopted towards those who favor Modernism either by extolling the Modernists or excusing their culpable conduct, by criticising scholasticism, the Holy Father, or by refusing obedience to ecclesiastical authority in any of its depositaries; and towards those who show a love of novelty in history, archaeology, biblical exegesis, and finally towards those who neglect the sacred sciences or appear to prefer to them the profane. (ibid., 93)

The careers of Catholic scholars were thus linked with their denunciation of modernism, and the groundwork was laid for the harassment or expulsion of anyone using critical methods in Catholic universities.

Publication was also to be strictly regulated by the church, thus sealing off all possibilities for Catholic scholars to use historical critical methods. "It is also the duty of the Bishops," the encyclical ordered,

to prevent writings infected with Modernism or favorable to it from being read when they have been published, and to hinder their publication when they have not. No book or paper or periodical whatever of this kind must ever be permitted to seminarists or university students. (ibid., 94)

The bishops were not only to eradicate modernism but to make that task a major priority as well: "We bid you do everything in your power to drive out of your dioceses, even by solemn interdict, any pernicious books that may be in circulation there" (ibid., 94). Catholic booksellers were prohibited from selling condemned works, and all were reminded that forbidden books and periodicals could be kept and read only with permission (ibid.).

Censors were to be appointed in each diocese to revise all works intended for publication (ibid., 94–95). Provisions were made for the scrutiny of all priests who were editors of papers or periodicals. Citing a previous ruling (Article XLII of the Constitution *Officiorum*) requiring all priests to obtain permission before undertaking editorships, the pope ruled that the bishops were to see that permission was withdrawn from priests who abused the privilege. No priests should publish in objectionable papers or periodicals (ibid., 95). Furthermore, congresses and public gatherings among priests were not allowed except on "very rare occasions," and then only "on condition that matters appertaining to the Bishops or the Apostolic See be not treated in them, and that no resolutions or petitions be allowed that would imply a usurpation of sacred authority, and that absolutely nothing be said in them which savours of Modernism, Presbyterianism or Laicism" (ibid., 95).

To implement the massive campaign against modernism, the pope called upon every diocese to establish a "Council of Vigilance" to meet in a secret session every two months in the presence of its bishop: "They shall watch most carefully for every trace and sign of modernism both in publications and in teaching, and to preserve from it the clergy and the young they shall take all prudent, prompt and efficacious measures" (ibid., 96). The councils were not to permit discussion of questions concerning sacred relics, dogmatic pronouncements, or pious traditions. A year after the publication of the encyclical, and every three years thereafter, the bishops of all dioceses were ordered to "furnish the Holy See with a diligent and sworn report on the prescriptions contained in . . . [this letter] and on the doctrines that find currency among the clergy, and especially in the seminaries and other Catholic institutions" (ibid., 97).

An additional proclamation on 1 September 1910—the *motu proprio, Sacrorum antistitum*—instituted an antimodernist oath to be taken by all clerics being promoted to major orders and by all clergy exercising ministerial functions (Pius X 1910). Among other things, the proclamation claimed that the existence of God can be demonstrated by natural reason, and that the church was immediately and directly instituted by Christ during his life on earth. The oath included a complete submission to *Lamentabili* and *Pascendi*. Despite predictions of resistance, the oath was taken without any major movements of protest, except in Germany, where university professors were exempted from taking the oath so as not to be "humiliated before their Protestant colleagues and to have their position as scholars hampered and restricted by the extravagant demands of the papacy" (Vidler 1934, 203; see Buonaiuti 1927, 159 ff.).

Despite the unequivocal condemnation, most modernists continued to consider their work justified and hoped that history would vindicate them. Fawkes wrote to Ward, saying, "I find that many simple people who have little or no sympathy with 'modernism' are shocked by the unchristian temper of recent Papal Documents and with their apologists in the press and pulpit."[23]

EXCOMMUNICATION

> If there are to be excommunications, the more the better.
> —Robert Dell to A. L. Lilley, 25 October 1907

The final act of the church hierarchy was to excommunicate the leading modernists who refused to submit unconditionally to the condemnations. The prime targets were Loisy and Tyrrell. Excommunication may not be a threatening measure for those whose identities are not caught up in the church, but for most of the modernists the possibility of excommunication was a grave matter indeed. Particularly for those in France and Italy, where there were few alternatives to "legitimate" religious associations, the possibility of excommunication—and therefore utter and complete exclusion from the Christian community—was a matter of ultimate importance. There are two kinds of excommunication: *vitandi* and *tolerati*. The former excludes from the church all who are mentioned by name as persons expelled from it, or those who violently attack the person of the pope; all other excommunicates are *tolerati*. The word "vitandus," from *vitare*, means literally "to shun," and all members of the church are to shun any contact with those so excommunicated, even in secular matters, unless they are a member of one's immediate family. A divine service may not be held if a *vitandus* is present, nor can the individual be buried in a Catholic cemetery (Attwater 1954, 520).

On 7 March 1908, the Holy Office announced that the sentence of excommunication was decreed for Loisy. It was never communicated to him personally because once it was pronounced, he did not exist as far as the hierarchy was concerned; he read about it in the newspapers the following day (Loisy [1913] 1968, 318). According to the language of the decree, he was to be "dutifully shunned by all" (ibid., 345), although many thought the procedure antiquated. Bishop Lacroix wrote to Loisy as soon as the excommunication was announced:[24]

I read this morning in La Croix, that one is forbidden to correspond with you. That inspires me with an irresistible desire to write to you, to tell you again of my lively and profound sympathy. It is beyond my comprehension that, in the twentieth century . . . such antiquated proceeding should be brought into play: it is childish, grotesque and odious.

Loisy's first impression, when the decree was finally issued,

was one of inexpressible relief. The Church restored to me—after no end of fracas, in the guise of disgrace and condemnation, by way of ostracism, and so far as possible by means of my extermination—nevertheless at last she restored to me the liberty which I had been so ill-advised as to alienate to her thirty years before. Despite herself, but effectually, she gave me back into my own keeping, and I was almost ready to bless her for it. (Loisy [1913] 1968, 318)

Tyrrell greeted the news of his excommunication quite differently: "As the excommunication principle is unChristian in itself," he wrote to von Hügel, "I feel bound to go against it in every possible way" (Petre 1937b, 173). Others were excommunicated either by name or in broad declarations (such as that against the entire *Rinnovamento* group), but since there was so little resistance to the Vatican's measures and opposition seemed hopeless, there were few specific excommunications. The specific, representative denunciations seemed sufficient. Some, like Butler, felt that a response of silence was honest and honorable.[25] Laity and clergy were treated differently in the matter; for example, both von Hügel and Petre[26] somehow escaped excommunication, despite the fact that neither of them publicly repudiated modernism.

Although the modernist movement was over by 1910 (or there-abouts), the antimodernist movement was not.[27] The modernists had created an active, thriving movement within the church, but it neither gained the organizational maturity of nor mobilized the level of resources obtained by the antimodernist movement. The Sapinière, a secret antimodernist organization, flourished until the outbreak of World War I in 1914, calling for an "integral Catholicism."

INTEGRAL CATHOLICISM

Obedience is the law of laws.
—Editorial in *Fede e Ragione* (an integralist review)

"Paulus" (from the name of the great apostle) is a fraternal alliance and a friendly correspondence among advocates of Catholicism in the full sense of that word; that is "papists and adherents of Rome," anti-revolutionaries, anti-liberals, anti-modernists. "Paulus" is not an association, nor a public organization. It does not employ anyone since its friends freely disseminate its ideas.

—from the charter of the "Amitié Paulus"

In 1909, with the support of the highest ranks of the ecclesiastical hierarchy, including the pope himself, the staunch antimodernist cleric Monsignor Umberto Benigni founded a group called the Sodalitium Pianum— or the Sapinière. Created explicitly for the purpose of combating modernism, the Sapinière worked through a network of sympathetic Catholic reviews—including Benigni's own *Correspondance de Rome* and, in France, *La Foi Catholique* and *La Vigie*—and an intricate system of internal correspondence. Violent anonymous attacks were launched against everyone suspected of heresy. The Sapinière served as a focal point for groups of "integral Catholics"—that is, Catholics who were primarily opposed to modernism, but also to all developments in the modern world which they felt were destroying the integral Catholic religion.

The integralist movement was particularly strong in France,[28] where it was aligned with the Action Française movement, founded in 1899 as an outgrowth of the Dreyfus affair. Charles Maurras and his collaborators were protesting Emile Zola and the defense of Dreyfus by the Ligue des Droits de l'Homme. Solidly behind the ancien régime—or what remained of it at the end of the century—the Action Française became increasingly royalist. Thus it picked up considerable support from conservative forces that sided with the church during the tumultuous period from 1903 until the Separation Law of 1906, during which time relations between the Roman Church and the French Republic grew increasingly hostile.

Benigni's Sapinière was a small, committed cadre of well-placed individuals. Papers seized by the Germans in Belgium during World War I lifted the veil of secrecy that covered the organization, although they were not published until 1969.[29] One of the documents outlines the program of the Sodalitium Pianum:

1. We are integral Roman Catholics. As the word indicates, the integral Roman Catholic accepts in toto the doctrine, the discipline and the directions of the Holy See along with all their legitimate consequences for the individual and society. He is a "papist," a "cleric," anti-modern, anti-liberal and anti-sectarian. Thus, he is completely counter-revolutionary, since he is not only an adversary of the Jacobin Revolution and radical sectarianism but also of religious and social liberalism. . . . 2. We are fighting for the principle and the fate of Authority, of Tradition, of religious and social Order in both the catholic meaning of these words and in their logical deductions. 3. We view the spirit and the fact of

so-called liberal and democratic Catholicism as well as intellectual and practical modernism, whether radical or moderate, and all their consequences as wounds on the human body of the Church. . . . 7. We are fighting against the Sect both within and without, always and everywhere, under all guises, by every upright and opportune method. (in Poulat 1969, 119–121)

A list of issues—and the Sapinière's stance on each of them—followed. The Sapinière opposed any reduction of the pope's influence in social affairs and advocated "the tireless claim of the Roman Question according to the rights and directives of the Holy See," as well as continued efforts to bring social life under the "legitimate and beneficent" influence of the papacy. The group was against "interconfessionalism, neutralism, and religious minimism," as well as syndicalism, which was areligious, individualistic "democraticism."

The Sapinière opposed "heathen nationalism" and favored healthy and moral patriotism. It denounced feminism, coeducation of the sexes, and sex education, while upholding the improvement of the material and moral conditions of women, youth, and the family. It railed against the "profoundly antichristian" separation of church and state, and against the separation between religion and civilization, science, literature, and art. The movement encouraged "ecclesiastic teaching inspired and guided by glorious, scholastic tradition, the holy elders of the Church and the best theologians" of the time of the Counter-Reformation (Poulat 1969, 121–123).

In 1921, Benigni claimed that the Sapinière had only about thirty-eight active members (see appendix E). It was directed by a diet or council responsible to the Consistorial, one of the Vatican congregations. The diet was composed of Benigni, Jules Saubat (1867–1949), Charles Maignen (1858–1937), and Monsignor Friedrich Speiser (1852–1913). Saubat, a long-time supporter of Benigni and a French Religious of the Congregation du Sacre-Coeur de Jesus de Betharram, became a consultant for the Congregation of the Religious in 1910, and served as secretary of the Sodalitium Pianum Diet. Saubat earned his "integralist credentials" when he became involved in a controversy among three religious orders in France in 1913–14—the Bon-Saveur de Caen, the Franciscaines de Villeurbanne, and above all, the brothers of Saint Vincent de Paul, to which Maignen belonged. Saubat was appointed by the Holy Office to make an "apostolic visit" to the three French congregations—as well as other visits (including one to America)—to investigate accusations about modernist forces at work in the church. He provoked a fierce controversy in France, including charges in the French press against "the police of the Church" (ibid., 419–422). In Rome, however, and among the integralists, he was warmly praised. The Saint Vincent de Paul superior and his assistants were removed, and nearly a third of the 250 religious, including two-thirds of those in France, asked to be secularized.

Maignen was the son of a professor at the Institut Catholique in Paris; after his ordination in 1884, he was appointed the first chaplain of the Catholic Action of French Youth. He wrote a series of books opposing Americanism (*Le Père Hecker est-il un saint?* 1898); democracy (*Nationalisme, Catholicisme, Revolution* 1901); Père Maumus, a Catholic Dreyfusard (*La Souveraineté du peuple est une hérésie* 1902); and modernism (*Nouveau Catholicisme et Nouveau clergé* 1902).[30] Speiser, a Swiss convert from Protestantism, was ordained a priest in 1893 and became professor of ecclesiastical law at the University of Fribourg in 1898. He became involved in a number of organizations,[31] and was "an ardent champion of papal instructions" (ibid., 139).

Benigni's list of participants fails to include several important persons associated with the Sodalitium Pianum (ibid., 594), including two assistants of the diet, Brunner and Falsacappa. As with the modernists, the Sapinière had a number of sympathizers, and its influence went far beyond the small group of identifiable participants. Unlike the modernists, the Sapinière had a formal organization with central coordination and the formal approval and encouragement of the Vatican establishment.

Benigni was a firm believer in papal infallibility as "le grand dogme" of Catholicism (see Poulat 1977, 130), and devoted his life to relentless combat against all enemies of the pope and "integral Catholicism." Born in Perouse, Italy, in 1862, Benigni had a remarkable career, entering the diocesan seminary at the age of eleven and becoming secretary to his archbishop at the age of eighteen. By the age of twenty-five he had been ordained, named a professor of history, and founded a bulletin, *Il Piccolo Monitore,* which assailed anticlericals and liberals. In 1891 he began publishing a journal called *Il Monitore Umbro,* announcing that it would maintain a program "always for the Pope and with the Pope!" (ibid., 63).

Benigni was not merely a conservative, but a counterrevolutionary. In 1894 he declared that he was opposed to both socialism and liberalism: "We are enemies of the two enemies. . . . Being merely anti-socialist, one can play the liberal's game; thus, to these terms, we should always add, both in word and deed, that of *antiliberalism*" (ibid., 88–89).

Although it was "social modernism" more than "modernisme savant" with which Benigni was most preoccupied, the campaign that he launched was directed against all who fell outside of his ever-narrowing definition of true Catholicism. Gradually, the whole world outside of a narrow circle was defined as the enemy. As one internal letter of the Sodalitium Pianum put it (January 1914), "we live by discipline and solidarity. Everyone who stands outside this discipline and solidarity is either an obvious enemy or a false friend. It is well-known how both such types are treated in time of war" (Poulat 1969, 399).

Benigni insisted upon absolute secrecy about everything, including the existence of the Sapinière,[32] in order to protect the organization and its members from sabotage by the French masonry, the modernists, and their accomplices (ibid., 579). The Sapinière created disruptions in the lives and careers of countless Catholics, introduced chaos into a number of institutions, and precipitated a strong undercurrent of suspicion, mistrust, and insecurity throughout the church, almost paralyzing scholarly inquiry within it. Eventually, the Sapinière itself came under suspicion. According to one Sapinière circular, the committees of vigilance, established to fight modernism, "became more and more machines in the service of modernism and of demo-liberalism, etc."[33] *La Vigie*, an integral Catholic daily in Paris, was denounced by the Paris Council of Vigilance.

Among the Sapinière's most formidable enemies were the Jesuits, who had shaped much of the earlier antimodernist campaign and were strategically placed in the Vatican. *Civiltà cattolica* was added to the Sapinière's secret code, and the Sapinière became engaged in bitter conflicts with the Viennese Sonntagsblatt and with the Jesuits associated with the journal *Etudes*.[34]

During Pius X's pontificate, a number of protests about the Sapinière were lodged by Cardinal Ferrari and Bishop Cazzani in Italy, and by Stimmen aus Maria Laach and the *Kölnische Volkszeitung* in Germany (see O'Brien 1967, 553). After Pius's death, Mignot prepared a memo to Cardinal Ferrato, the Vatican secretary of state, concerning the dangers of the Sapinière's excesses and outlining some of its activities, particularly in France. In Paris, Vienna, Brussels, Milan, Cologne, Berlin, and elsewhere, Mignot argued, the Sapinière moved to discredit faithful Catholics through a system of secret espionage.[35]

Opposition to the zealous integralists gradually swelled. Merry del Val, a staunch opponent of modernism, was instrumental in the suppression of Benigni's *La Correspondance de Rome* in 1913. Pope Benedict XV's first encyclical, *Ad beatissimi Apostolorum* (1 November 1914), called for an end to dissensions within the church. He declared that moderation should reign and denounced the escalating suspicions about orthodoxy among Catholics. Pius X was too sympathetic with the Sapinière to suppress it, but Benedict was more concerned about the negative implications of the Sapinière, the Action Française, and other integrist groups. Within Jesuit and Franciscan circles, there was a growing coolness toward the Action Française: it threatened to usurp some of the influence which those orders enjoyed. On 16 January 1914, the Congregation of the Index censured seven books by Action Française leader Maurras, although Pius X postponed publication of the news.[36] Benedict made some inquiries into the activities of both the Action Française and the Sodalitium Pianum, and finally both of them were suppressed.

The danger from the right had become almost as significant to the Vatican hierarchy as the danger on the left, despite the traditional alliance with conservative forces in Europe throughout the eighteenth and nineteenth centuries. Scholastic interpretations of the nature of Catholicism thus resulted in the suppression not only of modernism, but of extreme antimodernism as well.[37]

THE DYNAMICS OF CONTROL

In the final analysis, what was at issue was neither traditional Catholicism and scholasticism nor scientific research as it challenged those interests. As the conflict escalated, the focus of the controversy shifted from substantive issues surrounding the doctrines and history of the Christian faith to issues of authority and freedom. The modernist case demonstrates the complexity of social control and coercion, especially in a large bureaucratic organization. The control of dissidents is usually not as simple as authorities think it will be. Efforts to contain insurgency are complicated, first of all, by the dialectical relation between elites and insurgents, which inevitably creates unanticipated consequences. An attack on relatively isolated individuals, for example, may precipitate the mobilization of dissidents and the formation of a social movement.

A second major problem encountered by authorities who wish to squelch discontent arises from the nature of social institutions, especially when they are large and diversified. Agents of social control often play specialized roles—they are what Lofland (1969, 156) calls "imputation specialists," who are entrusted with labeling and dealing with deviants. Thus, as Wilson (1977, 471) rightly suggests, a triadic relationship emerges among the dissidents, the "target group," and the social control agents. Because the control agents may be relatively autonomous (or may seek autonomy) despite their structural links to the target group, their own special interests emerge, which may contradict those of the "target group" that authorized them to act in the first place.

In the modernist crisis (and, I suspect, in many other conflicts), even the triadic model masks the complexity of the situation. The modernist controversy emerged at a number of levels; alliances and enmities shifted and refocused as the crisis unfolded. Initially, the modernist scholars responded as part of a target group (Roman Catholics) that was assaulted by anticlerical forces outside of the church and by Protestants like Harnack.

Labeled as dissidents by quasi-official and self-appointed control agents (e.g., the *Civiltà cattolica* Jesuits and the right-wing Catholic press), the modernists mobilized to form a social movement. The Vatican responded by enacting its control mechanisms and creating new ones as well, such as the Sapinière. But there was considerable infighting within both elite and dissident groups, so that control, target, and dissident groups were identified differently by the various actors in the conflict. The Sapinière attacked the Jesuits, and vice versa; von Hügel became a control agent within the modernist movement, and was then challenged by Loisy. Eventually, the pope condemned one control group (the Sapinière) as dissidents. Even more ironically, half a century later, many of the "heretics'" ideas were declared orthodox by the Second Vatican Council, and one priest labeled Pope Paul VI a heretic.[38] In sum, the modernist controversy reveals both the inadequacies of a mechanistic model of social change and the need for a dynamic, dialectical approach to the study of social movements—an approach which accounts for the ironies and paradoxes of social life.

7

The Dialectics of Insurgency

Lester R. Kurtz and Stephen G. Lyng

Both the extent of the antimodernist campaign and the later suppression of Sapinière show that the real issue surrounding modernism— at least by the time of its condemnation—was much more than a series of specific objections to particular modernist ideas, or even the use of scientific methods per se. The crisis concerned a radical challenge to the institutional authority of the Catholic Church and the Catholic faith. It exemplifies the dialectical character of conflict and the dynamics of elective affinities between ideas and interests. This concluding chapter explores some implications of the modernist crisis when it is viewed as a case study of a social movement. It addresses some insights and problems raised by sociological studies of social movements—particularly what has been called "bureaucratic insurgency" (Zald and Berger 1978)—and proposes a dialectical model for the study of such phenomena. The implications of a dialectical approach for our understanding both of the modernist crisis and of contemporary conflicts within the Roman Church are also examined.[1]

The Roman hierarchy's misleading caricature of modernism was probably not a deliberate, malicious fabrication, but a genuine effort to save the church from what was perceived as a grave threat to the very existence of Catholicism. When the accuracy of the creation story in Genesis, the authorship of various parts of the Bible, and the authority of the pope began to be attacked in the name of science, the entire Catholic institutional framework and worldview were threatened. In addition, many anticlericals viewed scientific research as yet another tool in the battle against Catholicism and the ancien régime.

Efforts to maintain cognitive consistency emerge both within a cultural system and at the interface between cultural and social organization—that is, between the beliefs and attitudes that various groups of people hold and their respective life-styles and interests. Such attempts to maintain consistency are most clearly observable within the context of a bureaucratic institution, which has a well-defined division of labor based on the principle of office hierarchy and codified rules of procedure (see Weber [1925] 1968). When an institution's authority is challenged, organizational elites are more likely to demand consensus from their members. Thus, when the modernists claimed the right to hold opinions outside the boundaries of the officially sanctioned system, they were labeled insurgents by the institutional hierarchy.

As the conflict between the modernists and church authorities escalated, it became an institutional controversy more than a religious one, although the two types of issues were always interconnected. Both modernist scholars and Roman authorities claimed that they championed the Catholic faith and were defending it from demise in the modern world— that is, that they were on the side of good in a battle with evil forces. Each claimed legitimate authority in matters of mutual concern. Catholic scholars, oriented toward the norms of the scholarly community, demanded the right to do scientific research freely, even when their findings contradicted official doctrines. The church hierarchy responded by embellishing the Vatican's authority. Its organizational elites claimed to have the final word on all doctrinal matters and called for the silence of Catholic scholars who dared to oppose them. Because the institutional crisis seemed to require absolute consistency, Vatican authorities demanded that the scholars not only discontinue teaching and writing their false doctrines, but that they cease believing in them as well. The pattern of interaction between the Vatican and the modernists provides an instructive case study in the sociology of social movements and collective behavior within formal organizations.

THE SOCIOLOGY OF SOCIAL MOVEMENTS

Until recently, most sociological thinking has located "collective behavior" and "organizational behavior" at opposite ends of the continuum. Because of the emergent character of roles, norms, and other structural characteristics during episodes of collective action, such action appears to be the direct antithesis of highly structured bureaucratic activity (Pfautz 1961, 168). Yet recent work in both these areas highlights the similarities between collective and organizational behavior, rather than the differences. Berk suggests, for example, that much of the apparently chaotic behavior of crowds is actually rooted in rational decision-making procedures, and others argue that social movement formation is ultimately dependent upon rational self-interest and preexisting organizations (McCarthy and Zald 1973, 1977; Oberschall 1973; Tilly 1978).

In a complementary trend, some students of bureaucracy have recently moved beyond the traditional, rational model of formal organizations to perspectives that emphasize contradictions in organizational structure (Benson 1977) and the distortions of rational procedures by interest-oriented political action (Pfeffer 1981). As a result of these two trends, we now can conceive of collective behavior in more organizational terms, and vice versa.

Zald and Berger (1978) make a particularly important contribution to this new line of thought. They posit that change within bureaucratic organizations often results from "unconventional political activity" on the part of some group of organizational members. Hence, they suggest that it is heuristically useful to conceive of such organizational change in terms of "coup d'états," "bureaucratic insurgencies," and "mass movements." This social movements approach to organizational change breaks down the traditional distinction between collective and organizational behavior even further than do the two trends just mentioned.

Zald and Berger's analysis is provocative, especially when we consider the pervasiveness of bureaucratic organization as a contextual feature in most contemporary cases of collective protest. Unfortunately, no empirical evidence has been assembled to assess their theoretical model. This study of the Catholic modernist crisis helps to fill the gap by presenting data on an historical event that involved the growth and decline of a social movement within an organizational environment, or what Zald and Berger call a "bureaucratic insurgency within a hierarchical organization." The preceding examination of the modernist crisis supports aspects of the Zald and Berger approach, but also suggests some important modifications.

THE CONCEPT OF BUREAUCRATIC INSURGENCY

In approaching "unconventional activity" within organizations, Zald and Berger (1978) rely on the resource mobilization approach to social movement development, a perspective distinguished by its incorporation of two basic ideas. Departing from the traditional emphasis on the emergence of grievances and on the psychological states associated with such discontent, the resource mobilization approach first posits that there is always enough discontent in any social setting to fuel a social movement, but that the decision to participate depends on the actor's assessment of the risk–reward ratio (Oberschall 1973; McCarthy and Zald 1973, 1215). Second, it focuses on the social context rather than on the actor, emphasizing those infrastructural aspects of society that impinge on the risk–reward ratio. Researchers adopting this approach emphasize two factors: (1) preexisting networks and organizations, and (2) the relations between authorities and dissidents. It is the latter feature that concerns us most directly here.

In an important study of authority–partisan interaction, Gamson (1975) discussed the various options available to both groups. Partisans are chiefly concerned with mobilizing an operational resource base, which is used to bring about structural change and to maintain and develop the organization of the movement itself. Authorities then react to partisans' efforts to influence policy decisions by choosing from a range of strategic alternatives; most often, they respond by undertaking social control measures. In sum, Gamson's analysis suggests that the probability of collective action is increased by the various strategies that partisans use to generate positive resources, while it is decreased by authorities' use of negative or "coercive" resources.

Zald and Berger apply this general perspective to the analysis of organizational change. The concept of "bureaucratic insurgency" refers to the collective efforts of subordinate groups within a bureaucracy to usurp control or effect change in the organization. Consonant with the resource mobilization approach, Zald and Berger's model focuses on those contextual features that account for greater availability of resources for insurgency. They posit that insurgency is supported by factionalism in the organization or by sympathetic aid from organizational elites (1978, 838); insurgents may also benefit from "external supports such as advice on technical matters or ideological support" (ibid., 839–841).

Unfortunately, the problem of authority–partisan interaction receives short shrift in the bureaucratic insurgency model. Zald and Berger's treatment of this issue is limited to a simple affirmation of Gamson's proposition that social control produces "negative resources," which decrease the potential for insurgency (ibid., 841). Yet the modernist crisis reveals a pattern of interaction in which the opposition between authorities and potential partisans was, at a particular point in the controversy, necessary to the maintenance of both groups.

MODERNISM AND BUREAUCRATIC INSURGENCY

The modernist movement is clearly a case of what Zald and Berger (1978) call "bureaucratic insurgency," although two distinguishing features must be taken into account. First, the church bureaucracy is distinguished by the fact that one of its major organizational products is a specific ideological perspective, which it endeavors to elaborate and disseminate. Although the church bureaucracy shares with many other kinds of formal organizations a commitment to fulfilling certain "service" needs, the promotion of the religious perspective is its central goal. Second, the Roman Catholic Church is distinguished by the high degree of "professional commitment" exhibited by members of the organization, especially the clergy. Few professions require the level of commitment that is expected of Catholic priests, and this makes it very difficult for them to leave the organization, regardless of the ambivalence of their situation.

Despite these distinguishing characteristics, the empirical details of the modernist case lend some support to the Zald and Berger model. In particular, there is evidence of certain contextual features having a positive influence on the modernists' resource mobilization. The Catholic modernist movement coexisted with a broader modernist movement, which flourished for several decades in both Europe and America. Although there is no evidence of a transfer of monetary or technical support from the international movement to that of the Catholic modernists, the wealth of modernist literature emerging during this era constituted "an independent base for perspectives on goals, products and policies" (Zald and Berger 1978, 841). Despite this limited amount of support for the movement from sources outside of the organization, there is no evidence of the kind of intraorganizational support that Zald and Berger see as a stimulus to movement development.

Of primary importance in the modernist crisis was the response of the institutional authorities. By increasing the risks that accompanied participation in the movement, the adoption of social control measures did eventually undermine the modernists' vitality, so that in the final analysis, the movement was an apparent failure. Although insurgent activity flourished for a while, the repressive tactics of papal authorities gradually reduced the movement to a shambles. It is important to note, however, that the conventional sociological perspective on social movements applies only to the later stages of the modernist conflict. Papal authorities engaged in a vociferous campaign of repression against the Catholic modernists for a period of fifteen years, but it was only in the last three or four years that these efforts succeeded in thwarting the insurgency. Indeed, in the early stages of the conflict, the repressive efforts of church authorities precipitated an increase, rather than a decrease, in the development of the movement.

The sequence of interaction between authorities and insurgents in the early stages of the movement is the reverse of that predicted by Zald and Berger's model. The adoption of tactics of repression against the modernists did not evolve as a response to a clear-cut partisan challenge. Rather, papal authorities sought to repress what they labeled a "heretical movement" within the church well before the modernists themselves assumed the identity of insurgents.

In sum, the bureaucratic insurgency model can account for some aspects of authority–insurgent interaction, but it does not explain the pattern of interaction in the earliest stages of the modernist movement. Why did papal authorities mount an energetic campaign to repress a handful of scholars before any movement had actually taken shape? And why did these repressive measures have a stimulating rather than a retarding effect on the development of the modernist movement? Zald and Berger's model cannot answer these questions. Accordingly, we propose a theoretical model of authority–insurgent interaction that extends the existing model by accounting for the earliest stages of bureaucratic insurgency.

This model incorporates two basic themes. First, we attempt to build on Zald and Berger's contribution by analyzing the way in which certain bureaucratic imperatives influence the way that movements develop. Second, there are aspects of the process of conflict itself to which the student of social movements must attend. In an effort to deal with these features, we draw upon a body of literature (Simmel [1900] 1978, 1971; Coser 1956; Gerlach and Hine 1970; Coleman 1957; G. Marx 1979; Wilson 1977) that differs from the resource mobilization literature, in that it does not rely so heavily on utilitarian, rationalistic assumptions. This work consequently allows us to consider some of the more ironic, paradoxical aspects of movement development.

THE PERPETUATION OF POWER IN ORGANIZATIONS

As previously noted, the bureaucratic insurgency model emerges out of a more general, "political" approach to organizational analysis, which begins with the premise that "power and politics are fundamental concepts for understanding behavior in organizations" (Pfeffer 1981, 1; cf. Pfeffer 1978; Perrow 1970). This perspective focuses on the relationship between the distribution of power within the organization and factors such as organizational structure, resource allocation, administrative careers, and organizational choice. Zald and Berger's (1978) conception of social movements within organizations is an extension of a perspective that views political struggle, interests, coalitions, and strategy as important organizational variables.

Despite the concern for political dynamics, this approach avoids a one-sided emphasis on shifting power distributions and changing organizational structure by pointing out that "stability, not change, is descriptive of the power distributions in most organizations" (Pfeffer 1981, 289). Indeed, it suggests that under conditions of organizational failure or crisis, the most typical response is greater institutionalization of the existing power structure, rather than a shift in that distribution. The process by which authorities maintain their power under conditions of external threat is the key to understanding the interaction between authorities and insurgents during the modernist controversy.

When an organization confronts an external threat, as the Catholic Church did at the turn of the century, the problem of membership loyalty to the attitudes and beliefs of authorities assumes special significance. An atmosphere of "we versus they" develops, and any deviation from the party line is defined as an act of treason (Sherif et al. 1961). The lack of tolerance for deviance involves more than a simple effort to return wayward members to the fold, however. As Coser has pointed out, "the search for or invention of a dissenter within may serve to maintain a structure which is threatened from the outside (1956, 110; cf. Douglas 1966, ix). Conflict with an inner enemy (like conflict with any opposing force) can strengthen internal cohesion and increase centralization, make members more conscious of their group bonds, increase their participation, and reaffirm the group's value system.[2]

These propositions provide a way of theoretically organizing one of the anomalous findings of our case—namely, the fact that papal authorities instigated a campaign of repression against an "insurgent movement" long before such a movement actually existed. Here we would point to the authorities' concern for maintaining their power in the face of an external threat to the legitimacy of the church. The modernists' application of modern research techniques to the study of religious issues violated institutional norms enough to provide church authorities with the focus for a scapegoating campaign. Previously, the enemy had been external and beyond their control, but now the authorities had a basis for claiming that there was an "inner enemy" as well (see Simmel 1971, 172)—and hence an enemy who could be dealt with directly for the first time.

The campaign against modernism served an additional function: it clarified and reaffirmed the normative and ideological boundaries of the organization. Papal authorities made some major strides in establishing the "orthodox" Catholic perspective as a by-product of their effort to delegitimate the modernist perspective. A necessary part of their argument against the validity of certain modernist assumptions was specification of the "correct" assumptions upon which to base Catholic orthodoxy. Thus church authorities established orthodoxy in a reflexive fashion: they specified the outlines of the orthodox viewpoint by way of a response to modernist assertions. In other words, they established orthodoxy not by stating what it was, but by stating what it was not.

INSURGENT RESPONSE

Having examined the benefits of the "heretic hunt" to institutional authorities, we turn to the response of those who were labeled heretics. As with all social action, an individual does not respond to being called an insurgent in a rigidly determined way. The labeling actions of authorities are associated with a broad range of possible responses on the part of the individuals so labeled. It is therefore essential to identify the most likely response and, perhaps more importantly, to specify the environmental conditions that are correlated with each possible response. In a study of membership dissatisfaction within organizations,[3] Hirschman (1970) concludes that "exit" is the most likely choice. But if organizational loyalty or other factors militate against leaving an organization, members resort to what Hirschman calls the "voice" option—namely, undertaking attempts to change the "objectionable state of affairs" (ibid., 30).

This analysis provides a starting point for our effort to understand the process by which a specific partisan response emerges. For the modernists, as members of a religious institution (and in some cases as trained members of the profession), the exit option was extremely costly. Nor were the modernists simply members who had become unhappy with organizational "goals and products"; rather, they were members who had been labeled and sanctioned by church authorities as heretics.

The labeling process (discussed in chap. 6) is an important aspect of the modernist controversy. The modernist movement developed as a "self-fulfilling prophecy": the modernists existed as a loosely connected group of scholars in the initial stages of the controversy, and became a self-conscious insurgent movement only after ecclesiastical authorities branded them as heretics. As more and more sanctions were applied, the modernists became better and better organized. Each repressive measure was met by a collective effort to counter it. But at a certain point in the controversy, the major focus of the modernists' collective action shifted from how to defend themselves to how to mobilize a movement for reforming the Church. In other words, the structural features that developed from the modernists' efforts to defend themselves eventually became the basis for a reform movement.

For example, the application of sanctions against various modernist scholars produced a communication network that became an invaluable resource for the movement. During both major periods of crisis (1903–04 and 1907–08), von Hügel's correspondence with Loisy and Tyrrell increased dramatically. Initially, these exchanges were concerned with formulating an appropriate response to the Vatican's repressive acts, but as time passed, more and more attention was directed toward organizing and maintaining a movement to reform the church. With the publication of the modernist journal *Il Rinnovamento* toward the end of the conflict, reformist ideas were communicated to an even broader group.

Other resources were produced in a similar fashion. The ultimate effect of the *Index of Prohibited Books* was to make different scholars writing in the modernist vein aware of one another's work, thus facilitating an exchange of ideas among individuals who were to become the movement's ideologues. Also, the evidence indicates that although the various modernist meetings held during the controversy were formally committed to discussing responses to acts of repression, they ultimately became forums for discussing how to bring about major changes in the church. Hence, the effect of papal repression was to force a defensive response that eventually evolved into a self-conscious movement—a movement characterized by a well-defined agenda for reform, a division of labor (including a cadre of leaders), and an extensive communication network.

In the final analysis, these resources were not sufficient to sustain the modernist movement, which developed steadily as opposition from authorities increased, but only up to a certain level of repression. When opposition reached the "obliterating maximum"—excommunicating movement members, reassigning key members to less influential posts, and so on—repression began working as a negative force: it removed rather than produced resources (cf. Gerlach and Hine 1970, 188; Wilson 1977, 477). Ultimately, the modernists' resources were depleted to the point that organizing for collective action was no longer possible.

TOWARD A DIALECTICAL MODEL OF SOCIAL CHANGE

In the case of the modernist movement, Zald and Berger's (1978) bureaucratic insurgency model is valuable in explaining certain aspects of growth, but cannot account for the whole course of the movement's evolution. The present study reveals three major ways in which this model can be extended. First, it fails to account for the fact that the development of movements may involve distinct stages, and that these stages may be governed by different dynamics. Even in the event of the apparent failure of a movement, aspects of the insurgents' agenda for reform may be incorporated into the official definitions of the situation. The intense interaction between elites and dissidents often plants the seeds for subsequent changes in official policy. One generation's heresy is frequently the next generation's orthodoxy—a fact usually missed by studies of social movements which are limited to very short time frames. A significant revolt within an organization or a society may well identify a major contradiction within the system, and the short-term failure of efforts to address that contradiction can be a prelude to later change. Clearly, many of the modernists' conclusions have been adopted by the Catholic hierarchy since Vatican II (a development that is discussed in more detail shortly).

Second, the bureaucratic insurgency model overlooks how conditions outside of the organization influence the development of a movement. When an organization confronts an external threat, authority–insurgent interaction differs substantially from the patterns that evolve when no threat exists. It is therefore important to examine relationships among elites, inner enemies, and external enemies.

Finally, Zald and Berger's model cannot account for the paradoxes of authority–insurgent interaction. Our analysis indicates that under conditions of organizational crisis, the presence of a dissenting faction within the organization can enhance the prestige and power of the existing leadership. There is also a tendency for organizational authorities both to define as insurgency all cases of collective nonconformity among the membership and to engage in a campaign of repression against the labeled group.

A second paradox involves how the "insurgents" then respond to being identified and negatively sanctioned. In contrast to what organizational authorities expect, their campaign of repression can generate resources for the development of an actual social movement. The relationship between repression and the growth of an insurgent movement is curvilinear, rather than linear: mobilization is generally stimulated by increased repression, but only up to a certain level.

In light of this model's failure to include the paradoxes of authority–insurgent interaction, an alternative is required that emphasizes the paradoxes, ironies, negations, and unintended consequences of social phenomena. The "dialectical paradigm" provides just such a framework (see Schneider 1971; Friedrichs 1972*a*, 1972*b*; Albrow 1974; Appelbaum 1978; Benson 1977; Ball 1979). The central concept of the dialectical paradigm is the notion of "dialectical relation"—that is, a relationship in which the two "poles" are simultaneously necessary and opposed.[4]

The concept of dialectical relation can be applied to the pattern of inter-action between organizational authorities and insurgents found in our case study. The data show that each group engaged in action that threatened the existence of the other but that, paradoxically, this action contributed to the maintenance of both groups. In other words, their relationship was opposed but necessary; it was dialectical in character.

Implicit in this perspective is a new approach to the issue of the motivational basis of participation in a movement. Recent social move-ment perspectives generally posit that the individual's decision regarding participation depends on his or her assessment of the risk–reward ratio: if the individual perceives that the risks outweigh the rewards, then par-ticipation is unlikely (Oberschall 1973). This perspective neglects the phenomenon of intensified negative sanctions actually increasing the likelihood of participation.

Under these circumstances, the potential partisan's assessment of the rewards of joining the movement is still a crucial factor in his or her motivation to participate, but rewards are not measured against risks. Risk of participation acts as an independent causal factor, so that there is an unanticipated positive relationship between risk and the motivation to participate; as authorities increase the risk of participation through their use of repressive tactics, participants become more and more stig-matized and have less and less to lose by becoming full-blown insurgents. Under conditions in which organizational authorities label and sanction potential partisans, the latter have a dual motivation to become members of the movement: they not only envision the possibility of acquiring higher status in the organization if the movement succeeds, but they also view the movement's success as the only way to salvage their endangered status. If they participate and the movement succeeds, they win dramat-ically; if they participate and the movement fails, they will be no worse off than they would be if they did not participate in the first place.

A dialectical approach to the dynamics of insurgency and control thus elucidates significant aspects both of the social construction of reality and of how political conflicts unfold within institutions. A clear example is the identification of what Weber calls "elective affinities" between ideas and interests—a dialectical process that occurs within the effort to define appropriate normative expectations of roles and statuses.

Elective Affinities

There is nothing inherent in the role of a scholar—or perhaps even in that of a scholar-priest—which requires rebellion against ecclesiastical authority.[5] That is to say, cultural forms are not inevitably determined by social structural arrangements. Rather, cultural forms grow out of the definitions which people create when searching for ideas that have affinities with their perceived interests. Yet concrete structural arrangements do influence the way in which ideas are shaped, particularly in situations of social conflict, just as the ideas to which people adhere affect their selection of social networks, statuses, and roles. The modernists were faced with conflicting demands and sociological ambivalence. The emerging norms of scientific research required a suspension of judgment concerning the objects of their investigation, at a time when institutional authorities were most rigid in requiring adherence to official doctrines.

Similarly, there is nothing inherent in the role of an ecclesiastical leader that requires suppression of scholars. But Vatican officials were also faced with contradictory demands at the end of the nineteenth century. They believed it was their duty to demand total submission and to defend Catholic orthodoxy, while at the same time relying upon scholars for the development of Catholic teaching institutions. Modernists and antimodernists alike found themselves in ambivalent situations, and both sought ways of thinking and acting that were not ambivalent.

Modernism and antimodernism evolved out of the process by which certain Catholic scholars and certain Catholic officials defined their interests. Modernism and antimodernism were shaped from adaptations of scientific thought and scholasticism, respectively; those who did the shaping were those who found an affinity between their own interests and either scientific or scholastic thought. As the conflict expanded and those involved searched for consistency in their belief systems and social networks, social groupings and cultural formulations reinforced one another in a dialectical fashion.

In some ways, the conflict between modernist scholars and church officials manifested the perennial tensions between reformers and the guardians of tradition, between the heterodox and the orthodox. In another sense, however, the conflict was both qualitatively and quantitatively unique, because of the violent and widespread battles between clericals and anticlericals, religious and secular institutions, nineteenth-century science and Catholic doctrines. The origins of the modernist crisis were thus antecedent to specific questions raised by historical criticism. These origins are to be found in the constellation of events and strategies, coalitions and conflicts that surrounded anticlericalism and clericalism. To some extent, the roots of the conflict lie in the Protestant Reformation, which challenged the Roman hegemony in a radical way. Vatican authorities responded by promoting the infallibility of the church's teachings and the right of the Vatican to interpret scripture and tradition, which culminated in the doctrine of papal infallibility put forth in 1870 by the First Vatican Council.

Thus it was not simply the ambivalence of Catholic scholars or the conflict between science and scholastic theology that precipitated the modernist movement, although that ambivalence and conflict did set the stage for what was to follow. It was also the Vatican's posture of heresy hunting that, ironically, elicited a reform movement among scholars. The antimodernist campaign was waged in part because the antimodernists were not entirely cognizant of the consequences of their actions. More importantly, it was waged because the existence of the modernist movement was both a threat to the Roman hierarchy and a source of strength for it. This curious development is less baffling when one considers the central role that heresy plays both in the dialectical process of doctrinal formation and in mobilizing people in voluntary institutions.

Affinities and Heresies

Ideas can be viewed as having affinities with the interests of social groups not only in a positive sense, but in a negative way as well. Just as there are optimal constellations of ideas and interests which one affirms—and coalitions among groups with which one agrees—so there are affinities between orthodoxies and heresies, elites and heretics. It is more advantageous to disagree with some ideas and people than with others. As Simmel has pointed out, social organization is shaped not only by forces of attraction but also by repulsive forces: "Society, . . . in order to attain a determinate shape, needs some quantitative ratio of harmony and disharmony, of association and competition, of favorable and unfavorable tendencies. But these discords are by no means mere sociological liabilities or negative instances" (1971, 72).

It is in this sense that the modernists were an asset to the Vatican. They served as the negative model for the church's stance toward the modern world. Modernist ideas and intellectual formulations were defined as heretical, but their very existence provided the focus for a revitalization movement, motivated members of the church to rally to the faith's defense on the Vatican's terms, and set in motion an institutional reaction analogous to the flow of adrenaline in an endangered animal.

Not just any enemy, or any set of repulsive ideas, would have served that purpose effectively. For those guarding orthodoxy, the value of heresy lies in the fact that it is not diametrically opposed to but is an unacceptable variant of orthodoxy. Similarly, heretics are not persons outside of the institution, but inner enemies susceptible to mechanisms of control. Thus responses to heterodoxy are a function both of the critical social distance between the dissidents and the institution's authorities, and of the ideational distance between the beliefs of the elites and those of the insurgents.

There was a strong negative affinity between official Catholicism and the type of heresy presented by the modernists. Modernist criticism was a perfect symbol of heresy for the Vatican: modernists could be identified (however inaccurately) with rationalists, anticlericals, and other enemies of the church, yet they were "badly disguised" as defenders of the faith. Unlike external critics of the church, they used the language and codes of Catholicism. Thus an emphasis on the authority of the pope became the rallying point for the antimodernists, who recognized the symbolic importance of a battle with modernism.

The modernists, in contrast, increasingly defined "true Catholicism" in conscious opposition to what their Vatican adversaries claimed was the authoritative tradition. Whereas conflicts began with differences over specific doctrines, they were broadened and generalized to such an extent that church authorities and modernists could hardly communicate with one another, even when they attempted to do so.[6] What the modernists did not realize (although Rome did) was that they were not moving from subordination to freedom in rejecting Vatican restraints on their research; rather, they were exchanging one form of domination for another, albeit preferable, form. As Simmel (1971) suggests, different kinds of freedom emerge from rebellion against different forms of constraint. The church authorities, too, were seeking freedom in their own way—freedom from the invasion of scientific methods into the process of defining Christian doctrine.

The major difference between the two groups was that the Vatican elite was able to realize its claim because of its institutional bases of power, whereas modernist scholars lacked authority within the church. Ironically, the church authorities became captive to the very institutional mechanisms which they promoted as a means of ensuring their liberty. The modernists' opposition to papal authority grew largely out of the Vatican's embellishment of that authority, while the Vatican's accentuation of papal authority was facilitated by the modernists' continual efforts to limit it.

Much of the correspondence among the modernists was motivated by (and filled with discussions of) the campaign against them. Some modernists, such as Tyrrell, came to regard themselves as the true guardians of a Catholicism that was being destroyed by the authoritarianism of the Vatican and by ultramontane forces within the church. They assured one another that their opinions would at some point become Catholic orthodoxy and that "papism" would eventually be viewed as heresy.

In the final analysis, the modernist crisis involved much more than either the modernists or their adversaries could be held responsible for or could understand. Modernists and antimodernists alike were trapped in ambivalent situations, and when they attempted to find ways out of those situations—whether through Catholic historiography or scholastic theology, through the creation of a reform movement or through an institutional campaign to wipe out that movement—many unanticipated consequences resulted. Several questions inevitably arise at this point. What has happened in the church in the intervening years? What is the role of historical criticism in the creation of Catholic theology today? What is the relationship between critics and the Roman hierarchy? A full treatment of these questions is beyond the scope of this work, but a brief analysis of recent developments in the Roman Catholic Church reaffirms both the dialectical character of authority–insurgent conflicts and the need to examine such processes over extended periods of time.

IS CATHOLIC MODERNISM DEAD?

In 1910, the modernist movement seemed dead, and the science of biblical criticism appeared to be a closed chapter in the history of Roman Catholicism. By the 1980s, however (a mere 70 years later, in a 2,000-year-old institution), most of the modernists' program had been adopted. The "synthesis of all heresies" had, for the most part, been incorporated into Catholic orthodoxy. As Thomas Sheehan recently put it, "the dismantling of traditional Roman Catholic theology, by Catholics themselves, is now a *fait accompli*." That transformation has taken place through extensive use of the very methods of investigation for which the modernists were excommunicated. "The emergence of a radically new Catholic theology founded on modern exegesis of the Bible has altered the intellectual topography of what was, until a few years ago, a serene and uniform field" (Sheehan 1980, 34).

The dramatic change in Catholic biblical studies can be dated to Pope Pius XII's 1943 encyclical, *Divino Afflante Spiritu*, which sanctioned the use of scientific methods in scriptural studies. Pius XII (1939–1958) considered himself a scholar and approved of many modern intellectual trends, such as the theory of evolution and historical criticism. It was not until the Second Vatican Council (1962–1965), however, that the transformation became a full-scale revolution. Vatican II did not pronounce a single anathema (see Bourke 1970, 32), thus signaling a new spirit within the Roman Church. It differed from Vatican I in other significant ways. First, the Roman Church was not embroiled in any grave political crisis and there were no troops on the doorstep of Rome, as there had been in 1870. Tensions between the Vatican and various governments still existed, but the church had renounced the practice of governing secular states and had become more circumspect about its involvement in secular affairs, thus diffusing much of the opposition it had encountered in the nineteenth century.

Second, the conflicts between science and religion were not as acutely felt at the Second Vatican Council as they had been at the First. If the warfare between science and theology had not been won by either side, at least a truce had been called, and the rhetoric on both sides had cooled. This rapprochement was facilitated by increasing recognition of efforts by Catholic scientists (encouraged by Pius XII) to reconcile their scientific work and their faith. One of the most important of those scientists, the Jesuit paleontologist Pierre Teilhard de Chardin, offered bold, if controversial, efforts to develop a Catholic theory of evolution, which was much talked about in the hallways and back rooms of the Second Council (Lindbeck 1970, 12–13). Teilhard de Chardin may be the one demonstrably explicit link between the modernists and developments at Vatican II, in that he was a close colleague and friend of Edouard LeRoy. LeRoy confessed that the two had shared ideas to such an extent that he was not sure which ideas were originally his and which were Teilhard de Chardin's (Vidler 1970).

Third, the focus of controversy within the Roman Church shifted from doctrinal issues of faith (such as the Immaculate Conception and the infallibility of the Scriptures) to problems of morality (for example, birth control and abortion, justice for the poor, and the arms race).[7]

The clash between Christianity and the modern sciences is not easily resolved, however, and current disputes within the church contain residues of nineteenth-century conflicts. As Harvey (1966) claims, the conflict between the two is a one of moralities. Whereas traditional Christianity has required obedience to tradition and a loyalty to the church's beliefs, the ethics of science require adherence to methodological procedures and attention to the findings of research. In contrast to Christian morality, scientific morality demands the possibility—at least in principle—of the overthrow of methods, paradigms, and conclusions as a part of the natural process of science (see Tracy 1975, 6; Kuhn 1962). Whereas scientists consider methods as amoral (they are simply effective or ineffective), the church considers means and ends as inextricably linked—methods of inquiry may be inherently dangerous, even if they support official teachings. It is important to note how pervasive "scientific morality" has become in providing normative guidance for scholarly research. For example, it constricts the activity of theologians such as Hans Küng, who considers himself bound by rules of evidence and who uses the insights of scientific criticism to inform his theology, even though he is not a scientist (see the next section).

In evaluating the current situation in the Roman Catholic Church, the crucial question is not whether the conflict between science and religion has been or can be resolved, but whether the ecclesiastical hierarchy identifies its interests with an opposition to scientific research—particularly when it comes to matters of faith and doctrine, of the historicity of the scriptures and traditions of the church. How much scientific skepticism should be allowed at the expense of traditional doctrines? Such questions are not easily answered. Pope John Paul II, who is considered a conservative pope by most members of the contemporary church, does not view scientific criticism with the same distaste as did Pius IX and Pius X. There has been some effort since Vatican II to introduce a new pluralism into the church's theology (see Tracy 1975; Schillebeeckx 1970) and to redefine the nature of the magisterium (Gutwenger 1970; Sullivan 1983), but there is still conflict over the extent to which authority is allocated to scholars within the church, especially given the radical questions raised by most Catholic theologians and biblical scholars in recent years. The dialectical interaction between scholars and the Vatican continues, as can be seen most clearly in the controversies surrounding Hans Küng.[8]

THE KÜNG CONTROVERSY

Recent conflicts in the Roman Church—particularly those about the writings of Catholic scholars Hans Küng, Edward Schillebeeckx, and others—underscore the fact that neither the relationship between scholarship and religion nor the relative authority of scholars and officials within the church has been satisfactorily resolved. The church's organization remains highly differentiated, with considerable social distance between scholars and elites, despite recent efforts to bring scholars into consultative, decision-making roles. As in the modernist case, the Küng controversy revolves around the issues of papal authority, the magisterium, and the institutional hierarchy. In 1975, the Sacred Congregation for the Doctrine of the Faith, successor to the Holy Office of the Index, declared that two of Küng's books, *The Church* and *Infallible? An Inquiry*, contain views which "contrast with the doctrine of the Catholic Church" (Swidler 1981, 163). The congregation singled out three areas of concern, all of them involving the authority of the Roman hierarchy: the dogma of the infallibility of the church, the authenticity of the teaching office of the church, and the need for an ordained, baptized person for the celebration of the Eucharist.

Küng responded by charging that "neo-scholastic theology, . . . despite the Second Vatican Council, still dominates the Roman Curia." That theology takes all ecclesiastical propositions of faith literally—just as positivist jurists interpret and apply a law without asking where it came from, how it has changed, whether it has still another meaning. (in Swidler 1981, 192)

Following Küng's censure by the Sacred Congregation for the Doctrine of the Faith in December 1979, Joseph Cardinal Hoffner, president of the West German Bishops' Conference, told the press that "the chief issue is Küng's stand on infallibility" (Sheehan 1980, 40; *Frankfurter Allgemeine Zeitung* 19 December 1979, 4). In *Infallible?* and *Kirche— Gehalten in der Wahrheit?* Küng deliberately and openly challenged conventional interpretations of papal infallibility. In his preface to A. B. Hasler's *How the Pope Became Infallible* (1981, 5–6), Küng even went so far as to say that "the errors of the magisterium are a fact. Nowadays Catholic theologians concede with heretofore unwonted frankness that even the organs responsible for 'infallible' doctrinal decisions can err, at least in principle (though perhaps not in specific situations), and often have erred."

Because of his "contempt for the magisterium of the Church," as the congregation put it, on the issue of infallibility—and also because of his stands on the divinity of Jesus and the virginity of Mary—Küng was barred from his chair of dogma and ecumenical theology at the State University, Tübingen. There are striking differences, however, between Küng's censure and the censure of modernist scholars. First, the denunciation of Küng has been relatively mild, at least to date—he has not been declared a heretic, and there has been no public effort to excommunicate him.[9] The congregation simply revoked his authority to speak in the name of the church. It is impossible to know at this stage whether further, more sweeping actions will be taken against him and other scholars. One mitigating factor, which clearly separates his case from Loisy's earliest encounters with the Vatican, is the overwhelming public support expressed by both his colleagues and others. As Küng himself put it, "the number of doubters is too high" (Swidler 1981, 22).

The politics of heresy in the contemporary Roman Catholic Church are appreciably different from those at the turn of the century. Despite the presence of powerful conservative lobbies, such as the Opus Dei,[10] the Knights of Malta, and the Catholic Counter-Reformation,[11] mainstream Catholicism has shown considerable admiration for Küng. One conservative Catholic even charges that the "heresies of the twentieth century are those of the bishops" (Madiran 1968–1974, I:11). The day after the congregation's pronouncement against him, seventy-five American Catholic theologians published a statement to the effect that they considered Küng a "Roman Catholic theologian," even if they did not necessarily agree with him on all matters (see the text in Swidler 1981, 554–559). Fifty Spanish theologians issued a similar statement a few days later (ibid., 547–550), and his local bishop, Georg Moser, refused to serve the official notice of Küng's dismissal until prompted to do so by the pope, in consultation with other German bishops.

A major aspect of the controversy has been the procedures used by the Vatican versus Küng's rights. The Holy Office of the Index began a file on Küng in 1957, the year he obtained his doctorate at the Institut Catholique in Paris.[12] In 1967, its successor, the Sacred Congregation for the Doctrine of the Faith reprimanded the diocese of Rottenberg for giving *imprimatur* (approval) to Küng's *The Church*. Küng was called to Rome on very short notice, sparking off a series of conflicts between Küng and the congregation. At issue was Küng's demand to see his dossier,[13] the right to name his own "defense attorney," a delineation of competencies and a right of appeal, and mutual deadlines (ibid., 69 ff.).

After a censure for his introduction to Hasler's *How the Pope Became Infallible* (1981), Küng complained that "the Pope condemned a man whom he had not heard. The Roman motto *'audiatur et altera pars'* (the other side should also be heard) does not apply in papal Rome" (in Swidler 1981, 419). Similar protests were issued from other quarters, including a letter from Küng's colleagues, professors of Catholic theology at Tübingen. "Disputed questions within the realm of scholarly theology," the professors wrote,

as a rule cannot be settled through disciplinary measures without calling forth serious negative consequences. The anti-Modernist measures and the decisions of the Biblical Commission give testimony of that in manifold fashion. The proceedings against Hans Küng means unfortunately nothing other than the taking up again of a practice which has damaged the reputation of theology as a science and the Church as a whole. (in Swidler 1981, 99)

Similar controversies are brewing elsewhere, notably with progressive Flemish scholar Edward Schillebeeckx, at the University of Nijmegen in Holland, who was attacked by conservative theologian Jean Galot in a Vatican radio broadcast (4 December 1979), and in Galot's *Cristo contestato: Le cristologie non calcedoniane e la fede cristologica* (1979). It is too early to tell what else will occur, but there are a number of issues to watch, including the Vatican's attitude toward liberation theology.[14]

Some changes in procedure have been instituted in recent months, however, by Cardinal Ratzinger and the Congregation for the Doctrine of the Faith. Although not publicly acknowledged as such, the changes are probably a response to criticisms of the congregation's handling of the Küng case, and they reflect some new flexibility in the Vatican. For example, a theologian under investigation by the congregation will have access to a canon lawyer when he or she appears before the congregation (see Hebblethwaite 1983).

Another significant shift between the modernist period and the contemporary situation is that some powerful forces within the church hierarchy are now supportive of some controversial positions taken by the suspect scholars. In recent years, much of the conflict in the church has been over the orthodoxy of "liberation theology." This theological approach has been supported as "possible and necessary" by the Reverend Peter-Hans Kolvenbach, superior general of the Jesuit order (see Briggs 1984), despite sharp criticism of the idea in a Vatican document released 3 September 1984, entitled "Instructions on Certain Aspects of the 'Theology of Liberation'" (Kamm 1984). There has also been considerable support for the dissident clergy among many influential church officials in Latin America and elsewhere (see Riding 1984).

Whatever decisions the Vatican makes in the current conflicts, they will not be made simply with reference to particular issues, but will depend upon larger definitions—by both church authorities and scholars—of the nature of the church, its authority structure, and the relationship between its social organization and its teachings. Pope John Paul II has already demonstrated a style of papal governance which "can be soft and accommodating when dealing with outsiders, but as hard as he can be with those within" (Sheehan 1980, 39). Again, the relationship between internal and external matters of church governance can be seen in the new pope's tenure (as was the case with Pius IX, Leo XIII, and Pius X). In the midst of demands that he stand firm and defend the faith from attacks, John Paul II has often chosen to identify the enemy within the church, rather than outside of the institution. He has quarreled with heresies rather than with non-Christians—with the exception of Marxism, although here too he appears to be more concerned with Marxism within the church.[15]

It is significant that the theologian singled out by the Vatican in its recent condemnations of liberation theology is the Brazilian priest Leonardo Boff, whose book *The Church: Charisma and Power—Study of Militant Ecclesiology* attacks the church's authority structure. From the Vatican's perspective, use of Marxist analysis to criticize unjust social structures in Latin America is questionable, but it is much worse "to extend liberation theology's analysis to the very structure of the Roman Catholic Church."[16]

In a document made public 20 March 1985, the Congregation for the Doctrine of the Faith objected to Boff's contention "that there was a historical process of expropriation of the means of religious production on the part of the clergy and to the detriment of the Christian people" (Dionne 1985, 6). As in the modernist crisis, the controversy between the Vatican and certain scholars within the church has escalated to a level at which the issue is not a particular dogma or set of doctrines but the authority of the institutional hierarchy to define orthodoxy. Although the congregation affirms that criticism and prophecy have a role within the church, it claims that the "judgement of the authenticity of the prophetic denunciation belongs to the hierarchy."

The future relationship between the Vatican and scholarship will depend largely upon how scholars and Vatican authorities, especially the pope, define their situations. In other words, it will depend on what ideas and belief systems each group finds to sustain its faith and its interests. The use of scientific research for the pursuit of truth is too widely recognized now for the Vatican simply to sweep contradictory findings under the rug, as Pius X did at the beginning of the century.

One possibility is an effort by the pope to focus on issues other than historical criticism and scholarship when defining orthodoxy in the contemporary period. This has already occured, to some extent, with John Paul II's emphases on traditional family issues—particularly abortion and divorce—and on questions of peace and justice. The area of sexual morality may become an important new battleground. The Roman Church is also becoming increasingly identified with the poor, rather than with the powerful, especially in the Third World, where much of its growth is currently taking place. Thus the specific issues of the nineteenth century, when the church tended to be identified with the aristocracy of the ancien régime, may be fading into the background. Increasingly in Latin America, and recently in the United States (with the bishops' pastoral letters on the nuclear arms race and economics), the Roman Church is identifying anti-Christian forces outside of the church (and often in places of power), rather than focusing on heretics within the institution.

Furthermore, democratic models of organization have replaced earlier monarchical models in most institutions, including the church (at least to some extent). This makes it difficult for the Vatican simply to evoke the traditional authority of the papal office. Yet it does not mean that it will not do so, since it is frequently when a form of government is most threatened that elites cling most vociferously to the status quo. The Roman Catholic Church has not seen the end of conflicts between Catholic orthodoxy and modernist heresies.

APPENDIXES

Appendix A.
Von Hügel Correspondence

TABLE 1

NUMBER OF LETTERS TO AND FROM VON HÜGEL: GREAT BRITAIN

Correspondent	Occupation	Catholic?	Relation to modernism	Number of letters		
				1903–1904	1907–1908	Total 1903–1909
Edmund Bishop	scholar; civil servant	yes	somewhat sympathetic	11	12	56
F. C. Burkitt	scholar (Oxford)	no	sympathetic	15	21	46
E. C. Butler	scholar-priest	yes	active interest	14	13	65
Adeline Chapman			active	18	24	90
G. B. Coore	senior examiner, Board of Education	yes	active interest	6	21	53
H. C. Corrance	justice of the peace	yes	active interest	20	7	44
Angelo Crespi	scholar	yes	very active	0	25	48
Robert Dell	journalist, *Daily Telegraph*	yes	active involvement	46	37	127
Charles Dessoulavy	scholar	yes	active	34	19	91
Alfred Fawkes	priest	yes	active	36	27	73
Cesare Foligno	scholar's spouse (Oxford)	yes	active	0	33	57
Percy Gardner	scholar (Oxford)	no	rather sympathetic	8	18	40
Lord Halifax (Wood)	scholar	no	rather critical	11	5	23
James Hastings	scholar; editor, *Encyclopedia of Religion*	no	interested	1	13	33
A. C. Headlam	principal, King's College, London	no	active, then hesitant	11	9	21
T. A. Lacey	chaplain, London Diocesan Penitentiary	no	active interest	3	9	20
Eveline Lance		yes	active	0	34	49
D. C. Lathbury	editor, *Guardian; Pilot*	no	usually sympathetic	17	1	19
A. L. Lilley	Anglican canon	no	very active	38	42	119

Claude Montefiore	editor, *Jewish Quarterly Review*	no	active interest	0	17	49
G. E. Newsom	warden, King's College, London, hostel	no	somewhat interested	9	6	39
Carlton Parker	author	?	some interest	19	0	21
Maude Petre	author, scholar	yes	very active	25	53	192
G. C. Rawlinson	Anglican curate	no	active interest	0	16	32
Bailey Saunders	scholar	no	active interest	2	22	28
Ida Taylor	author	yes	active interest	0	12	13
Sylvanus Thompson	scholar	no	sympathetic	0	13	17
George Tyrrell	scholar-priest	yes	very active	78	148	341
C. van den Biesen	scholar (St. Joseph's)	yes	active at first	33	8	55
James Ward	scholar (Cambridge)	no	sympathetic	4	12	24
Wilfrid Ward	scholar; editor, *Dublin Review*	yes	skeptically sympathetic	51	33	143
Clement Webb	scholar (Oxford)	no	sympathetic	14	10	59
Joseph Wickstead		no	skeptical	27	35	108
William J. Williams	publisher		active	7	21	41
G. W. Young	scholar (Oxford)	no	active	11	16	47

SOURCE: Von Hügel Diaries, St. Andrews University Library.

TABLE 2

NUMBER OF LETTERS TO AND FROM VON HÜGEL: FRANCE

Correspondent	Occupation	Catholic?	Relation to modernism	Number of letters		
				1903–1904	1907–1908	Total 1903–1909
Maurice Blondel	scholar (Aix)	yes	hostile	28	3	42
Jacques Chevalier	scholar (Grenoble)	yes	active	8	42	74
Charles Denis	scholar-priest	yes	active	12	(deceased)	14
George Fonsegrive	scholar; editor, *La Quinzaine*	yes	active	19	3	26
Albert Houtin	scholar-priest	yes	mixed	9	2	17
Pierre Imbart de la Tour	scholar (Bordeaux)	yes	sympathetic	0	6	8
Lucien Laberthonnière	scholar; editor, *Annales*	yes	cautiously sympathetic	15	6	46
Augustin Leger	scholar (Nantes)	yes	active	4	20	54
Edouard LeRoy	scholar (Collège de France)	yes	active	0	22	49
Alfred Loisy	scholar-priest	yes	extremely active	91	82	173
Monsignor Mignot	Roman bishop (Albi)	yes	extremely active	37	25	79
Auguste Picard	publisher	yes	sympathetic	4	16	32
Paul Sabatier	scholar-clergyman	no	active	14	15	64
François Thureau-Dangin	scholar; curator (Louvre)	yes	sympathetic	15	1	19
Jacques Zeiller	scholar (Freiburg)	yes	active	1	11	16

SOURCE: Von Hügel Diaries, St. Andrews University Library.

TABLE 3
NUMBER OF LETTERS TO AND FROM VON HÜGEL: ITALY

Correspondent	Occupation	Catholic?	Relation to modernism	Number of letters		
				1903–1904	1907–1908	Total 1903–1909
Antonio Aiace Alfieri	scholar; editor, *Il Rinnovamento*	yes	very active	0	88	130
Ernesto Buonaiuti	scholar-priest	yes	very active	0	8	14
Alessandro Casati	scholar-priest; editor *Il Rinnovamento*	yes	very active	0	5	13
Brizio Casciola	scholar-priest	yes	active	5	8	15
Antonio Fogazzaro	scholar, novelist, statesman	yes	very active	6	18	47
Tommaso Gallarati Scotti	scholar; editor, *Il Rinnovamento*	yes	very active	13	27	50
G. Gallavresi	scholar	yes	rather sympathetic	8	16	34
Giovanni Genocchi	scholar-priest	yes	moderate involvement	16	9	32
Concetta Ginntini		yes	active interest	0	12	18
Germain Morin	scholar-priest (Benedictine)	yes	somewhat sympathetic	16	6	34
Contessa Lillian Priuli-Bon		yes	active interest	0	10	13
Giovanni Semeria	scholar-priest (Barnabite)	yes	very active	43	29	134

SOURCE: Von Hügel Diaries, St. Andrews University Library.

TABLE 4

Number of Letters to and from von Hügel: Germany

Correspondents	Occupation	Catholic?	Relation to modernism	Number of letters		Total
				1903–1904	1907–1908	1903–1909
Rudolf Eucken	scholar (Jena)	no	active interest	12	21	65
Heinrich Holtzmann	scholar (Strassburg)	no	active interest	10	9	34
Odilo Rothmanner	scholar-priest	yes	active interest	15	1	22
Joseph Sauer	scholar	yes	active	23	8	55
Ernst Troeltsch	scholar	no	active interest	8	14	28
Hans Vaihinger	scholar (Kantsgesellschaft)	no	some interest	5	9	24

SOURCE: Von Hügel Diaries, St. Andrews University Library.

Appendix B.
Loisy Correspondence

TABLE 5

Von Hügel–Loisy Correspondence

Year	Number of letters von Hügel to Loisy	Number of letters Loisy to von Hügel	Total
1900	9	11	20
1901	19	12	31
1902	11	17	28
1903	17	19	36
1904	21	26	47
1905	6	6	12
1906	4	6	10
1907	15	17	32
1908	22	23	45
1909	10	9	19
1910	12	7	19

SOURCE: Loisy Papers, Bibliothèque nationale, Paris.

TABLE 6

NUMBER OF LETTERS TO LOISY

Correspondent	Country	Occupation	Catholic	Letters to Loisy 1900–1910	Total
Albert I	Monaco	Prince of Monaco	yes	1	1
Don Amelli	Italy	scholar-priest	yes	7	7
Marie Peyrot Arconati-Visconti	France		yes	50	191
Ernst Babut	France	scholar	no	10	38
Henri Bergson	France	scholar	no	5	29
Maurice Blondel	France	scholar	yes	7	9
C. J. P. Bolland	Holland	scholar		7	7
Henri Bremond	Belgium	scholar-priest	yes	18	99
Louis Canet	France	scholar	yes	3	127
Jacques Chevalier	France	scholar-priest	yes	4	4
Arthur Chuquet	France	scholar-priest; editor, *Revue critique*	yes	5	6
Franz Cumont	Belgium	scholar		15	160
E. J. Dillon	Britain	journalist	yes	40	88
Louis Duchesne	France, Italy	scholar	yes	8	28
Alfred Fawkes	Britain	scholar-priest	yes	28	142
Giovanni Genocchi	Italy	scholar-priest	yes	15	17
Louis Havet	France	scholar	yes	28	36
Marcel Hébert	France, Belgium	scholar-priest	yes	18	21
Albert Houtin	France	scholar-priest	yes	69	149
Friedrich von Hügel	Britain	scholar	yes	146	189
Monsignor La Croix	France	bishop	yes	19	23
Paul Lejay	France	scholar-priest	yes	21	31
Édouard LeRoy	France	scholar	yes	7	5
A. L. Lilley	Britain	Anglican canon	no	7	7
Hyacinthe Loyson	Switzerland	clergyman-scholar	no	17	25

Name	Country	Occupation			
Herbert Lucas	Britain	Jesuit scholar	yes	6	6
Charles Michel	Belgium	scholar	yes	10	10
Monsignor Mignot	France	bishop	yes		8
Frédéric Monier	France	scholar	yes	6	
Alfred Morel-Fatio	France	scholar		10	10
Maude Petre	Britain	author	yes	6	129
Salomon Reinach	France	scholar	no	43	101
Hippolyte Renaudin	France	scholar-priest	yes	20	20
Albert Reville	France	scholar		9	9
Cardinal Richard	France	bishop	yes	8	10
Richard's secretary				5	6
Abbé Rousselot	France	priest	yes	6	6
Paul Sabatier	France	scholar-priest	no	30	40
Bailey Saunders	Britain	journalist, scholar	no	5	5
Giovanni Semeria	Italy	Barnabite scholar	yes	6	14
Joseph Turmel	France	scholar-priest	yes	17	55
George Tyrrell	Britain	Jesuit scholar	yes	15	15
Abbé Vacandard	France	scholar-priest	yes	9	9
A. Veronnet	France	priest	yes	10	11
George W. Young	Britain	scholar	no	10	10

SOURCE: Loisy Papers, Bibliothèque Nationale, Paris.

Appendix C.
Lilley Correspondence

TABLE 7

NUMBER OF LETTERS TO A. L. LILLEY

Correspondent	Country	Occupation	Letters to Lilley	Number of references to in letters to Lilley
Maurice Blondel	France	scholar	0	5
Henri Bremond	Belgium	scholar-priest	6	28
Alfred Caldecott	Britain	scholar	1	6
Jacques Chevalier	France	scholar-priest	1	6
Thomas Cheyne	Britain	scholar	8	0
Robert Dell	Britain	journalist	9	10
A. Fogazzaro	Italy	novelist, scholar	0	7
H. S. Holland	Britain	precentor, St. Paul's Cathedral	11	3
F. von Hügel	Britain	scholar	70	46
L. Laberthonnière	France	scholar	0	10
Alfred Loisy	France	scholar-priest	10	47
S. Minocchi	Italy	scholar-priest	0	6
Maude Petre	Britain	author	43	21
Hastings Rashdall	Britain	clergyman-scholar	12	1
Paul Sabatier	France	scholar-priest	10	9
Lisa Scopoli	Italy		0	5
T. Gallarati Scotti	Italy	scholar	0	5
Norah Shelley	Britain		7	0
George Tyrrell	Britain	Jesuit scholar	120	57

SOURCE: Lilley Papers, St. Andrews University Library.

Appendix D.
Books on the *Index of Prohibited Books*

TABLE 8

BOOKS ON THE *INDEX OF PROHIBITED BOOKS*

Author	Work condemned	Year condemned
Henri Bremond	Sainte Chantal	1913
Ernesto Buonaiuti	Saggi di filologia e storia del nuovo testamento	1910
	La genesi della dottrina agostiniana intorno al peccato originale	1918
	Sant' Agostino	1918
	Opera et scripta omnia	1925
Paul Bureau	La crise des temps nouveaux	1908
Henri Bergson	Essai sur les données immédiates de la conscience	1914
	L'évolution créatrice	1914
	Matière et mémoire; essai sur la relation du corps à l'esprit	1914
Charles Denis	Un carême apologetique sur les dogmes fondamentaux	1903
	L'église et l'état; les leçons de l'heure presente	1903
Ernest Dimnet	La pensée catholique dans l'Angleterre contemporaine	1907
Ernest Havet	Le christianisme et ses origines	1879
Albert Houtin	Mes difficultés avec mon évêque	1908
	La question biblique chez les catholiques de France au xixᵉ siècle	1903
	L'américanisme	1904

TABLE 8 *(Continued)*

Author	Work condemned	Year condemned
	La question biblique au xxᵉ siècle	1906
	La crise du clergé	1907
Lucien Laberthonnière	Essais de philosophie religieuse	1906
	Le réalisme chrétien et l'idéalisme grec	1906
	Sur le chemin du Catholicisme	1913
	Le témoignage des martyrs	1913
Édouard LeRoy	Dogme et critique	1907
Alfred Loisy	Etudes évangeliques	1903
	L'Évangile et l'Église	1903
	Le quatrième Évangile	1903
	Autour d'un petite livre	1903
	La religion d'Israël	1903
Romolo Murri	I problemi dell-Italia contemporanea; vol. I: la politica clericale e la democrazia	1909
	Battaglie d'oggi	1909
	Democrazia e cristianesimo; i principii comuni: Programma della societa nazionale di cultura	1909
	La filosofia nuova e l'enciclica contro il modernismo	1909
	La vita religiosa nel cristianesimo; discorsi	1909
Maude Petre	Autobiography and Life of George Tyrrell	1913
Paul Sabatier	Vie de s. François d'Assise	1894
Joseph Turmel	L'eschatologie à la fin du ivᵉ siècle	1909
	Histoire du dogme de la papauté; des origines à la fin du ivᵉ siècle	1909
	Histoire du dogme du péché originel	1909
	Histoire de la théologie positive depuis l'origine jusqu'au concile de Trente	1910
	Saint Jérôme	1910
	Tertullien	1910
	Histoire de la théologie positive du concile de Trente au concile du Vatican	1911
Reviews	Annales de philosophie chrétienne	1913
	Rivista di scienza delle religioni	1916
	Rivista storico-critica delle scienze teologiche	1910
	Il Rinnovamento	1910
	Ricerche religiose	1925

SOURCE: *Index of Prohibited Books* (1930).
NOTE: This list is intended to be representative rather than exhaustive, although all works by the authors listed that are in the 1939 edition of the *Index* are included.

Appendix E.
Members of the Sapinière

TABLE 9

MONSIGNOR BENIGNI'S LIST OF SAPINIÈRE MEMBERS

Italie: Abbé Giovanni Boccardo, de Genes . . . , Abbé Giovanni Menara, de Padoue . . . ; Baron Luigi De Matteis et Baronne Ersilia Pitocco, de Naples . . . ; le Chanoine Alberto Destantins, de Pise . . . ; Mgr. Pesenti, de Milan . . . ; M. Publio Roesler Franz, de Rome. . . .

France: RR. PP. George, Castelain, Herbaux et Dupuis, redemptoristes; RR. PP. Rollin et Hello, des frères de Saint-Vince de Paul; Abbé Boulin, à Paris; M. Rocafort, a Pàris; Comte et Comtesse de Calan, de Rennes; Mlles. Lucien-Brun et Rollin, de Lyon; M. Merlier, d'Amiens.

Belgique: l'avocat Jonckx, de Gand.

Suisse: Mgr. Speiser, de Fribourg

Allemagne: Baron Franz von Savigny; Comte Oppersdorff; Abbé Fournelle, de Berlin; Rev. Schulte, de Breslau, et Rev. Baron, de Berlin; Baronne Adrian Werburg, de Munich.

Ex-Empire Russe: Chanoine Majewski, de Wilna; Abbé Kajewski, curé à Moscou; Comte Jules Ostrowski, de Varsovie.

Ex-Empire Austro-Hongrois: Rev. Antoine Mauss, de Vienne; Rev. Manjaric et Strigic, de Osick.

États-Unis: M. Fritz Simon, du Texas. . . .

SOURCE: Poulat (1969, 582–583).

Appendix F.
Chronology

1633	Galileo summoned to Rome
1651	Thomas Hobbes: *Leviathan*
1678	Richard Simon: *Critical History of the Old Testament*
1789	The French Revolution
1834	Pope Gregory XVI condemns liberal Catholicism in *Singulari nos*
1835–36	David Strauss: *Das Leben Jesu kritisch bearbeitet*
1846	Pius IX replaces Gregory XVI
1848	Revolution of 1848; Pius IX forced to flee Rome
1859	Charles Darwin: *The Origin of Species*
1863	Ernest Renan: *La Vie de Jésus*
1864	Pius IX issues the encyclical *Quanta Cura* and a *Syllabus of Errors*
1869	The First Vatican Council begins (8 December)
1870	Approval of the constitution *Pastor aeternus* on papal infallibility
1871	Charles Darwin: *The Descent of Man*
1875	Catholic Institutes established in Paris, Lille, Lyon, Angers, and Toulouse
1878	Leo XIII replaces Pius IX (20 February)
1879	Encyclical *Aeterni Patris* sanctions Thomism
1880	Jules Ferry secularizes French schools
1888	Leo XIII condemns 40 propositions from the works of Antonio Rosmini

1891	Leo XIII issues *Rerum Novarum*
1892	International Scientific Congress of Catholics held in Paris
1893	Encyclical *Providentissimus Deus* issued on biblical studies
1896	Loisy begins publishing the *Revue d'histoire et de littérature religieuses*
1897	W. Elliott: *Vie du père Hecker* published in French; translation by Félix Klein
	First meeting between von Hügel and George Tyrrell
1899	"Americanism" condemned in *Testem benevolentiae*
1900	Adolf von Harnack: *Das Wesen des Christentums*
1902	Albert Houtin: *La question biblique chez les catholiques de France au XIX siècle*
	Civiltà cattolica attacks *Studi religiosi*
	Alfred Loisy: *L'Evangile et l'Eglise*
1903	Cardinal Richard of Paris condemns Loisy's *L'Evangile et l'Eglise*
	Pius X replaces Leo XIII
	Alfred Loisy: *Autour d'un petit livre*
	Books by Loisy placed on the *Index of Prohibited Books*
1904	*Diplomatic relations broken between France and the Vatican*
	Lettres romains published anonymously in the *Annales de philosophie chrétienne*
1905	Edouard LeRoy: "Qu'est-ce qu'un dogme" published in *La Quinzaine*
	Antonio Fogazzaro: *Il Santo*
1906	George Tyrrell expelled from the Society of Jesus
	Fogazzaro's *Il Santo* placed on the *Index*
	Lucien Laberthonnière's *Essais de philosophie religieuse* and *Le réalisme chrétien et l'idéalisme grec* put on the *Index*
	The Biblical Commission decrees the Mosaic authenticity of the Pentateuch
	Von Hügel refutes the decree in *The Papal Commission and the Pentateuch*
	George Tyrrell: *A Much-Abused Letter*
	Loisy says his last Mass (1 November)
1907	First issue of *Rinnovamento* published in Milan (January)
	Don Romolo Murri suspended *a divinis* (15 April)
	Lamentabili sane exitu condemns 65 propositions, the majority of them from Loisy's work (3 July)
	Works by LeRoy and Houtin put on the *Index* (26 July)
	Meeting at Molveno with von Hügel and the Italian modernists (27–29 August)

Encyclical *Pascendi dominici gregis* condemns modernism (8 September)

Il programma dei modernisti, Risposta all'enciclica di Pio X Pascendi dominici gregis appears anonymously in Rome (28 October)

The Pope excommunicates the authors of *Il programma dei modernisti* (29 October)

Cardinal Ferrari forbids *Il Rinnovamento* to be bought or read (6 November)

Cardinal Ferrari excommunicates the editors, directors, authors, and collaborators of *Il Rinnovamento*

1908   Salvatore Minocchi suspended *a divinis*

Alfred Loisy excommunicated (7 March)

Friedrich von Hügel: *The Mystical Element of Religion*

1909   Loisy elected to the Collège de France

Umberto Benigni founds the Sapinière

Romolo Murri excommunicated (22 March)

Works by Turmel, Murri, and Tyrrell placed on the *Index*

George Tyrrell dies (15 July)

Il Rinnovamento ceases publication (December)

1910   Loisy resumes publication of *Revue d'histoire et de littérature religieuses*

Pius X requires an antimodernist oath by all clergy engaged in pastoral or instructional work

1914   Benedict XV suppresses the Sapinière and the Action Française

Notes

1. CATHOLIC ORTHODOXY AND THE DYNAMICS OF HERESY

1. This chapter is a substantially revised version of Kurtz, "The Politics of Heresy," *American Journal of Sociology* 88 (May 1983):1085–1115.

2. The idea of the combination of nearness and remoteness is suggested by Georg Simmel in his essay on the "stranger" as one who is "near and far at the same time" (1971, 148). What is interesting about the stranger is that despite his or her presence, there is a distance that characterizes his or her relationship with others present. "The stranger is an element of the group itself, not unlike the poor and sundry 'inner enemies'—an element whose membership within the group involves both being outside it and confronting it" (ibid., 144). Thus the heretic is a stranger, in Simmel's sense of the term. This is a social form that provides a certain degree of freedom and objectivity, which grow out of the distance between the stranger and others, and it is precisely this freedom which heretics seek and which elites refuse to grant. Similar dynamics can be found in the deviance literature, notably Erikson (1966) and Szasz (1975).

3. Merry del Val to Ward, 5 June 1899; St. Andrews University Library, Wilfrid Ward Family Papers VII 205a, ms. deposit 21.

4. The notion of "elective affinities" (*Wahlverwandtschaften*) is an analogy used by Weber to describe the relationship between ideas and interests (Weber 1947, 83; cf. Howe 1979). For a more detailed discussion, see chapter 7.

5. Erikson, following Durkheim, has noted that institutions created to suppress deviant behavior (e.g., prisons and mental hospitals) often promote the type of behavior that they are supposed to mitigate (Erikson 1966; cf. Ben Yehuda 1980).

Durkheim has pointed out that even in a society of saints, there will be crime and punishment: "Faults which appear venial to the layman will create there the same scandal that the ordinary offense does in ordinary consciousness" ([1895] 1938, 69). Violations of social norms can only be evaluated vis-à-vis that which is valued in the society.

6. "Therefore, you shall keep his statutes and his commandments, which I command you this day, that it may go well with you, and with your children after you, and that you may prolong your days in the land which the Lord your God gives you forever" (Deut. 4:40; cf. Weber 1968, 399–400). All quotations from scripture are from the *Oxford Annotated Bible, Revised Standard Version,* edited by Herbert G. May and Bruce M. Metzger (New York: Oxford University Press, 1962).

7. As Weber points out (1968, 480), *coge intrare* or *compelli intrare,* "to force [them] to join," justifies the use of force against heretics, and is derived from an allegorical interpretation of Luke 14:23, in which a servant is told, "go out to the highways and hedges, and compel them to come in."

8. In Simmel's sense of the concept of social forms (1971). The crucial observation is that religious dogmas and canons (see Weber 1968, 459) are usually fashioned in situations of conflict, in order to oppose persons and ideas that religious elites perceive as threatening.

9. The concept of "relative deprivation" refers to situations in which one feels deprived because of one's perception of the conditions of others or of past conditions, rather than as a consequence of absolute deprivation at the given moment.

10. On the importance of social networks for the recruitment of membership in social movements, see Snow, Zurcher, and Ekland-Olson (1980).

11. The term "status ethic" is suggested by Weber (1968, 213). Although not defined, it presumably refers to a normative belief which is related to and somehow legitimates the status of a group of adherents to that ethic.

12. See Merton ([1949] 1968, 601–602) and Harvey (1966).

13. For more information on the internal workings of the Roman hierarchy, see Turvasi's important work (1979), which includes translations of and comments on the correspondence between Loisy and the well-placed Roman priest, Giovanni Genocchi.

14. "No taste or moderation in statement," von Hügel wrote to the moderate editor of the *Dublin Review,* "will make the militant scholastics tolerant of what you and I have got in common" (von Hügel to Ward, 10 October 1907; St. Andrews University Library, Wilfrid Ward Family Papers VII 143).

2. THE MODERNIST CRISIS

1. See, for example, Leff (1967), Moore (1975); compare Congar (1978).

2. With scientism, the organized skepticism of the scientific method is turned into a worldview that calls into question "the validity of tradition as such; it insists on the testing of everything which is received and on its rejection if it does not correspond with the 'facts of experience'" (Shils 1972, 18).

3. The statement by the Council of Trent soon after the Protestant Reformation

was in direct opposition to the Protestants' reliance on scriptures (*sola scriptura*) rather than on both scripture and tradition as the sufficient source of revelation. All quotations from the Council of Trent are from translations in Neuner and Roos (1967, 59–63).

4. In a letter from Rousseau to Voltaire ([1756] 1924–34, II:324).

5. The context of Loisy's remarks was his interview with the Parisian archbishop, Cardinal Richard, who charged that he had submitted to the influence of German authors. Loisy responded by saying, "Monseigneur, it is a myth and, I might dare add, an unpleasant joke. I devoted myself conscientiously to my work as it was assigned me. My studies of the Bible were based on the Bible itself, which is precisely where I learned of the problems that are to be found there (1930–31, II:16).

6. The argument is similar to objections made against Copernicus and Galileo, who claimed that the earth was not the center of the universe.

7. The term "anticlericalism" was in some use in Europe from the twelfth century, but is usually associated with the nineteenth century, following the French Revolution; it connotes opposition to clerical privileges established by feudalism and to clerical alliances with the monarchy.

8. "Ultramontanism" denotes showing deference to the power of the papacy "over the mountains."

9. One reassessment of the reform government of the early days of the Republic (Rebérioux 1975) claims that the educational changes produced the only lasting effects of late nineteenth-century radicalism in France.

10. Realizing the apparent inevitability of the French Republic, Leo XIII became the first pope to recognize its legitimacy. He did not express a preference for democratic government; rather, he declared that it should be respected because it was the duly constituted authority in the country, and therefore a representative of the power of God. The policy was no doubt intended to reconcile the church with the new regime and to mitigate anticlericalism.

11. Gregory VII not only established a parallel political structure within the church but also asserted its superiority to secular monarchies. The imperial crown, for example, was only to be worn by the pope, and secular kings were forbidden to wear it (see Ullmann [1955] 1970, especially pp. 310 ff.).

12. Gallicanism refers to a movement within the French church to limit the power of the pope, due to conflicts between the French and the pontiff. A set of four propositions called "The Gallican Liberties," which were drawn up in 1682, denied that Peter and his successors had received any authority from God in civil affairs, affirmed the supremacy of the councils over the pope, emphasized the authority of the Gallican and other local or national churches, and contended that although the pope has a principal role in questions of doctrine, the consent of the church is necessary if his decisions are to be considered irreformable (see Palanque 1962). Febronianism was a form of Gallicanism developed by Bishop John Nicholas von Hontheim (1701–1790), who called himself "Febronius" and claimed that the bishops should restrain the activities of the Holy See.

13. Not to be confused with the encyclical by the same name that was issued by Leo XIII in 1879, calling for a revival of Thomistic studies.

14. For more details, see the account in Coppa (1979, 169 ff.).

15. One interesting example of the vicious and sometimes personal (as well as sexist) nature of the attacks is Petrucelli's *Popery Exposed,* which charges that "Pius IX is as full of vanity as a poet, and as fond of dress as a woman. The vicar of Christ is, besides, very womanish. He has their mobility, their exaltation, their freedom on intimacy, their little coquetries, their gossiping, talking by fits and starts, their neatness, their absolute need of luxury, of silk, of perfumes, of flowers, for the brilliant and costly, inconstancy in taste" and so on (Petrucelli 1875, 273). Such attacks help to explain the motivations behind Pio Nono's oppressive administration.

16. Hughes (1961, 398) warns that although there was an opposition movement, it should not be interpreted—as he claims Butler (1936) does—as constituting an organized opposition party such as those that exist in modern parliaments.

17. Hasler (1981, 69) claims that although the minority bishops protested restrainedly in public, they did so vehemently in private: "The Roman Archbishop Vicenzo Tizzani spoke of inquisitorial practices. Archbishop Georges Darboy of Paris called it the grave of the bishops."

18. One bishop wrote a letter to one of his priests criticizing the proceedings of the First Vatican Council, and its recipient allowed it to be printed anonymously in the London *Times.* When the bishop's identity was revealed, the pope was reported to be looking for him; the bishop promptly threw his scheme into the Tiber and escaped from Rome (Butler 1936, II:107). After the final vote was taken, the two dissenting bishops (out of a total of 535) reportedly made their way to the foot of the papal throne, announcing solemnly, "Holy Father, now I believe" (Hughes 1961, 364).

19. One opposition bishop, the French bishop Félix Dupanloup, wrote in his diary on 28 June 1870, "I'm not going to the Council anymore. The violence, the shamelessness, and even more the falsity, vanity, and continual lying force me to keep my distance" (Hasler 1981, 136). Hasler claims that on the day of the vote on infallibility, some bishops became "conveniently sick" (ibid., 187). Reprisals were apparently taken against dissident bishops, such as the refusal to grant marriage dispensations for the dioceses of Bishop Joseph Hefele of Rottenburg and Bishop Johannes Beckmann of Osnabruck, Germany (ibid., 201).

20. The treatment of the neo-Thomist movement that follows relies heavily on Gerald McCool's important analysis of *Catholic Theology in the Nineteenth Century* (1977) and on Thomas J. A. Hartley's *Thomistic Revival and the Modernist Era* (1971).

21. That is, the Apostolic Constitution on Faith; see Butler 1936, I:200, II:129, 131.

22. See Hartley (1971, 31). Hasler (1981, 121) claims that the public campaign for the doctrine of infallibility was initiated in February 1869 in the pages of the *Civiltà cattolica.*

23. The *Civiltà cattolica* was the first Italian Catholic review to champion Thomism, and an article in the 18 May 1872 issue called for the creation of a Thomist academy in every diocese (Hartley 1971, 5).

24. Liberatore, a member of the *Civiltà cattolica* editorial staff, coordinated the campaign for infallibility at the Vatican Council (Hasler 1981, 72).

25. Sanks is using the term "paradigm" as it was developed by Thomas Kuhn. His thesis is that in the period between the First and Second Vatican Councils, there was a shift in the paradigms of the theology of the magisterium. That change is analogous, Sanks argues, to Kuhn's notion of changing paradigms in scientific communities. Although Sanks tends to confuse "theories" with "paradigms," I have found his treatment extremely insightful. I would argue that paradigm changes occurred in the nineteenth century which were similar to those that Sanks found between the two councils—that is to say, new paradigms were developed by the Roman establishment to confront the church's nineteenth-century antagonists.

26. For example, the pope had opened portions of the Vatican archives to scholars.

27. Diaries of von Hügel, 8 February 1903, St. Andrews University Library. According to Briggs, "the Commission is singularly destitute of biblical critics; and hence its Opinion, standing for that of the average member, or even for that of the majority of the members, can, whatever its importance in ecclesiastical circles, be of but little or no consequence before the tribunal of Biblical scholarship" (Briggs and von Hügel 1906, 7).

28. See McAvoy (1963, x), a major source of information for the discussion that follows.

29. Bishop Carroll, for example, argued for a return to the ancient practice of electing bishops (see Greeley 1977, 33).

30. In Maignen, "Les ideés du P. Hecker," *La Verité*, 19 March 1898.

31. The condemnation served not only to consolidate the Vatican's power in Europe but also to make the American church more careful in its relations with Rome. Greeley (1977, 35) even argues that the American church has still not recovered, "in part because the apostolic delegates who came after the encyclical . . . have consistently supported the appointment of 'sate' bishops who lack the initiative and ingenuity of the nineteenth-century pioneer-intellectual bishops."

32. The doctrine of the Immaculate Conception is sometimes erroneously confused with that of the Virgin Birth. The former refers to Mary's being born without sin, whereas the latter refers to Jesus's birth.

33. See "La *Civiltà cattolica* Nei suoi inize e nelle prime prove," in the second volume of *Civiltà cattolica* (1924, 19).

34. Vaughan to von Hügel, 1 October 1896, St. Andrews University Library.

35. In Pius X's first encyclical, *E supremi apostolatus*, 4 October 1903.

3. FROM SCHOLARSHIP TO SCANDALS

1. By 1556 three-fourths of the Jesuits were engaged in teaching and teaching-related duties in 46 colleges. By 1579 there were 144 colleges; in 1626, 444 colleges, 56 seminaries, and 44 houses of training. By 1749 there were 669 colleges (used primarily for secondary education), 176 seminaries, 61 houses of study for Jesuits, and 24 universities.

2. This is not to say that structural ambivalence does not have psychological consequences; it can certainly be examined from that point of view. Psychological ambivalence can also have an impact on social structures, especially when people holding positions of power and influence experience such ambivalence. Like all social and psychological variables, sociological ambivalence and psychological ambivalence are dialectically interrelated.

3. Yet Vidler's earlier book (1934) was entitled *The Modernist Movement in the Roman Church*.

4. See Thierry's (1963) account of daily life in Rome, which is in the form of a fictional diary written by a member of the Curia of modest rank.

5. I do not mean to imply that all of those mentioned (e.g., Ward and Blondel) should be identified as modernists, but rather that they were subject to similar ambivalences and were in some way associated with the modernists. A number became quite cool toward the modernists after conflicts between the modernists and the Vatican escalated. It is because of those conflicts that it is sometimes impossible to say who was and who was not a modernist.

6. It was common for bright young men from poorer families to be channeled into the priesthood, since it provided a means for obtaining an excellent education without undue strain on the family's limited resources.

7. The situation at the Institute Catholique changed later on, when the rector was reproved by Leo XIII, who ordered him to abandon Cartesianism and promote Thomism (Riet 1963–1965, I:188; Baudrillart 1912–1914, II:62).

8. As Vidler has pointed out, the charge of subversive influence by rationalist critics "is one of the commonest methods by which the orthodox account for 'the errors of modernism'" (1934, 73). See also Loisy (1930–31, III:83 ff.); Rivière ([1913] 1929, 96); Lagrange (1932, 23 ff.); and Mercier (1910).

9. Arthur Galton attributed the attack on Duchesne to the Jesuits in a letter to Houtin (1 January 1912; Bibliothèque nationale, Nouvelles acquisitions françaises 15705).

10. Loisy was not without support among the bishops. Four of them spoke in his favor: Monsignor Pagis, Bishop of Verdun, and Monsignor Hugonin, of Bayeux, both subscribers to Loisy's *Enseignement biblique*; Monsignor Lagrange, Bishop of Chartres; and Monsignor Renon, Bishop of Amiens (Loisy 1930–31, I:272).

11. At one point, Loisy wrote that he could not accept any article of the Catholic creed, at least in its official interpretation, except that Jesus had been "crucified under Pontius Pilate" (Loisy 1930–31, I:363).

12. This tactic is not uncommon within bureaucratic and institutional hierarchies. Shared understandings and behind-the-scenes maneuvering can make it appear that a powerful individual is "above" participation in a particular action, particularly if it is somewhat "messy." One of the most thorough documentations of how the process works is the set of transcripts of White House conversations that were made public during the Watergate affair. The official's actual power is increased by maintaining social distance from a questionable activity or group. By using a tactic of impression management that Goffman (1959) calls "mystification," the individual fosters the impression that he or she is not involved in activities which are in reality under his or her control.

13. Cardinal Richard was kept informed as to Loisy's teaching, and a summary of one of Loisy's lectures was found among the papers of Monsignor Montagnini, the papal nuncio of Paris.

14. Mignot to Loisy, 13 November 1900; Bibliothèque nationale, n.a.f. 15659.

15. Mignot to Loisy, 26 January 1902; Bibliothèque nationale, n.a.f. 15659.

16. Mathieu to Loisy, 20 November 1902; Bibliothèque nationale, n.a.f. 15659.

17. Some Protestants simply dismissed Loisy's work because of its critique of Protestantism. Gardner, for example, appreciated "his merits on the historic side," but felt that Loisy did "not in the least understand the facts of the reformed theology: and one could scarcely expect it in a Frenchman. Comte also quite fails in this matter" (Gardner to von Hügel, 18 March 1903, St. Andrews University Library, 2591).

18. Quoted in Poulat (1962, 270), Maignen's article was entitled "Autour de *L'Evangile et l'Eglise*" and appeared in the 4 March 1903 edition of the *Verité française,* and previously in the *Patriote* (Brussels). As Poulat noted, the Apollinaire is the diocesan seminary of Rome.

19. Von Hügel was the behind-the-scenes organizer of the movement, whose role is discussed in more detail in the next section.

20. Montefiore wrote to von Hügel in April of 1903 that "Loisy is *splendid and brilliant*" (St. Andrews University Library, 2837, emphasis in the original); and on 14 March 1903, von Hügel received a long letter from Troeltsch in which he expressed his admiration (St. Andrews University Library, 3026; Diaries of von Hügel, 14 March 1903).

21. An article entitled "Un scandale" appeared in the *Verité française* on 14 January 1903; it denounced the errors in *L'Evangile et l'Eglise* as new forms of Arianism and Nestorianism (Poulat 1962, 129–130).

22. Siegfried (1932, II:408). Loisy assured Abbé Marfoix that if he had known that Rome intended to put his work, *La Religion d'Israël,* on the *Index,* he would have printed 5,000 copies instead of 500 (ibid., II:409).

23. The index to Loisy's *Mémoires,* for example, has 182 references to letters from von Hügel. It is possible, however, that the von Hügel–Loisy correspondence was omitted because it was in French.

24. Von Hügel to Petre, 13 March 1918, British Library, Additional Manuscripts 45362; see also von Hügel 1927, 248.

25. Petre, a chronicler of the movement and confidant of von Hügel and Tyrrell, probably knew more about the scope of the movement than anyone, with the exception of von Hügel himself.

26. An important source of information on Tyrrell is the two-volume work edited by Maude Petre after his death; the first volume consists of Tyrrell's autobiography up to 1884 and of Petre's biography, which finishes the story. The most comprehensive study of Tyrrell is David Schultenover's excellent study, *George Tyrrell: In Search of Catholicism* (1981b).

27. Tyrrell to von Hügel, 1 November 1903, British Library, Add. Mss. 44928.

28. See Vidler (1970, 171). Tyrrell's scholastic training later proved helpful, in that it gave him insight into the scholastics' way of thinking. He was attracted to Thomism as a method, but not as a compendium of knowledge (Root 1981,

71). As Tyrrell later wrote to Laberthonnière, for example, "I am fighting scholastics with their own weapons & must leave no point unguarded" (14 March 1907, University of San Francisco Archives).

29. Tyrrell to von Hügel, 30 September 1904, British Library, Add. Mss. 44928.

30. Ranchetti is inaccurate when he claims that Tyrrell "was little influenced by new books and by what von Hügel and others told him of what was going on" (1969, 136). Although he was highly original in his thought and went beyond the works of those he studied, such as Newman, Tyrrell was also deeply influenced by his relationship with von Hügel (see Barmann 1972). Vidler received a letter from Maude Petre after the publication of his *Modernist Movement in the Roman Church* (1934), in which she remarked that his history contained a gap—namely, the "pervasive and persistent influence of the Baron. . . . He is essential to any account. Without him Father Tyrrell would have been a spiritual and moral pioneer, but not strictly a Modernist" (Vidler 1970, 111). Tyrrell was also greatly influenced by Loisy, who was the subject of many letters.

31. For a discussion of the relevant documents in the Jesuit archives, see Schultenover (1981*a*).

32. See Tyrrell to Bremond, 26 July 1900, University of San Francisco Archives.

33. This is not to say that Tyrrell and von Hügel did not have their differences. In a letter to Bremond, for example, in discussing a recent piece by Blondel, Tyrrell complains that "the dear Baron is too deaf & too transcendental to understand my questions on this subject" (11 January 1899, University of San Francisco Archives).

34. Schultenover (1981*b*, 249) points out that although Tyrrell's *The Church and the Future* doesn't mention Loisy by name, Tyrrell "began and ended with Loisy."

35. Loisy wrote in his *Mémoires* that "one could say that modernism as a party of open resistance to Roman absolutism died with Tyrrell" (1930–31, III:127).

36. See Haight (1974, 636, 662). Although I have perused many of the writings and letters of Blondel, Laberthonnière, and LeRoy, I have relied a great deal on Haight's guidance; see his study of the three (1974).

37. See Haight (1974, 639) and Blondel and Laberthonnière (1961, 134–138). Several collections of Blondel's letters have been published and provide insight into these and other issues surrounding the controversies. On the question of his audience, and his lack of consideration of the impact of his work on the scholastic theologians, see his letters to Valensin, 11 July 1912 (Blondel and Valensin 1957, III:175–181), and to Picard, 19 December 1896 (Blondel and Laberthonnière 1961, 121–123); see also Haight (1974), whose study draws upon these and other documents.

38. Tyrrell, in writing to Laberthonnière, suggested that he would like to publish something in *Annales*, "which is the proper organ of our party" (2 March 1907, University of San Francisco Archives); compare Laberthonnière and Blondel (1905).

39. "Blondel uses these words in a pejorative sense to designate not the use

but 'the abuse of exclusively historical or exclusively dogmatic preoccupations'"
(Haight 1974, 645; cf. Marlé 1960, 205).

40. LeRoy claimed not to use the word "pragmatist" in the same sense as
William James (Vidler 1965, 66).

41. LeRoy to Loisy, 12 March 1908, Bibliothèque national, n.a.f. 15658.
LeRoy also supported Loisy's candidacy for a chair at the Collège de France
(Loisy 1930–31, III:42).

42. In a letter to his bishop on 18 August 1907, Tyrrell said, "I feel sure that
LeRoy . . . is right; and what we need is a new conception of the very nature of
dogma" (Petre 1912, 409).

43. Mignot to Loisy, 3 September 1910, Bibliothèque nationale, n.a.f. 15659.

44. See Flammarion 1927; E. Weber 1962; Thomas 1965.

45. Although in his memoirs, Minocchi recalls von Hügel's presence at the
Fribourg conference, and Ranchetti assumes that he is accurate (1969, 77, 86),
it is clear from the baron's diaries (24–27 July and 1–5 August 1897) that he
did not attend the conference, but rather asked Semeria to read the paper for
him (cf. Barmann 1972, 68).

46. Buonaiuti was apparently the original author of *The Programme of Modernism* (1908), and Tyrrell the principal translator (see the Petre Papers, British
Library, Add. Mss. 44930, and Schultenover 1981*b*, 446).

47. On the modernists' uses of Newman's work, see Burke and Gilmore (1982).

48. In Fogazzaro's letter to L. M. Billia, editor of the *Nuovo Risorgimento*,
which was published under the title of "Pro Libertat," in vol. IV, no. 2 (see
Ranchetti 1969, 105, n. 2).

49. Von Hügel to Ward, 28 May 1907, St. Andrews University Library; see
also Barmann 1972, 183.

50. Von Hügel to Petre, 15 October 1909, British Library, Add. Mss. 45361.

4. COPING WITH AMBIVALENCE

1. The best reviews of the Loisy controversy—and some attempts at resolving
the enigma—are in Vidler (1970, chaps. 2 and 3) and Poulat (1962). Attempts
to solve the mystery are still thwarted by the conflicts of the period and by the
charges and countercharges that emerged at the time. For example, attacks on
Loisy by Houtin and Sartiaux are particularly suspect and are not always entirely
credible.

2. Vidler (1970, 41–42) suggests that the title is best translated as *A Clerk
who has not played false*. As he pointed out, the title is suggested by Julien
Benda's well-known *La trahison des clercs* (1927).

3. The inscription read: "Alfred Loisy, Priest, Retired from the ministry and
from teaching, Professor at the Collège de France, Tuam in votis tenuit volun-
tatem" (see Dagens and Nedoncelle 1968, 92). Bremond contended that Loisy
continued to be a priest even after his excommunication. As Vidler put it, "as
long as he was allowed to do so he exercised his priesthood within the Church.
After his excommunication he continued to be a priest, in the religious though

not in the ecclesiastical sense: he was still constantly concerned with the religious well-being of mankind, and not only with the historical study of religions, and also he exercised a pastoral ministry" (1970, 44).

4. Cardinal Richard to Loisy 8, 21 February 1904; 11, 17 March 1904, Bibliothèque nationale, n.a.f. 15661; see also Loisy (1930–31, II:339ff.).

5. Compare Loisy (1930–31, I:302–330, II:62–90). See also von Hügel to Loisy, 3 January 1902, and Loisy to von Hügel, 6 January 1902, both in the Bibliothèque nationale, n.a.f. 15645.

6. This was not published until Emile Poulat brought out an edition in 1960.

7. That is, the Divine Office—or the service of prayer and praise, hymns, lessons, and so on—which all priests are required to say daily. The offices are contained in a breviary, or compendium, of such services (cf. Attwater 1954, 152).

8. The text of the letter was published in Turmel's *Semaine religieuse* ("Religious Weekly") on 30 May 1908. It was reproduced in Turmel (1935, 31).

9. That is, he was to be shunned by the faithful; *vitandus* is from the Latin *vitare*, "to avoid."

10. Turmel to Loisy, 16 November 1930, Bibliothèque nationale, n.a.f. 15662; see also Vidler (1970, 62).

11. Loisy was referring to a letter from Houtin's mother published in *Ma vie laique* (Houtin 1927, 300–301; Loisy 1930–31, III:257).

12. Von Hügel, for example, tried to negate the impact of Houtin's publications. In 1912, von Hügel wrote to Maude Petre that he was asking Rawlinson "to say what he tactfully can to make a Houtin book appear quite uncalled for" (von Hügel to Petre, 29 October 1912, British Library, Add. Mss. 45362).

13. Loisy to von Hügel, 7 June 1912, Bibliothèque nationale, n.a.f. 15645.

14. It is at this point that one can see the connection between Bremond, who was almost always circumspect in his relationships with the church authorities, and the other modernists—particularly von Hügel and Tyrrell, but also Loisy and Fogazzaro.

15. See Bremond to Loisy, 7 April 1916, Bibliothèque nationale, n.a.f. 15650.

16. Félix Klein, a close friend of Loisy's during the stormy modernist crisis, concludes that Loisy tended to project into the past his subsequent lack of faith (see Vidler 1970, 46), thus calling into question some of Loisy's harshest self-criticism in *Choses Passées* and *Mémoires* (1930–31).

17. When M. and Mme. Boyer de Sainte Suzanne graciously allowed me to visit with them in their home in Paris (March 1978), they explained that Loisy was an extremely religious man who lived an ascetic existence. He lived very simply, ate little, remained faithful to his vow of celibacy, and seldom even traveled far from his home.

18. According to church law, the service cannot proceed when someone who has been declared *vitandus* is present.

19. "Ah! It is not true." (See Vidler 1970, 46–47; Poulet 1962, 452.)

20. Vidler also concludes that, even though Loisy later came to believe that his hopes for the renewal of Catholicism had been based on an illusion about what the church might tolerate, "yet at the time, particularly in 1902 when he published *L'Evangile et l'Eglise,* which was the watershed of his career as a

modernist, he was sincerely Catholic" (1970, 40). Another interesting statement in support of Loisy is in an article written by J. Ernest-Charles entitled "Le Professor Loisy," which was sent to Loisy by Mme. Arconati-Visconti in 1909, and is now in Loisy's papers (Bibliothèque nationale, n.a.f. 15645).

21. Bremond reportedly commented that in his *Mémoires*, Loisy "says nothing which isn't deeply respectful of Monsignor Mignot" (Bécamel 1969, 271).

22. Mignot to Loisy, Bibliothèque nationale, n.a.f. 15659; see also Loisy 1930–31, I:395.

23. Mignot to Loisy, 13 March 1898, Bibliothèque nationale, n.a.f. 15659.

24. Mignot to von Hügel, 3 January 1903, St. Andrews University Library, 2793.

25. Compare Mignot to von Hügel, 24 May 1896 [?], St. Andrews University Library, 2793; Vidler 1970, 96.

26. Mignot to Loisy, 13 September 1896, Bibliothèque nationale, n.a.f. 15659.

27. Mignot to Loisy, 17 September 1903, Bibliothèque nationale, n.a.f. 15659.

28. One indicator of those relationships is the frequency with which Bremond is referred to in the modernists' correspondence (e.g., by Lilley, St. Andrews University Library).

29. See for example a letter in which Tyrrell warns Bremond that "for your own sake I don't think you ought to quote me, as I may become exceedingly 'infamous' before they are done with me, and you will need everything to make you respectable" (26 July 1900, University of San Francisco Archives).

30. In this respect, Petre resembled von Hügel, who was never forced to submit to the condemnations of modernism, at least publicly.

5. A MOVEMENT EMERGES

1. The eminent scholar Nathan Soderblom, later archbishop of Stockholm, referred to von Hügel as a "most revered layman-bishop" and "a teacher within the various parts of piety and Church as few are in our times" (Soderblom to von Hügel, 26 April 1922, St. Andrews University Library, 3071).

2. Soderblom to von Hügel, 26 April 1922, St. Andrews University Library, 3701.

3. Vatican Secretary of State Merry del Val wrote to Ward on 5 June 1899, complaining that "some Catholics . . . seem to be attracted by the glamour and popularity of appearing what is so vaguely described as broad mindedness (sic). I am not in the least surprised at what you say of Baron von Hügel: indeed I should have been surprised had it been otherwise" (St. Andrews University Library, Wilfrid Ward Family Papers, VII 205a[3]). Unfortunately, Merry del Val continues on another subject without further elaboration.

4. Von Hügel (1927, 143–144); Diaries of von Hügel, 24 October 1907, St. Andrews University Library.

5. Lilley's articles appeared in *The Guardian* (25 February 1903) and *The Commonwealth* (March 1903); see Barmann (1972, 101–102).

6. Von Hügel to Lilley, 6 April 1903, St. Andrews University Library, 30513.

7. Diaries of von Hügel, 8 April 1903, St. Andrews University Library.

8. On the Synthetic Society, see von Hügel (1927, 34).

9. Von Hügel to Lilley, 6 April 1903, St. Andrews University Library, 30513. The book was Tyrrell's *Oil and Wine* (1902).

10. Von Hügel to Lilley, 19 April 1903, St. Andrews University Library, 30513.

11. This is the number of letters contained in the Lilley papers in the St. Andrews University Library (see manuscripts 30503–30561). There are an additional twenty-one letters from the baron for the years 1910–1925 (St. Andrews University Library, 30562–30582).

12. Lilley's papers include ten letters from Loisy between 1903 and 1910 (St. Andrews University Library, 30654–30695) and, most importantly, 120 letters from Tyrrell between 1903 and 1909 (St. Andrews University Library, 30762–30882). The letters from Tyrrell are full of information about events that were taking place in the church, articles and books being written, and general developments in attempts to reform the church. During some periods of considerable activity, Tyrrell wrote to Lilley about every other week—for example, during 1904, when rumors of condemnation were flying and Tyrrell's relationship with the Jesuits was becoming increasingly perilous (see especially St. Andrews University Library, mss. 30772, 30777, 30779, 30783).

13. See appendix A. Letters from von Hügel's two most important correspondents, George Tyrrell and Alfred Loisy, are in the British Library and the Bibliothèque nationale. In the Von Hügel–Tyrrell correspondence (British Library, Add. Mss. 44927–44931), there are a total of 166 letters from Tyrrell, from the first, written on 10 October 1897, until Tyrrell's death in 1909. During that same period, there are 195 letters from von Hügel to Tyrrell, constituting an extensive exchange of ideas and information that sustained their friendship and collegiality in between their frequent meetings.

14. Von Hügel to Petre, 23 May 1907, British Library, Add. Mss. 45361; see also von Hügel 1927, 138–140.

15. Concerning advice received from von Hügel on one occasion in 1902, Loisy comments that he himself never liked to have someone prescribe a particular line of conduct (1930–31, II:105).

16. See Resch's (1983) discussion of von Hügel and Blondel's correspondence in 1903–04.

17. Von Hügel to Bishop, 16 September 1904; reprinted in the *Dublin Review* 227 (April 1953):182.

18. Diaries of von Hügel, 19 November 1903, St. Andrews University Library.

19. Von Hügel to Tyrrell, 4 March 1900, British Library, Add. Mss. 44927; emphasis in the original.

20. Diaries of von Hügel, 10 November 1902, St. Andrews University Library. For a detailed account of von Hügel's relationship to the controversies surrounding *L'Evangile et l'Eglise,* see Barmann (1972, chap. 6).

21. Gardner to von Hügel, 30 November 1902, St. Andrews University Library, 2589.

22. Both Butler and Kent wrote letters to *The Tablet* following the publication in that journal of a list of errors compiled from Loisy's book and printed by the Jesuit Palmier (Barmann 1972, 102–103).

23. See the Diaries of von Hügel, 5 May 1907, 26 September 1907, and 9 October 1907ff., respectively (St. Andrews University Library).

24. Von Hügel to Tyrrell, 22 June 1903, British Library, Add. Mss. 44928.

25. See, for example, the Diaries of von Hügel, 19 January 1907, St. Andrews University Library.

26. Unfortunately, I have been unable to find further information about Mrs. Cancellor, who is not referred to in any other accounts of modernism I have read. She apparently lived in the London area, and von Hügel had occasional contact with her (see Diaries of von Hügel, 24 May 1907, St. Andrews University Library).

27. A young Oxford tutor, George W. Young, responded immediately (see von Hügel to Young, 18 April 1907, St. Andrews University Library, 30504).

28. Von Hügel complained that "deafness means crippledness and a handsome crop of little humiliations during . . . social attempts" (von Hügel to Tyrrell, 30 June 1904, British Library, Add. Mss. 44928). At meetings, he passed around an electric box from speaker to speaker (Lilley 1937, ix).

29. Loisy (1930–31, I:293 ff.). Compare this to von Hügel (1918) and Barmann (1972, 38–39).

30. Von Hügel to Tyrrell, 28 May 1901, British Library, Add. Mss. 44927; compare Petre (1937, 78).

31. See the Diaries of von Hügel, 8–14 April 1907, in which he records meetings with LeRoy, Houtin, Loisy, Desjardin, Huvelin, Chevalier, Boutroux, Fonsegrive, Legendre, Laberthonnière, Zeiler, Bergson, and others (St. Andrews University Library).

32. Loisy (1930–31, II:559–560). See also von Hügel to Loisy, Bibliothèque nationale, n.a.f. 15656.

33. Loisy (1930–31, I:529). In 1907, von Hügel also offered to contribute ten to twenty pounds to print Loisy's *Synoptics*, an offer which Loisy did not refuse (Diaries of von Hügel, 13 July 1907, St. Andrews University Library).

34. Diaries of von Hügel, 25 November 1907, St. Andrews University Library.

35. Von Hügel to Tyrrell, 4 December 1899, British Library, Add. Mss. 44927.

36. See the Diaries of von Hügel, 6 March; 26, 31 August; 2, 3, 7, and 15 September, and 2 and 30 October 1908 (St. Andrews University Library). As Barmann (1972, 217) points out, there is some confusion as to Hammersley's Christian name, which is listed as Raymond in *The Catholic Directory* of 1907, but noted as W. H. in von Hügel's diaries (7 September 1908); it is clear, however, that he was a curate at Chatham in Kent.

37. See appendix A for the frequencies of von Hügel's correspondence with major figures in each country.

38. As von Hügel put it in a letter to Tyrrell (30 September 1900, British Library, Add. Mss. 44927), "one does long for the sympathy and stimulation of fellow-watchers. In England, among Catholics, I feel that at present I have got *two* such, Miss Maude Petre and yourself."

39. Von Hügel's diaries also have numerous references to conversations with Lilley on a regular basis. The Lilley Papers in St. Andrews University Library contain forty-nine letters from von Hügel between 1903 and 1909, full of references to Loisy, Tyrrell, Petre, Laberthonnière, and others.

40. Despite the infrequent amount of correspondence between Rawlinson and von Hügel during the modernist period, Vidler claims that "after L. Lilley, he was the Anglican priest who was the most attached to the modernists" (1970, 178–179).

41. On William J. Williams, see Root (1982), which includes a discussion of Williams' involvement in the Synthetic Society and his defense of Tyrrell to the very end, including a scathing letter to *The Times*.

42. See Diaries of von Hügel, 24 May 1907 and 1 June 1907, for example (St. Andrews University Library). Chapman was the wife of Lord Hugh Richard Heathcote Gascoyne Cecil, First Baron of Quickswood, and she was an active promoter of *Il Rinnovamento*.

43. Clutton's strong views were expressed in a letter written to G. W. Young at Oxford, probably in 1907, in which she said, "I am returning 'what we want' with many thanks. Poor things—if they want it they will have to take it—that is a law of nature—that applies in the spiritual world too—if we can call religious government spiritual" (Clutton to Young, 27 July 1907 [?], St. Andrews University Library 30500–30501).

44. In his section on "Lesser Lights and Fellow Travelers" (1970, 167), Vidler suggested that "Robert Dell was a 'lesser light' of lighter weight." Although Dr. Vidler's position on Dell is certainly a plausible one, I fear that his emphasis on the sincerity of the modernists may occasionally lead him to de-emphasize the involvement of some of the movement's less "faithful" participants (in the religious sense)—notably Dell and Fawkes.

45. Von Hügel's diaries record 127 letters from Dell between 1903 and 1909.

46. See Vidler (1970, 167) and von Hügel's letters to Bishop (Abercrombie 1953, 186 ff., 291 ff.). After Tyrrell had criticized the *Pascendi* in *The Times*, Dell wrote to Lilley that "what is wanted, as you say, is a manifesto involving excommunication for all who sign it; if there are to be excommunications, the more the better; I have always thought that" (25 October 1907, St. Andrews University Library, 30607). Von Hügel later noted in his diary that he wrote to Dell, warning against (1) publishing part of Tyrrell's article on excommunication, (2) developing an address of support for Tyrrell, or (3) "enlisting ex-R. C.s of any kind in our ranks" (Diaries of von Hügel, 25 October 1907, St. Andrews University Library).

47. Tyrrell to Lilley, 8 August 1908, British Library, Add. Mss. 52368.

48. Von Hügel to Loisy, 30 April 1893, Bibliothèque nationale, n.a.f. 15655; compare Loisy (1930–31, I:287).

49. The von Hügel papers at the St. Andrews University Library contain fifty-three letters from Mignot.

50. See, for example, von Hügel to Mignot, 19 March 1903, St. Andrews University Library, 30306.

51. On Mignot's support for Loisy, see von Hügel to Gardner, 14 March 1903, St. Andrews University Library, and von Hügel (1927, 115–116).

52. LeRoy to von Hügel, 1 August 1907, St. Andrews University Library, 2756.

53. See the correspondence between Chevalier and George Young, St. Andrews University Library, 30499.

54. Chevalier to Young 1907, St. Andrews University Library.

55. Zeiller is not mentioned by Vidler (1970), Barmann (1972), or Poulat (1960), and only appears without comment in a list of names in Poulat (1962, 275).

56. See Houtin's list of the principal collaborators of the review (1913, 285).

57. There are nine references to Alfieri in Loisy's *Mémoires* (1930–31, II:497, 520, 557, 593, 613, 633; III: 42, 45, 137), but they contain almost no substance about Alfieri except in the last reference (Loisy 1930–31, III:137), in which Loisy discusses a conflict between Alfieri and Casati over the administration of *Il Rinnovamento*. Ranchetti's (1969) first allusion to Alfieri does not come until page 173 of his work, and there are only four references to Alfieri in the entire work, all of them merely as one of the editors of *Il Rinnovamento*. Vidler (1970) does not name Alfieri at all, and Houtin mentions him only twice (1913, 157, 285), both of which are merely references. Only Barmann emphasizes Alfieri's role to any extent (1972, 184–186, 194, 199, 208).

58. Diaries of von Hügel, 6–7 August 1907, St. Andrews University Library.

59. Loisy thought that this conflict may have provoked the ruin of the review. He suggested (or it may have been a quotation from von Hügel; there is a typographical error which makes it difficult to discern whether it is Loisy's or von Hügel's opinion) that "Alfieri, an excellent director, was from a general point of view a mediocre administrator" (Loisy 1930–31, III:137). Despite von Hügel's defense of Alfieri, Casati assumed the direction of the review, assuring von Hügel on 3 October 1907 that the review was in good financial shape, only to announce three days later that "le *Rinnovamento* allait disparaître et qu'il ne fallait rien tenter pour le garder en vie" (Loisy 1930–31, III:137).

60. Diaries of von Hügel, 14 November 1894, St. Andrews University Library. See also Barmann 1972, 55.

61. See von Hügel's notes for his introduction of Semeria on that occasion (St. Andrews University Library, 2657; Barmann 1972, 55–56).

62. In a letter to Tyrrell, von Hügel wrote,

Semeria has been talking much to me, and (I think) extraordinarily well, as to the present situation in the church, the right and wise course for us to take, and the conditions under which we can expect to get and keep the largest amount of such elbow-room as we require if our life-work is to continue. . . . And he and his friends have got their troubles and trials—not uninstructive even for yourself. . . . and why his arguments impress me, is no doubt, that *they but enforce and re-awaken my own deepest impressions and misgivings.* (von Hügel 1927, 132)

63. Scotti and von Hügel remained friends after the movement's condemnation (see von Hügel to Webb, 16 September 1912, in von Hügel 1927, 197).

64. Von Hügel to Ward, 18 October 1907, St. Andrews University Library, 30498.

65. For example, Genocchi wrote to von Hügel in 1903, advising him that he would be in Rome during the following month and would get together with Mignot. "We will look together at what to do, if anything can be available in the present state of things" (31 December 1903, St. Andrews University Library, 2605). Again on 19 January 1904, Genocchi wrote, "My inquiries—on the sly—

about Laberthonnière, made me know for the present that his denunciation, *if true*, is ignored by those consultors that presumably should know of [*sic*]. I will look better on the matter" (St. Andrews University Library, 2606).

66. For example, von Hügel noted in his diary on 29 October 1907 that he received a letter from Morin that was "cold" and "discreet."

67. See the Diaries of von Hügel, 31 July 1907, St. Andrews University Library.

68. Priuli-Bon, a friend of Italian modernist Padre Gazzola, wrote to von Hügel about once a year. Alfieri brought the Contessa to the von Hügels', and the baron gave her copies of Tyrrell's "Letter to a Professor" and the Italian translation of the Briggs–von Hügel correspondence (Diaries of von Hügel, 13 July 1907, St. Andrews University Library).

69. This is an influence on von Hügel which has been analyzed in depth by Peter Neuner (1977); compare Loome (1973) and Rollmann (1978, 1979).

70. After reading Troeltsch's "Geschichte und Metaphysik," sent to him by von Hügel, Tyrrell wrote to the baron that it dealt with precisely the issues he himself was moving toward—namely, "the relation of Christianity to other religions" (Tyrrell to von Hügel, 11 January 1903, British Library, Add. Mss. 44928).

71. When Troeltsch died, the baron wrote to Clement Webb that he had found that Troeltsch's death "and all it has involved for me has been a very big thing even merely physically" (von Hügel 1927, 365).

72. Von Hügel to Tyrrell, 4 June 1902, British Library, Add. Mss. 44928.

73. See von Hügel's diaries, 23 April to 18 May 1902, St. Andrews University Library.

74. In the discussion that follows, I have drawn upon Rollmann's careful two-part article on von Hügel and modernism (1978, 1979).

75. "Like all Protestant interpreters of Modernism," Rollmann suggests, Holtzmann "finds himself in the awkward situation of assessing a self-conscious group of less than stable existence, which in turn denies Protestantism its right to existence" (1979, 143).

76. Loisy charged that he was "condemned without [being] read" by the Board of Bishops that oversaw the Institut Catholique, because of his work that had appeared in *L'Enseignement biblique* (Loisy [1913] 1968, 147 ff.).

77. According to Emile Poulat (1962, 671–672), the most likely author of the "Lettres Romain" was Genocchi, the person whom Loisy surmised had written them (Loisy 1930–31, II:298). As Barmann points out, however, there were some practical problems with Genocchi's having written the letters—problems suggested by a letter written to von Hügel by Genocchi (Barmann 1972, 107).

78. Von Hügel noted in his diary (28 July 1907) that he wrote a long letter to Jay following the demise of *Demain*.

79. An interesting sidelight of Buonaiuti's participation in *Studi religiosi* is that his first article in the review, in 1904, was a look at Herbert Spencer and his work from the religious point of view (see Ranchetti 1969, 88)—an indicator of the modernists' fascination with the notion of evolution.

80. *Vita religiosa* was a monthly review created by some *Studi religiosi* writers; it was founded and edited by Minocchi (Ranchetti 1969, 220).

81. Loisy Papers, Bibliothèque nationale, n.a.f. 15632–15633, 15655–15657.

82. Houtin Papers, Bibliothèque nationale, n.a.f. 15718.

83. There were nineteen letters between Loisy and Houtin before 1908, and 149 in total; they sometimes wrote several times a week (e.g., there are letters from Houtin to Loisy dated 1, 4, 9, 14, 16, 19, 22, and 25 February 1909!).

84. Marquise Marie-Louise Arconati-Visconti was a wealthy patron of the arts and scholarship and the daughter of the republican Senator Alphonse Peyrat. It was not until the modernist movement was in its final days that Loisy and Arconati-Visconti became acquainted and developed a very close friendship. Her first letter was written on 24 June 1908; in it, she introduces herself as a friend of Mme. Alfred Marel-Fatio, Joseph Bedier, and Abel Lefrancs, all of whom intend to vote for Loisy for a chair at the Collège de France. The marquise, who was a generous benefactor of the Collège de France (as well as the Louvre), was influential in behind-the-scenes lobbying on Loisy's behalf.

85. Houtin (1913, 390) insisted that "any accusation that there exists some masonic intrigue is based on pure fantasy: it isn't ever possible to unearth a plausible cause for such humbug. The origin of a so-called Jewish conspiracy is easier to unravel. It was apparently born in a spontaneous manner in the editing offices of the anti-semitic journals *Libre Parole* and *Action Française.*"

86. Loisy Papers, Bibliothèque nationale, n.a.f. 15652.

87. Lejay was a close collaborator of Loisy's who taught Latin literature at the Institut Catholique and was secretary of Loisy's review. Nonetheless, he remained only narrowly involved in the modernist controversy, because his academic specialization was only marginally relevant to modernism (Poulat 1960, 373). Loisy wrote that "I was never on exactly intimate terms with him, but we did have a good relationship right up to the time of his death (1930–31, III:389).

88. Loisy wrote about Bremond's association with Tyrrell in a little book entitled *George Tyrrell and Henri Bremond* (1936).

89. Loisy Papers, Bibliothèque nationale, n.a.f. 15662.

90. See Tyrrell's letter of 27 January 1904, after the condemnation of Loisy's *L'Evangile et l'Eglise:*

I have only this moment heard of this most painful development. It seems to me that you must hold fast to your distinction between the religious and the scientific aspects and approaches of the same questions, allowing the Church's jurisdiction over the former, firmly denying it over the latter. . . . As to the purely scientific interest it is out of the Church's jurisdiction. You are bound by your presuppositions and methods. You teach in the Sorbonne not *qua* priest but *qua* critic and expert. . . . If they excommunicate you for that, the whole world will give it against them. . . . You will no doubt be overwhelmed with conflicting counsels, and I only offer this opinion as the best that now occurs to me. Whatever you do, I will always believe to be dictated by the sincerest and most disinterested love of truth and of religion. With every sentiment of affection and loyalty. (Bibliothèque nationale, n.a.f. 15662; Tyrrell 1920, 84–85)

91. See Loisy Papers, Bibliothèque nationale, n.a.f. 15649, which contains an equal number of letters from Loisy to Babut.

92. See appendix C. Personal traits, such as letter-writing habits, would interfere with the accuracy of such an indicator.

93. Some, like Rashdall and Cheyne, were linked with Lilley but were not

involved in the modernist movement; Rashdall did not ever refer to any of the modernists in his letters to Lilley, except one reference to LeRoy (Rashdall to Lilley, 14 February 1910, St. Andrews University Library, 20705). Cheyne, in contrast, was very interested in the movement and visited Loisy in 1904 (Cheyne to Lilley, 21 February 1904, St. Andrews University Library 30596). His letters were full of references to modernism (St. Andrews University Library, 30594–30601). Others were frequently referred to, but did not correspond with Lilley frequently (e.g., Bremond), or did not correspond with him at all (e.g., Fogazzaro, Chevalier, Scopoli, and Scotti).

94. Thus Vidler wrote that his own "interest is not modernism but the modernists (1970, 15), and Poulat suggested that he himself prefers to provide an "ensemble of individual profiles" (1962, 10).

95. Blondel laid down two rules for himself: first, "never to forget that the 'reactionaries' can and often do act in good faith and with good intentions, and are zealous and virtuous people," and second, "never to stop applying to oneself the demands, warnings, and criticisms one makes of others, for anti-Pharisaism is always in danger of becoming a new Pharisaism" (translation in Ranchetti 1969, 59–60).

96. Tyrrell to von Hügel, 3 May 1908, British Library, Add. Mss. 44930.

97. Von Hügel to Houtin, 27 May 1903, Bibliothèque nationale, n.a.f. 15711.

98. Tyrrell to Petre, June 1903, British Library, Add. Mss. 52367.

6. INSTITUTIONAL CONTROL OF MODERNIST DISSIDENTS

1. Wilson (1977, 470); compare Gibbs (1972) and Gamson (1968). The concept of "social control," as developed by E. A. Ross and the Chicago sociologists, originally "referred to the capacity of a society to regulate itself according to desired principles and values" (Janowitz 1975, 82). Its meaning has unfortunately narrowed in recent years, so that it now refers to the control of an individual or group by other social forces or institutions.

2. The documents were carefully analyzed and reproduced in part by Poulat (1969, 1977).

3. The author of the pamphlet, Reverend Arsene Pierre Millet, received with a note of thanks from Cardinal Merry del Val, on behalf of the pope (Petre 1918, 190).

4. *Civiltà cattolica,* IV (November 1905):464 ff.; Ranchetti 1969, 148.

5. For a detailed summary of reactions to the work, see Poulat (1962, 125 ff.).

6. Tyrrell to von Hügel, 26 January 1903; compare Tyrrell to von Hügel, 14 February 1903, British Library. Add. Mss. 44928.

7. Maignen's essays in *La Verité Française* on 11, 12, 13, 17, 23, 26 November and 2, 6, 12, 16, 23 December 1903.

8. Especially Abbé Vigouroux; compare Loisy (1908*a*, 117).

9. This charge was made in two articles by M. Gaudeau in *La Foi catholique:*

"Les Etudes, assure-t-il, ne l'y ont ni vue ni signalée à temps, ni combattue avec l'énergie nécessaire" (5 January 1914), and "De la méthods à employer dans la lutte contre les erreurs modernes" (25 March 1914).

10. Von Hügel wrote to Tyrrell (4 December 1899) that friends of Semeria told him that, as early as 1899, "Laberthonnière has been denounced to Rome, and that some censure might well come of it" (von Hügel 1927, 81).

11. Schell's assertions about the procedures of the Holy Office of the Index were strenuously refuted by Merry del Val, who claimed that they were "nothing less than a hideous calumny. Yet some pious ladies and others repeat those assertions like parrots, to the edification of many as you may suppose!" (Merry del Val to Ward, 5 June 1899, St. Andrews University Library, Wilfrid Ward Family Papers, VII 205a[3]).

12. Merry del Val to Ward, 9 January 1901, St. Andrews University Library, Wilfrid Ward Family Papers, VII 205a(7).

13. See the text in Loisy ([1913] 1968, 262).

14. "An encyclical letter is one addressed by the pope to the patriarchs, primates, archbishops, bishops, and other ordinaries of the whole Church or, less often, to the hierarchy of a particular country. . . . Encyclicals are not necessarily infallible documents, though the pope could choose to speak *ex cathedra* by means of them if he wished to do so; but if they contain doctrinal teaching Catholics are bound to give to them interior as well as exterior assent and obedience" (Attwater 1954, 169).

15. Tyrrell to Jesuit General Martin, quoted in Petre 1912, II:248.

16. That is, he was prohibited from saying mass; Bremond to Lilley, 8 August 1909, St. Andrews University Library, 30590–30591.

17. The letter was published in *Il Rinnovamento* 1 (May 1907) and is translated in Ranchetti (1969, 198).

18. Von Hügel to Ward, 28 May 1907, St. Andrews University Library, Wilfrid Ward Family Papers, VII 143(172).

19. See Loisy's *Simples réflexions* (1908b), in which he discusses the probable source of the propositions.

20. Von Hügel to Ward, 8–9 August 1907, St. Andrews University Library, Wilfrid Ward Family Papers, VII 143(174).

21. Von Hügel to Ward, 10 February 1908, St. Andrews University Library, Wilfrid Ward Family Papers, VII 143(177).

22. Bazin (1928, 230) explains that the encyclical exposed a "subtle heresy" and required the "entire rebuilding of a heresy which had been purposely produced piece-meal, hidden and camouflaged."

23. Fawkes to Ward, 1 December 1908 (?), St. Andrews University Library, Wilfrid Ward Family Papers, VII 97(12).

24. Lacroix to Loisy, 10 March 1908, Bibliothèque nationale, n.a.f. 14548; translation in Vidler (1970, 108).

25. Butler to von Hügel, 8 March 1904 and 12 May 1907, St. Andrews University Library, 2367, 2368.

26. Petre was, however, disciplined in her own diocese and denied communion.

27. In 1910, for example, Mignot wrote a letter to von Hügel predicting further excommunications (28 October 1910, St. Andrews University Library, 2822).

28. It is no accident that in 1908, the name of Benigni's review was changed from its original Italian *Corrispondenza di Roma* to the French *Correspondance de Rome.*

29. They were compiled by Poulat (1969) and remain the only authoritative source on the movement except for Poulat's study of Benigni (1977).

30. For more on Maignen, see Poulat (1969, 273 ff.).

31. These included the Federation internationale des ligues catholique feminines and the Association catholique internationale des oeuvres de protection de la jeune fille, for which Speiser served as ecclesiastical director of the international committee.

32. See Benigni's letter to Jonckx, 4 March 1912, in Poulat (1969, 429). Benigni and his colleagues were so concerned about secrecy that they developed an elaborate system of secret codes to use in their correspondence (Poulat 1969, 364–366).

33. From the *Circularie de mai* (1913); see Poulat (1969, 561).

34. De Grandmaison, writing in *Etudes* in 1914, deplored the integralist custom of denouncing their critics as "enemies of God, hypocrites, and false brethren" (O'Brien 1967, 553).

35. Mignot complained that:

It is no exaggeration to say that these journalists exercised in the European Catholic world a sort of tyranny whose effect among believers of delicate conscience was to create an impression of pure terror which often manifested itself in discouragement and an abandoning of the struggle. . . . Benigni, the great artisan behind this demoralization enterprise . . . decided to create a network of periodicals which he would inspire and control, in Vienna, Paris, Ghent, Cologne, Milan and elsewhere. . . . Both abroad and in a great number of French dioceses, there appeared to be organized a spy ring. Bishops, priests, active citizens, rectors and professors at universities, all were watched. . . . The most innocuous words and actions were odiously transformed and presented as treason towards the faith or the hierarchy. The victim was obliged to repent since it was quite impossible to establish one's innocence against anonymous and secret libel. This system which according to venerated prelates went on in Paris, Milan, Freiburg, Vienna and in several other dioceses, was referred to in France by the name "combisme ecclésiastique," after the hypocritical persecution levelled against Catholics by the minister Combes. (Mignot [1914] 1969, 516–519)

36. Pius X strongly supported the Action Française and refused to condemn the movement. He is quoted as having said, "While I am living, the *Action Française* will never be condemned" (Flammarion 1927, 208).

37. For details on the condemnation of the Action Française in 1926–1927, see Flammarion (1927); on the Sapinière, see Poulat (1969).

38. See "The Abbé de Nantes Disavowed by the Pope," in the July 1977 issue (Number 88) of the newsletter, *The Catholic Counter-Reformation in the XXth Century.* The July 1978 issue (Number 100) spoke of the "fumes of Satan" which were let in through the Vatican Council.

7. THE DIALECTICS OF INSURGENCY

1. The first sections of this chapter include a revision of "Bureaucratic Insurgency: The Vatican and the Crisis of Modernism" (Lyng and Kurtz 1985).

2. See Coser (1956, 87–90); compare Bergesen (1977), Erikson (1966); and Durkheim ([1893] 1933).

3. And of consumer dissatisfaction with products.

4. Unfortunately, there is still no general definition of the concept of "dialectical relation." Our use of the term is consistent with Appelbaum's (1978) interpretation of the Marxian definition of the dialectic.

5. Nevertheless, as already suggested, some tensions are inevitable between institutional authorities and those in scholarly roles, especially in cultural institutions.

6. In a literal sense, then, the excommunication of various modernists during the movement's final stages was simply formal recognition of something that had actually occurred much earlier.

7. I am indebted to Teresa Sullivan for her stimulating insights into the nature of that shift.

8. This controversy is amply documented in Swidler's (1981) *Küng in Conflict,* which provides a relatively comprehensive collection of correspondence between Küng and the hierarchy, public statements and official documents, and so on (in English translation).

9. Indeed, Küng claims that Pope Paul VI protected him against excommunication during his tenure as pope, allowing his work to be investigated, but within guidelines stating that the "attempt to find a solution—in any case, to avoid an open break" (Swidler 1981, 369).

10. A powerful organization, the Opus Dei ("Work of God") enjoys the favor of the pope and has 72,000 members in more than 80 countries. See Kamm (1984), Hebblewaite (1983), and James (1982). The Sovereign Military Order of Malta, founded in 1113, assumed a military role in the Crusades and is now the world's smallest nation-state. The Knights of Malta have powerful connections in the Vatican and around the world. Its members include Alexander Haig, William Casey, J. Peter Grace, Lee Iococca, and William Simon (see Lee 1983).

11. The Catholic Counter-Reformation is a conservative French organization whose members think that Mgr. Lefebvre is too liberal! In an editorial in its newsletter, *The Catholic Counter-Reformation in the XXth Century* (March 1978, 15), the editors charge that "slowly and insidiously Protestant criticism is regaining lost ground and conquering the schools of Catholic theology."

12. Küng had argued that Barth's doctrine of justification and the Council of Trent's were fundamentally the same (Swidler 1981, 3).

13. In their statement of 16 June 1974, the Swiss bishops complained that the congregation's proceedings do not even grant the human rights granted to individuals in the United Nations Charter, Articles 10 and 11.

14. One interesting case, related by Swidler (1981, 33–34) surrounds a 1968 book by Dutch bishop Francis Simons, who questioned the doctrine of infallibility by claiming that there was a lack of biblical support for it. He was visited by a

delegation from the Doctrinal Congregation "with the suggestion that he resign because of ill health. His response was that he never felt better in his life. After that he kept public silence on the matter, and so did the Vatican."

15. See Kamm (1984). In a letter to John Paul II on 30 March 1979, Küng raised the issue of having different policies toward authority within and outside of the church, asking: "Of what value is all the preaching to the world for conversion if the Church itself does not practically lead in such conversion?" (Swidler 1981, 371).

16. Dionne (1985, 6); Simons (1985) reports that "according to a key advisor of the Brazilian Bishops' Conference, Father Boff's interrogation in Rome last September [1984] 'revolved largely around the question of authority and hierarchy in the church.'"

Selected Bibliography

A. ARCHIVAL COLLECTIONS

London. British Library. Maude D. Petre Papers. Includes: (a) entire correspondence between Friedrich von Hügel and George Tyrrell (Additional Manuscripts 44927–44931); (b) letters from von Hügel to Petre (Additional Manuscripts 45361); (c) letters to Petre from various correspondents (Additional Manuscripts 45744–45745); (d) Petre's manuscript diaries (Additional Manuscripts 52372–52379); (e) miscellaneous correspondence and documents, including letters from Tyrrell to Petre (Additional Manuscripts 52367); Tyrrell's correspondence with his Jesuit superiors (Additional Manuscripts 52368); other Tyrrell correspondence and clippings (Additional Manuscripts 52368); and (f) other correspondence with Petre, including letters from Henry Bremond and James Walker, and other items (Additional Manuscripts 52370–52371, 52380–52382).

Paris. Bibliothèque nationale. William Gibson, Lord Ashbourne Papers. Nouvelles acquisitions françaises 16318. Letters from various correspondents, including Duchesne, Fonsegrive, Loisy.

———. Marcel Hébert Papers. Nouvelles acquisitions françaises 15752. Various letters to and from Hébert, including Denis, LeRoy, Loyson, Martin du Gard, Sartiaux, Loisy, Duchesne, and Buonaiuti.

———. Albert Houtin Papers. Nouvelles acquisitions françaises 15688–15737. Large number of letters to Houtin from Loisy, von Hügel, Petre, Tyrrell, and others; miscellaneous papers, clippings, and letters.

———. Félix Klein Papers. Nouvelles acquisitions françaises 15677. Letters to Klein from Bureau, La Croix, and others.

———. Lucien Laberthonnière Papers. Nouvelles acquisitions françaises 15658, 15712, 16806. Letters, including those from Loisy and Houtin.

———. Lucien La Croix Papers. Nouvelles acquisitions françaises 16806, 15658, 15677, 15712, 15713. Various letters and documents.

———. Félix Sartiaux Papers. Nouvelles acquisitions françaises 15753–15754. Sartiaux's correspondence from Hébert, Loisy, Turmel, and others.

———. Louis Scarpatett Papers. Nouvelles acquisitions françaises 16804, 16806. Miscellaneous letters from J. Chevalier, Denis, Fogazzaro, Houtin, d'Hulst, Klein, Laberthonnière, La Croix, La Grange, Le Camus, Mignot, and others.

———. Joseph Turmel Papers. Nouvelles acquisitions françaises 15756. Manuscript copy of *Apres cinquante ans d'études* (*Mémoires*).

St. Andrews, Scotland. St. Andrews University Library. Von Hügel Papers. Includes (a) von Hügel's personal library; (b) more than a thousand letters received by von Hügel (see appendix A); (c) 43 volumes of manuscript diaries, 1877–1924 (lacking volumes 1880–1883, 1901); (d) copies of letters from von Hügel to various correspondents, including Mignot and Bremond; and (e) miscellaneous manuscripts and papers.

———. Juliet Mansel Papers. Includes letters from von Hügel and miscellaneous items.

———. Lilley Family Papers. Letters from a number of correspondents, with a valuable index.

———. Wilfrid Ward Family Papers. Numerous miscellaneous papers and letters, including 203 letters and cards from von Hügel.

San Francisco. University of San Francisco. The Tyrrell/Modernist Collection. A large collection of correspondence and documents, most of them photocopies and microfilms of originals. Includes correspondence from Tyrrell, von Hügel, and others.

Note: Because of the massive volume of the above sources, I consulted some of them only superficially. For more detailed analysis I obtained copies of a number of documents, which will be deposited in the Regenstein Library at the University of Chicago:

Loisy Papers: Loisy–von Hügel correspondence, 1893–1924; Loisy–Mignot correspondence; all other letters to Loisy in the Bibliothèque nationale archives for 1903–04 and 1907–08; drafts of Loisy's letters to a number of correspondents.

Houtin Papers: selections from volume 15718.

Hébert Papers: selections from volume 15752.

Petre Papers: complete von Hügel–Tyrrell correspondence (361 letters); miscellaneous letters to Maude Petre (1903–04, 1907–08 letters from von Hügel, Tyrrell, and others).

Von Hügel Papers: all letters from Mignot to von Hügel; all letters to von Hügel for 1903–04, 1907–08.

Wilfrid Ward Family Papers: miscellaneous letters from Fawkes, Halifax, Merry del Val, and Leger.

Miscellaneous letters to Young.
Index to the Lilley Family Papers.
Abbreviations: Add. Mss.   Additional Manuscripts
n.a.f.   Nouvelles acquisitions françaises

B. PUBLISHED WORKS

Abercrombie, Nigel. 1953. "Friedrich von Hügel's Letters to Edmund Bishop." *Dublin Review* 227:66–78, 179–189, 419–438.

———. 1959. *The Life and Work of Edmund Bishop.* London: Longmans, Green, and Co.

Acomb, Evelyn Martha. 1941. *The French Laic Laws (1879–1889): The First Anti-Clerical Campaign of the Third French Republic.* New York: Columbia University Press.

Albrow, Martin. 1974. "Dialectical and Categorical Paradigms of a Science of Society." *Sociological Review* 22 (May):183–201.

Alexander, Jon. 1979. "*Aeterni Patris,* 1879–1979: A Bibliography of American Responses." *Thomist* 43 (July):480–481.

Appelbaum, Richard P. 1978. "Marx's Theory of the Falling Rate of Profit: Towards a Dialectical Analysis of Structural Social Change." *American Sociological Review* 43 (February):67–80.

Aquinas, Thomas. [1267–1273] 1952. "Summa Theologica." In *The Great Books of the Western World,* edited by Robert M. Hutchins, vols. 19–20. Chicago: Encyclopedia Britannica.

Aron, Raymond. 1970. *Main Currents in Sociological Thought.* 2 vols. Translated by R. Howard and H. Weaver. Garden City, N.Y.: Doubleday Anchor.

Arquilliere, H. X. 1955. *L'Augustinisme politique.* 2d ed. Paris: J. Vrin.

Attwater, Donald, ed. 1954. *A Catholic Dictionary.* New York: Macmillan.

Aubert, Roger. 1952. *Le pontificat de Pie IX (1846–1878).* Paris: Blond et Gay.

Augustinus, Aurelius. 1956. *De Haeresibus.* Translated by L. G. Muller. Washington, D.C.: Catholic University of America Press.

Bacon, Francis. [1605] 1952. "Of the Proficience and Advancement of Learning: Divine and Human." In *Great Books of the Western World,* edited by R. M. Hutchins, vol. 30, 1–101. Chicago: Encyclopedia Britannica.

Bainton, Roland H. 1950. *The Reformation of the Sixteenth Century.* Boston: Beacon.

Ball, Richard A. 1979. "The Dialectical Method: Its Application to Social Theory." *Social Forces* 57 (May):785–799.

Barbier, Emmanuel. 1907. *Le progrès du libéralisme Catholique en France sous le Pape Leon XIII.* 2 vols. Paris: Lethielleux.

———. 1924. *Histoire du Catholicisme liberal et du Catholicisme social en France.* 5 vols. Bordeaux: Y. Cadoret.

Barbour, Ian. 1960. "The Methods of Science and Religion." In *Science Ponders Religion,* edited by Harlow Shapley, 196–215. New York: Appleton-Century-Crofts.

Barmann, Lawrence F. 1972. *Baron Friedrich von Hügel and the Modernist Crisis in England*. Cambridge: Cambridge University Press.

Barraclough, Geoffrey. 1968. *The Medieval Papacy*. London: Thames and Hudson.

Battersby, William John. 1968. *History of the Institute of the Brothers of the Christian Schools in the Eighteenth Century, 1719–1798*. 3 vols. London: Waldegrave.

Baudrillart, Alfred. 1912–1914. *Vie de Mgr. d'Hulst*. 2 vols. Paris: Ancienne Librairie Poussielgue.

Baur, Ferdinand. 1847. *Kritische Untersuchungen über die kanonischen Evangelien, ihr Verhältnis queinander, ihren Charakter und Ursprung*. Tübingen: Fues.

Bayle, Pierre. 1697. *Dictionnaire historique et critique*. Rotterdam: Leers.

Bazin, René. 1928. *Pius X*. London: Sands & Co.

Bécamel, Marcel. 1966. "Lettres de Loisy à Mgr. Mignot: A propos de la crise moderniste." *Bulletin de littérature ecclésiastique (Toulouse)* 67:3–44, 81–114, 170–194, 257–286.

———. 1968a. "Autres lettres de Loisy à Mgr. Mignot." *Bulletin de littérature écclesiastique (Toulouse)* 69 (October–December):241–268.

———. 1968b. "Lettres du Père Hyacinthe à Monseigneur Mignot." *Bulletin de littérature ecclesiastique (Toulouse)* 69 (April–June):98–114.

———. 1969. "Monseigneur Mignot et Alfred Loisy." *Bulletin de littérature ecclésiastique (Toulouse)* 70 (October–December):267–286.

———. 1970. "Le P. Joseph Bonsirven, S.J. et Monseigneur Mignot." *Bulletin de littérature ecclésiastique (Toulouse)* 71 (October–December):262–273.

———. 1971. "La politique religieuse au début de ce siècle vue par Henri d'Urcle, correspondant de Mgr. Mignot." *Bulletin de littérature ecclésiastique (Toulouse)* 72 (July–September):187–199.

———. 1973. "Comment Monseigneur Batiffol quitta Toulouse, à la Noël 1907." *Bulletin de littérature ecclésiastique (Toulouse)* 74 (April–June):109–138.

Becker, Howard. 1960. "Normative Reactions to Normlessness." *American Sociological Review* 25 (December):803–810.

Bedeschi, Lorenzo. 1959. *Le origini della gioventu cattolica, dalla caduta del Governo pontificio al primo congresso cattolico de Venezia su documenti inediti d'archivio*. Bologna: Capelli.

———. 1968. *La curia romana durante la crisi modernista. Episodie metodi di governo*. Parma: Guanda.

———. 1970. *Lettere ai Cardinali di don Brizio*. Bologna: Edizioni dehoniane.

———. 1975. *Interpretazioni e sviluppo del modernismo cattolico*. Milano: Bompiani.

Bedoyere, Michael de la. 1951. *The Life of Baron von Hügel*. London: J. M. Dent & Sons.

Bellow, Saul. 1977. "Writers and Literature in American Society." In *Culture and Its Creators: Essays in Honor of Edward Shils*, edited by Joseph Ben-David and Terry Nichols Clark, 172–196. Chicago: University of Chicago Press.

Ben-David, Joseph. 1977. "Organization, Social Control, and Cognitive Change in Science." In *Culture and Its Creators: Essays in Honor of Edward Shils,* edited by Joseph Ben-David and Terry Nichols Clark, 244–265. Chicago: University of Chicago Press.

——, and Terry Nichols Clark, eds. 1977. *Culture and Its Creators: Essays in Honor of Edward Shils.* Chicago: University of Chicago Press.

Benda, Julien. 1927. *La trahison des clercs.* Paris: Grasset.

Bendix, Richard. 1962. *Max Weber: An Intellectual Portrait.* Garden City, N.Y.: Doubleday Anchor.

Benson, J. Kenneth. 1977. "Organizations: A Dialectical View." *Administrative Science Quarterly* 22 (March):1–21.

Bentley, Richard. 1699. *A Dissertation upon the Epistles of Phalaris: With an Answer to the Objections of Charles Boyle, Esquire.* London: Mortlock.

Ben Yehuda, Nachman. 1980. "The European Witch Craze of the 14th to 17th Centuries." *American Journal of Sociology* 86 (July):1–31.

Berger, Peter. 1969. *The Sacred Canopy: Elements of a Sociological Theory of Religion.* Garden City, N.Y.: Doubleday Anchor.

Bergesen, Albert James. 1977. "Political Witch Hunts: The Sacred and the Subversive in Cross-National Perspective." *American Sociological Review* 42 (April):220–232.

Bernard-Maitre, Henri. 1968. "Lettres d'Henri Bremond à Alfred Loisy." *Bulletin de littérature ecclésiastique* 69 (October–December):269–289.

Blanchet, André. 1967. *Histoire d'une mise à l'Index, la "Sainté Chantal" de l'abbé Bremond, d'après des documents inédits.* Paris: Aubier, Editions Montaigne.

——, ed. 1971. *Henri Bremond et Maurice Blondel Correspondance.* Paris: Aubier, Editions Montaigne.

Blondel, Maurice. [1893] 1970. *L'Action: Essai d'une critique de la vie et d'une science de la pratique.* Paris: Alcan.

——. [1896, 1904] 1964. *"Letter on Apologetics" and "History and Dogma."* Translated by Alexander Dru and Illtyd Trethowan. London: Harvill.

——. 1904. "Histoire et dogme: Les lacunes philosophique de l'exégèse moderne." *Quinzaine* 56:45–67, 349–373, 433–458.

Blondel, Maurice, and Auguste Valensin. 1957. *Correspondance (de Maurice Blondel et Auguste Valensin).* 3 vols. Text annotated by Henri de Lubac. Paris: Aubier.

Blondel, Maurice, and Lucien Laberthonnière. 1957. *Correspondance philosophique (de) Maurice Blondel (et) Lucien Laberthonnière.* Publiée et presentée par Claude Tresmontant. Paris: Editions du Seuil.

——. 1961. *Correspondance philosophique (de) Maurice Blondel (et) Lucien Laberthonnière.* Paris: Editions du Seuil.

Blunt, J. H. 1874. *Dictionary of Sects, Heresies, Ecclesiastical Parties, and Schools of Religious Thought.* London: R. Vingtons.

Bodley, John Edward Courtenay. 1906. *The Church in France: Two Lectures Delivered at the Royal Institute.* London: Archibald Constable & Co.

Boff, Leonardo. *The Church: Charisma and Power—Study of Militant Ecclesiology.*

Bourke, Myles M. 1970. "Should the Church Impose Sanctions for Errors of Faith?" In *Dogma and Pluralism,* edited by Edward Schillebeeckx, 21–32. New York: Herder and Herder.

Boyer de Sainte Suzanne, Raymond de. 1968. *Alfred Loisy: Entre la foi et l'incroyance.* Paris: Editions du Centurion.

Bremond, Henri. 1901. *L'Inquiétude religieuse.* Paris: Perrin.

———. 1907. *The Mystery of Newman.* Translated by H. C. Corrance, with an introduction by George Tyrrell. London: Williams and Norgate.

———. [pseud. Sylvain Leblanc]. 1931. *Un clerc qui n'a pas trahi: Alfred Loisy d'après ses "Mémoires."* Paris: Nourry.

———. 1970–71. *Correspondance (d'Henri Bremond et Maurice Blondel).* 3 vols. Etablie, presentée, et annotée par André Blanchet. Paris: Aubier, Editions Montaigne.

Briggs, Charles A., and Friedrich von Hügel. 1906. *The Papal Commission and the Pentateuch.* London: Longmans, Green, and Co.

Briggs, Kenneth A. 1984. "Jesuit Chief Defends Liberation Theology and Social Activism." *New York Times,* 28 October 1984.

Brucker, Joseph. 1914. *"Les Etudes" contre le modernisme de 1888 à 1907.* Paris: Bureaux des Etudes.

Buckley, G. A. 1967. "Sin of Heresy." In *The New Catholic Encyclopedia,* vol. 6, 1069. New York: McGraw-Hill.

Buehrle, Marie Cecilia. 1957. *Rafael Cardinal Merry Del Val.* Milwaukee, Wis.: Bruce Publishing Co.

Buonaiuti, Ernesto. 1908. *The Programme of Modernism: A Reply to the Encyclical of Pius X, "Pascendi dominici gregis."* Translated by A. L. Lilley. London: T. Fisher Unwin. (First published as *Il Programma dei modernisti: Riposta all'enciclica di Pio X "Pascendi dominici gregis."* Rome: Societa internazionale scientifico-religiosa, 1908.)

———. 1927. *Le modernisme catholique.* Translated by René Mannot. Paris: Rieder.

———. [1945] 1969. "Pellegrino di Roma: La generazione dell'esodo a cure di Mario Niccoli." In *Pilgrim of Rome: An Introduction to the Life and Work of Ernesto Buonaiuti,* edited by C. N. Nelson and Norman Pittenger, 43–74. London: Nisbet.

Burke, Kenneth. [1945] 1969. *A Grammar of Motives.* Berkeley and Los Angeles: University of California Press.

Burke, Ronald. 1980. "Loisy's Faith: Landshift in Catholic Thought." *Journal of Religion* 60:138–164.

———. 1981. *Three Discussions: Biblical Exegesis, George Tyrrell, Jesuit Archives.* Mobile, Ala.: Spring Hill College.

———. 1982. *Modernist Uses of John Henry Newman.* Mobile, Ala.: Spring Hill College.

———. 1983. *Regarding Modernism.* Mobile, Ala.: Spring Hill College.

Burke, Ronald, and George Gilmore, eds. 1980. *Current Research in Roman Catholic Modernism.* Mobile, Ala.: Spring Hill College.

Burton, Edward. 1829. *An Inquiry into the Heresies of the Apostolic Age, in Eight Sermons Preached before The University of Oxford, in the Year 1829.* Oxford: By the author.

Butler, Cuthbert. 1936. *The Vatican Council.* 2 vols. London: Longmans, Green and Co.

Butterfield, Herbert. 1949. *The Origins of Modern Science.* London: Bell.

Campbell, Joseph. 1972. *The Flight of the Wild Gander: Explorations in the Mythological Dimension.* Chicago: Henry Regnery.

Cannon, Susan Faye. 1978. *Science in Culture: The Early Victorian Period.* Kent: Dawson.

Canon, Walter F. 1964. "The Normative Role of Science in Early Victorian Thought." *Journal of the History of Ideas* 25:487–502.

Caron, Jeanne. 1966. *Le Sillon et la démocratie chrétienne, 1894–1910.* Paris: Plon.

Chadwick, Owen. 1960. *The Mind of the Oxford Movement.* London: Black.

———. 1966. *The Victorian Church.* New York: Oxford University Press.

———. 1975. *The Secularization of the European Mind in the Nineteenth Century.* Cambridge: Cambridge University Press.

Chalendar, X. de. 1969. *Les prêtres du journal officiel: 1887–1907, I. Milieu-Taches Relations.* Paris: Les Editions du Cerf.

Chateillon, S. 1935. *Concerning Heretics.* Translated by Roland H. Bainton. New York: Columbia University Press.

Clark, Terry Nichols. 1973. *Prophets and Patrons: The French University and the Emergence of the Social Sciences.* Cambridge, Mass.: Harvard University Press.

Cock, Albert A. n.d. *A Critical Examination of von Hügel's Philosophy of Religion.* London: The Cambrian News (Aberystwyth) Ltd.

Coleman, James S. 1957. *Community Conflict.* New York: Free Press.

Colenso, Bishop John William. 1862–1879. *The Pentateuch and the Book of Joshua Critically Examined.* London: Longmans, Green, and Co.

Congar, Yves. 1962. "The Historical Development of Authority in the Church: Points for Reflection." In *Problems of Authority,* edited by John M. Todd, 119–156. Baltimore, Md.: Helicon.

———. 1967. *Tradition and Traditions: An Historical and a Theological Essay.* New York: Macmillan.

———. 1976. *Challenge to the Church: The Case of Archbishop Lefebvre.* Huntington, Ind.: Our Sunday Visitor, Inc. (First published as *La Crise dans l'Eglise et Mgr. Lefebvre.* Paris: Les Editions du Cerf, 1976.)

———. 1978. *Eglise Catholique et France Moderne.* Paris: Hachette.

Conrad, Joseph. 1953. *The Secret Agent: A Simple Tale.* Garden City, N.Y.: Doubleday Anchor.

Coppa, Frank J. 1979. *Pope Pius IX: Crusader in a Secular Age.* Boston: Twayne Publishers.

Coser, Lewis A. 1956. *The Functions of Social Conflict.* Glencoe, Ill.: Free Press.

Couchoud, P.-L., ed. 1928. *Congrès d'histoire du Christianisme: Jubilé Alfred Loisy.* 3 vols. Paris: Editions Rieder.

Coulton, G. G. [1929] 1974. *The Inquisition.* London: Ernest Benn Ltd.

———. 1938. *Inquisition and Liberty.* London: William Heinemann Ltd.

Cross, George. 1925. "Heresy (Christian)." In *The Encyclopedia of Religion and Ethics,* edited by James Hastings, vol. 6, 614–622. New York: Scribner's.

Dagens, J., and M. Nedoncelle, eds. 1968. *Entretiens sûr Henri Bremond.* Paris: La Haye, Mouton & Co.

Dakin, A. Hazard, Jr. 1934. *Von Hügel and the Supernatural.* London: Society for Promoting Christian Knowledge.

Dansette, Adrien. 1961. *Religious History of Modern France.* 2 vols. Freiburg: Herder.

Darnton, Robert. 1980. *The Business of Enlightenment: A Publishing History of the "Encyclopedie."* Cambridge, Mass.: Harvard University Press.

Darwin, Charles. [1859] 1952. "The Origin of Species by Means of Natural Selection." In *Great Books of the Western World,* edited by Robert M. Hutchins, vol. 49, 1–251. Chicago: Encyclopedia Britannica.

———. [1871] 1952. "Descent of Man." In *Great Books of the Western World,* edited by Robert M. Hutchins, vol. 49, 253–600. Chicago: Encyclopedia Britannica.

David, A. L. 1971. *Lettres de George Tyrrell à Henri Bremond.* Paris: Aubier.

Delassus, Henri. 1899. *L'Americanism et la conjuration antichrétienne.* Lille: Desclee, De Brouwer.

Delcor, M. 1969. "A propos de la question biblique en France." *Bulletin de littérature ecclésiastique (Toulouse)* 70 (July–September):199–219.

Dell, Robert. 1904. "The Crisis in the Catholic Church." *Fortnightly Review* 455: 846–860.

De Maria, Amalia. 1979. *Il Pensiero Religioso di Friedrich von Hügel.* Torino: Giappichelli.

Dickens, A. G. 1966. *Reformation and Society in Sixteenth-Century Europe.* New York: Harcourt, Brace and World.

Dickens, Charles. [1859] 1957. *A Tale of Two Cities.* New York: Washington Square.

Digeon, Claude. 1959. *La crise allemande de la pensée française (1870–1914).* Paris: Presse universitaires de France.

Dikijian, Diradour Avedis. 1911. "Modernism as an Ecclesiastical Movement." M.A. thesis, University of Chicago.

Dillon, E. J. 1894. "The Papal Encyclical on the Bible." *The Contemporary Review* 65:567–608.

———. 1902. "Catholicism versus Ultramontanism." *Contemporary Review* 82:776–807.

———. 1903. "The Abbé Loisy and the Catholic Reform Movement." *Contemporary Review* 83:385–412.

Dionne, E. J., Jr. 1985. "Vatican Criticizes Brazilian Backer of New Theology." *New York Times,* 21 March 1985, 1, 6.

Douglas, Mary. 1966. *Purity and Danger: An Analysis of Concepts of Pollution and Taboo.* London: Routledge & Kegan Paul.

———. 1975. *Implicit Meanings: Essays in Anthropology.* Boston: Routledge & Kegan Paul.

———. [1970] 1982. *Natural Symbols: Explorations in Cosmology.* New York: Pantheon.

Dru, Alexander. 1962. "The Importance of Maurice Blondel." *Downside Review* 80:118–129.

———. 1963. *The Church in the Nineteenth Century: Germany 1800–1918.* London: Burns and Oates.

———. 1964. "Modernism and the Present Position of the Church." *Downside Review* 82:103–110.

Duchesne, Louis. 1915–1924. *Early History of the Christian Church, from its Foundations to the End of the (Fifth Century).* Translated by Claude Jenkins. London: Longmans, Green, and Co.

Dunham, Barrows. 1967. *Heroes and Heretics: A Social History of Dissent.* New York: Alfred Knopf.

Durkheim, Emile. [1893] 1933. *The Division of Labor in Society.* Translated by G. Simpson. New York: Free Press.

———. [1895] 1938. *The Rules of Sociological Method.* New York: Free Press.

———. 1961. *Moral Education: A Study in the Theory and Application of the Sociology of Education.* Translated by Everett K. Wilson and Herman Schnurer; edited, with an introduction by E. K. Wilson. New York: Free Press of Glencoe.

Eiseley, Loren. 1961. *Darwin's Century: Evolution and the Men Who Discovered It.* Garden City, N.Y.: Doubleday Anchor.

Elliott, Walter. 1898. *The Life of Father Hecker.* New York: Columbus Press.

Erikson, Kai. 1965. "The Sociology of Deviance." In *Social Problems: Persistent Challenges,* edited by Edward C. McDonagh and Jon E. Simpson, 457–464. New York: Holt, Rinehart, and Winston.

———. 1966. *Wayward Puritans.* New York: John Wiley.

Eyt, Pierre. 1967. "Un témoin catholique de la primauté de l'Ecriture au XVI siècle." *Bulletin de littérature ecclésiastique (Toulouse)* 68 (July–September): 161–179.

Fawkes, Alfred. 1909*a*. "Modernism: A Retrospect and a Prospect." *Hibbert Journal* 8:67–82.

———. 1909*b*. "Father George Tyrrell." *Nation* 24 (July):601–602.

———. 1913. *Studies in Modernism.* London: Murray.

———. 1925. "Baron Friedrich von Hügel." *Modern Churchman* 14:662–666.

Fee, Joan L., Andrew M. Greeley, William C. McCready, and Teresa A. Sullivan. 1981. *Young Catholics: A Report to the Knights of Columbus.* Los Angeles: Sadlier.

Ferry, Jules. [1879] 1967. "The Two School Systems." In *Anticlericalism,* edited by J. S. Schapiro, 153–154. Princeton, N.J.: Van Nostrand.

Festinger, Leon. 1957. *A Theory of Cognitive Dissonance.* Evanston, Ill.: Row, Peterson.

Firey, Walter. 1948. "Information Organization and the Theory of Schism." *Sociological Review* 13 (February):15–24.

First Vatican Council. [1870] 1967. "Dogmatic Constitution on the Catholic Faith." In *The Teaching of the Catholic Church,* edited by Josef Neuner and Heinrich Roos, 31–41. Staten Island, N.Y.: Alba House.

———. [1870a] 1967. "The First Draft of the Constitution of the Church of Christ." In *The Teaching of the Catholic Church,* originally prepared by Josef Neuner and Heinrich Roos, edited by Karl Rahner, 211–220. Translated by Geoffrey Stevens. Staten Island, N.Y.: Alba House.

———. [1870b] 1967. "Dogmatic Constitution on the Catholic Faith." In *The Teaching of the Catholic Church,* edited by Josef Neuner and Heinrich Roos, 31–41. Staten Island, N.Y.: Alba House.

Flammarion, Ernest, ed. 1927. *"L'Action Française" et le Vatican.* Preface by Charles Maurras and Leon Daudet. Paris: By the Author.

Flaubert, Gustave. 1857. *Madame Bovary: Moeurs de province.* Paris: Levy.

Fogarty, Michael. 1957. *Christian Democracy in Western Europe 1820–1953.* London: Routledge & Kegan Paul.

Fogazzaro, Antonio. [1904] 1906. *Il Santo.* Translated into English (as *The Saint*) by Prichard-Agnetti. 3d ed. London: Hodder and Stoughton.

Fonsegrive, Georges. 1903. "A propos d'exégèse." *Quinzaine* 16 (December):441–453.

Forg, Ludwig. 1932. *Die ketzerverfolgung in Deutschland unter Gregor IX.* Berlin: Ebering.

Fremantle, Anne. 1963. *The Papal Encyclicals in Their Historical Context.* New York: Mentor-Omega.

Friedrichs, Robert W. 1972a. "Dialectical Sociology: An Exemplar for the 1970s." *Social Forces* 50 (June):447–455.

———. 1972b. "Dialectical Sociology: Toward a Resolution of the Current 'Crisis' in Western Sociology." *British Journal of Sociology* 23 (September): 263–274.

Galea, Ferdinandus. 1964. *Religious Freedom: A Study of Its Historical and Legal Developments in France.* Rome: Tomasetti.

Galilei, Galileo. [1615] 1957. "Letter to the Grand Duchess Christina." In *Discoveries and Opinions of Galileo,* translated and edited, with an introduction and notes, by Stillman Drake, 173–216. Garden City, N.Y.: Doubleday Anchor.

Galot, Jean. 1979. *Cristo contestato: Le cristologie non calcedoniane e la fede cristologica.* Florence: Libreria Editrice Fiorentina.

Gambetta, Leon. [1877] 1967. "Le Clericalisme, voila l'ennemi." In *Anticlericalism,* edited by J. S. Schapiro, 152–153. Princeton, N.J.: Van Nostrand.

Gamson, William. 1968. *Power and Discontent.* Homewood, Ill.: Dorsey Press.

———. 1975. *The Strategy of Social Protest.* Homewood, Ill.: Dorsey Press.

Garvin, J. N., and J. A. Corbett. 1958. *The Summa contra haereticos Ascribed to Praepositinus.* Notre Dame, Ind.: University of Notre Dame Press.

Gay, Peter. 1966–1969. *The Enlightenment: An Interpretation.* 2 vols. New York: Alfred Knopf.

Geertz, Clifford. 1973. *The Interpretation of Cultures.* New York: Basic Books.

Gennep, Arnold van. [1909] 1960. *The Rites of Passage.* Translated by Monika B.

Vizedom and Gabrielle L. Caffee. Chicago: University of Chicago Press.

Gerlach, Luther P., and Virginia M. Hine. 1970. *People, Power, Change: Movements of Social Transformation.* Indianapolis, Ind.: Bobbs-Merrill.

Gerth, Hans H., and C. Wright Mills. [1946] 1958. "Introduction: The Man and His Work." In *From Max Weber,* edited by H. H. Gerth and C. Wright Mills, 1–74. New York: Oxford University Press.

Gibbons, James Cardinal. 1893. "Address of H. E. Cardinal Gibbons." In *World's Columbian Catholic Congresses,* 15–17. Chicago: Hyland.

Gibbs, Jack. 1972. *Social Control.* Andover, Mass.: Warner Module.

Gibson, William Ralph B. 1907. *Rudolf Eucken's Philosophy of Life.* 2d ed. London: Black.

Gillet, Marcel. 1964. "La philosophie d'Edouard LeRoy." *Archives de philosophie* 27:530–533.

Goethe, Johann Wolfgang von. [1832] 1952. "Faust." In *Great Books of the Western World,* edited by Robert M. Hutchins, vol. 47. Translated by George Madison Priest. Chicago: Encyclopedia Britannica.

Goffman, Erving. 1959. *The Presentation of Self in Everyday Life.* Garden City, N.Y.: Doubleday Anchor.

Greeley, Andrew M. 1977. *The American Catholic.* New York: Basic Books.

Gregory XVI, Pope. [1834] 1963. "Singulari nos." In *The Papal Encyclicals,* edited by Anne Fremantle, 128. New York: Mentor-Omega.

Guerin, Pierre. 1957. "La Pensée religieuse d'Alfred Loisy." *Revue d'histoire et de philosophie religieuses* 37:294–330.

———. 1961. "La Vie et l'oeuvre de Loisy à propos d'un ouvrage récent." *Revue d'histoire et de philosophie religieuses* 37:334–343.

Gusfield, Joseph R. 1963. *Symbolic Crusade: Status Politics and the American Temperance Movement.* Urbana: University of Illinois Press.

Gutwenger, Engelbert. 1970. "The Role of the Magisterium." In *Dogma and Pluralism,* edited by Edward Schillebeeckx, 43–55. New York: Herder and Herder.

Haight, Roger. 1974. "The Unfolding of Modernism in France: Blondel, Laberthonnière, LeRoy." *Theological Studies* 34:632–666.

Hales, E. E. Y. 1958. *The Catholic Church in the Modern World: A Survey from the French Revolution to the Present.* Garden City, N.Y.: Hanover House.

Hanotaux, Gabriel. 1903. *Contemporary France.* Translated by J. C. Tarver. London: Constable.

Harnack, Adolf von. [1900] 1957. *Das Wesen des Christentums.* Translated into English (as *What is Christianity?*) by Thomas B. Saunders. New York: Harper and Row.

Hartley, Thomas J. A. 1971. *Thomistic Revival and the Modernist Era.* Toronto: Institute of Christian Thought, University of St. Michael's College.

Harvey, Van A. 1966. *The Historian and the Believer: The Morality of Historical Knowledge and Christian Belief.* New York: Macmillan.

Haskins, Charles Homer. 1957. *The Rise of Universities.* Ithaca, N.Y.: Cornell University Press.

Hasler, August Bernhard. 1981. *How the Pope Became Infallible: Pius IX and the Politics of Persuasion.* Translated by Peter Heinegg. Garden City, N.Y.: Doubleday & Co.

Healey, Charles J. 1977. "Aspects of Tyrrell's Spirituality." *Downside Review* 95:133–148.

Heaney, John J. 1965. "The Enigma of the Later von Hügel," *Heythrop Journal* 6:145–159.

————. 1969. *The Modernist Crisis: von Hügel.* London: Chapman.

Hebblewaithe, Peter. 1983. "'A Glimmer of Hope' in CDF's Regulations; A More 'Human Face.'" *National Catholic Reporter,* 21 January 1983.

Hecker, Isaac. 1869. *Is Romanism the Best Religion for the Republic? Six Papers from "The American Churchman."* New York: Pott and Anery.

————. 1887. *The Church and the Age: An Exposition of the Catholic Church in View of the Needs and Aspirations of the Present Age.* New York: Catholic World.

Heiler, Friedrich. 1947. *Der Vater des katholischen Modernismus: Alfred Loisy (1857–1940).* Munchen: Erasmus-Verlag.

Hirschman, Albert O. 1970. *Exit, Voice, and Loyalty: Responses to Declines in Firms, Organizations, and States.* Cambridge, Mass.: Harvard University Press.

Hobbes, Thomas. [1651] 1952. "Leviathan." In *Great Books of the Western World,* edited by Robert M. Hutchins, vol. 23, 39–283. Chicago: Encyclopedia Britannica.

Hoffner, Joseph Cardinal. 1979. "Damit sind die unausweichlichen Konsequenzen gezogen worden." *Frankfurter Allgemeine Zeitung.* 19 (December):4.

Holland, Bernard. 1927. "Memoir." In *Baron Friedrich von Hügel: Selected Letters 1896–1924,* edited by Bernard Holland, 1–68. London: J. M. Dent & Sons.

Holtzmann, Heinrich Julius. 1903. "Das Urchristentum und der Reformkatholizismus." *Protestantische Monatshefte* 7:165–196.

Houtin, Albert. 1901. *Les origines de l'église d'Angers: La légende de Sainte René.* Laval: Goupil.

————. 1902. *La question biblique chez les catholiques de France au xixe siècle.* Paris: Picard.

————. 1904. *L'Americanisme.* Paris: Nourry.

————. 1907. *La Crise du clergé.* Paris: Nourry.

————. 1913. *Histoire du modernisme catholique.* Paris: By the Author.

————. 1920–1924. *Le Père Hyacinthe.* 3 vols. Paris: Nourry. (Vol. 1: *Le Père Hyacinthe dans l'église romaine, 1827–1869;* vol. 2: *Le Père Hyacinthe réformateur catholique, 1869–1893;* vol. 3; *Le Père Hyacinthe prêtre solitaire, 1893–1912.*)

————. 1925. *Un prêtre symboliste, Marcel Hébert (1851–1916).* Paris: Nourry.

————. 1927. *The Life of a Priest: My Own Experience, 1867–1912.* Translated by W. S. Whale. London: Watts.

————, and Félix Sartiaux. 1960. *Alfred Loisy: Sa vie, son oeuvre.* Paris: Editions du centre nationale de recherche scientifique.

Howe, Richard Herbert. 1979. "Max Weber's Elective Affinities: Sociology within the Bounds of Pure Reason." *American Journal of Sociology* 84 (September): 366–385.

Hügel, Friedrich von. 1894–95. "The Church and the Bible: The Two Stages of Their Inter-Relation." 3 parts. *Dublin Review* 115:313–341, 116:306–337, 117:275–304.

———. 1904*a*. "The Case of the Abbé Loisy." *Pilot* 9:30–31.

———. 1904*b*. "The Case of M. Loisy." *Pilot* 9:94.

———. 1904*c*. "The Abbé Loisy and the Holy Office." *The London Times*, 2 March 1904, 15.

———. 1906*a*. "Experience and Transcendence." *Dublin Review* 138:357–379.

———. 1906*b*. *The Papal Commission and the Pentateuch*. London: Longmans, Green, and Co.

———. 1908*a*. "The Abbé Loisy." *Tablet* 111:378–379.

———. 1908*b*. *The Mystical Element of Religion as Studied in Saint Catherine of Genoa and Her Friends*. 2 vols. London: J. M. Dent & Sons.

———. 1909. "The Death-Bed of Father Tyrrell." *Tablet* 114:182.

———. 1912. "The Religious Philosophy of Rudolf Eucken." *Hibbert Journal* 10:660–677.

———. 1918. "Julius Wellhausen." *The London Times Literary Supplement* 7 March 1918, 117.

———. 1927. *Selected Letters 1896–1924*. London: J. M. Dent & Sons.

Hughes, Philip. 1961. *A Church in Crisis: A History of the General Councils 325–1870*. Garden City, N.Y.: Hanover House.

Hulshof, Jan. 1973. *Wahrheit und Geschichte: Alfred Loisy, Zwischen Tradition und Kritik*. Essen: Ludgerus Verlag Hubert Wingen.

Hume, David. [1757] 1956. *Natural History of Religion*. London: A. and C. Black.

Index of Prohibited Books. 1930. Rome: Vatican Polyglot Press.

Ireland, John [J. St. Clair Etheridge]. 1900. "The Genesis of Americanism." *North American Review* 170:679–312. (Reprinted in *Americanism: A Phantom Heresy*, edited by Félix Klein, 299–312. Cranford, N.J.: Aquin Book Shop, 1951.)

Ivaldo, Marco. 1977. *Religione e Christianesimo in Alfred Loisy*. Firenze: Felice Le Monnier.

James, Constantin. 1877. *Du darwinism; ou, L'homme-singe*. Paris: Plon.

James, Barry. 1982. "Catholicism's Opus Dei Controversy: Powerful Conservative Group Gains Church Power." *Houston Post*, 16 October 1982, 10 ff.

Janowitz, Morris. 1975. "Sociological Theory and Social Control." *American Journal of Sociology* 78 (July):105–135.

Kamm, Henry. 1984. "Vatican Censures Marxist Elements in New Theology." *New York Times*, 4 September 1984.

Kelly, J. J. 1979. "On the Fringe of the Modernist Crisis: The Correspondence of Baron Friedrich von Hügel and Abbot Cuthbert Butler." *Downside Review* 97: 275–303.

———. 1981. "The Modernist Controversy in England: The Correspondence between Friedrich von Hügel and Percy Gardner." *Downside Review* 99 (January):40–58.

Kittel, G. 1964–1976. *Theological Dictionary of the New Testament.* 10 vols. Translated and edited by G. W. Bromiley. Grand Rapids, Mich.: Eerdmans.

Klein, Félix. 1950. *La Route du petit Morvandiau.* Paris: Plon.

———. 1951. *Souvenirs. Vol. 4, Americanism: A Phantom Heresy.* Cranford, N.J.: Aquin Book Shop.

Kleutgen, Joseph. 1868. *La philosophie scholastique exposée et défendue, introduction.* Paris: Gaume Frères et J. Duprey.

———. 1869. *La philosophie scholastique exposée et défendue, comment nous connaissons l'essence des choses réelles.* Paris: Gaume Frères et J. Duprey.

———. 1870. *La philosophie scholastique exposée et défendue, de la création.* Paris: Gaume Frères et J. Duprey.

Kuhn, Thomas. 1962. *The Structure of Scientific Revolutions.* Chicago: University of Chicago Press.

Kümmel, Werner Georg. 1972. *History of the Investigation of the New Testament.* Translated by S. M. Gilmour and H. C. Kee. Nashville, Tenn.: Abingdon Press.

Küng, Hans. 1980. *The Church—Maintained in Truth?* New York: Seabury Press.

Kurtz, Lester R. 1980. "Scholarship and Scandal: Catholic Modernism at the Turn of the Century." Ph.D. thesis, University of Chicago.

———. 1983. "The Politics of Heresy." *American Journal of Sociology* 88 (May): 1085–1115.

Laberthonnière, Lucien. 1897. "Le problem religieux." *Annales de philosophie chrétienne* 132:497–511, 615–632.

———. 1903. *Essais de philosophie religieuse.* Paris: Plon.

Laberthonnière, Lucien, and Maurice Blondel. 1905. "Nôtre programme," *Annales de philosophie chrétienne* 151:5–31.

Lacey, T. A. 1904. *Harnack and Loisy.* Introduction by Lord Halifax. London: Longmans, Green, and Co.

Lagrange, M.-J. 1907. "Le decret 'Lamentabili' et la critique historique." *Revue biblique* 16:542–554.

———. 1919. "Critique biblique. Reponse à l'article de la 'Civiltà cattolica': Venticinque anni dopo l'enciclica 'Providentissimus.'" *Revue biblique* 28: 593–600.

———. 1932. *Monsieur Loisy et le modernisme: A propos des 'Mémoires' d'Alfred Loisy.* Juvisy: Editions du Cerf.

Lamennais, Felicité Robert de. [1837] 1967. "Political and Economic Freedom." In *Anticlericalism,* edited by J. S. Schapiro, 141–143. Princeton, N.J.: Van Nostrand.

Lampe, G. W. H., ed. 1961. *A Patristic Greek Lexicon.* Oxford: Oxford University Press.

Lawlor, F. X. 1967. "Heresy." In *The New Catholic Encyclopedia,* vol. 6, 1062–1063. New York: McGraw-Hill.

Lea, Henry Charles. 1887. *A History of the Inquisition of the Middle Ages.* 3 vols. New York: Harper.

Lee, Martin A. 1983. "Who are the Knights of Malta?" *National Catholic Reporter* 19 (14 October):1, 5–7.

Lecanuet, Edouard. 1910. *L'Eglise de France sous la troisième république.* Rev. ed. Paris: Gigord.

Leff, Gordon. 1967. *Heresy in the Later Middle Ages: The Relation of Heterodoxy to Dissent c. 1250–c. 1450.* Manchester, England: Manchester University Press.

Leo XIII, Pope. [1879] 1931. "Aeterni Patris." In *Acta Sanctae Sedis,* 97–115. Rome: Typis Polyglottae Officinae S. C. de Propagande Fide.

———. [1891] 1956. "Rerum Novarum." In *The Papal Encyclicals in Their Historical Context,* edited by Anne Fremantle, 165–195. New York: Mentor-Omega.

———. [1893] 1981. "Providentissimus Deus." In *The Papal Encyclicals, edited by Claudia Carlen, vol. 2,* 325–339. Raleigh, N.C.: McGrath Publishing Co.

———. 1899. *"Testem Benevolentiae." In Leonis XIII Pontificus Maxima Acta,* vol. 19, 5–20. Rome: Ex Typographia Vaticana.

LeRoy, Edouard. 1904. "Lettres Romaines." *Annales de philosophie chrétienne* 3:349–359, 473–488.

———. [1905] 1918. "Qu'est-ce qu'un dogme?" *Quinzaine* 63:495–526. Translated into English (as *What is a Dogma?*) by Lydia G. Robinson, Chicago: Open Court.

———. 1906. "Essai sur la notion du miracle." *Annales de philosophie chrétienne* 3:5–33, 166–191, 225–259.

———. 1907. *Dogme et critique.* Paris: Bloud.

Lill, Rudolf. 1970. *Vatikanische Akten zur Geschichte des Deutschen Kulturkampfes: Leo XIII.* Tübingen: Niemeyer.

Lilley, A. L. 1903*a.* "Biblical Criticism in France." *Guardian* 25 (February):267–268.

———. 1903*b.* "L'Affaire Loisy." *Commonwealth* 8:73–76.

———. 1906. "A Roman Catholic Protest Against the Recent Vatican Policy." *Commonwealth* 11:216–220.

———. 1908. *Modernism: A Record and Review.* London: Pitman.

———. 1916. "Modernism." In *Encyclopedia of Religion and Ethics,* edited by James Hastings, vol. 8, 763–768. Edinburgh: Clark.

———. 1937. "Preface." In *Von Hügel and Tyrrell: The Story of a Friendship,* by Maude D. Petre, v–xii. New York: Dutton & Co.

Lindbeck, George. 1970. *The Future of Roman Catholic Theology.* Philadelphia: Fortress.

Lipset, Seymour Martin. 1965. "The Sources of the Radical Right." In *The New American Right,* edited by Daniel Bell, 166–234. New York: Criterion Books.

Locke, John. [1695] 1823. "The Reasonableness of Christianity as Delivered in the Scriptures." In *The Works of John Locke,* by John Locke, vol. 7, new ed., corrected. London: Printed for Thomas Tegg et al.

———. [1705–1707] 1824. "An Essay of the Understanding of St. Paul's Epistles, by Consulting St. Paul Himself." In *The Works of John Locke, by John Locke, vol. 7, 12th ed. London: Rivington et al.*

Loisy, Alfred. 1892. "De la critique biblique." *Etudes biblique* 6:1–16.

———. 1898. "Le Developpement chrétien d'après le Cardinal Newman." *Revue du clergé français* 1 (December):5–20.

———. 1899. "La théorie individualiste de la religion." *Revue du clergé français* 1 (January):202–214.

———. 1900*a.* "L'idée de la revelation." *Revue du clergé français* 1 (January): 250–271.

———. 1900*b.* "La lettre de Leon XIII au clergé des France et le études d'Ecriture

Sainté." *Revue du clergé français* (June):5–17.

———. 1900*c*. "Un nouveau dictionnaire biblique." *Revue d'histoire et de littérature religieuses* 6:534–551.

———. 1901*a*. *Les mythes babyloniens et les premiers chapîtres de la Génèse.* Paris: Picard.

———. 1901*b*. *La religion d'Israël.* Paris: Letouzey et Ane.

———. 1903*a*. *Autour d'un petit livre.* Paris: Picard.

———. [1903*b*] 1976. *L'Evangile et l'Eglise.* Bellevue: By the Author. Translated into English (as *The Gospel and the Church*) by Christopher Home. Philadelphia: Fortress.

———. 1906. "Sûr l'Encyclique de Pie X." *Correspondance de l'union pour la verité* 2:162–175.

———. 1907–08. *Les Evangiles synoptiques.* 2 vols. Ceffonds: By the Author.

———. 1908*a*. *Quelques lettres sûr des questions actuelles et sûr des événements récents.* Ceffonds: By the Author.

———. 1908*b*. *Simples réflexions.* Ceffonds: By the Author.

———. 1910. "Magie, science et religion." *Revue d'histoire et de littérature religieuses.* 2:144–174.

———. [1913] 1968. *Choses Passées.* Paris: Nourry. Translated into English (as *My Duel With the Vatican*) by R. W. Boynton, New York: Greenwood.

———. 1930–31. *Mémoires pour servir à l'histoire religieuse de notre temps.* 3 vols. Paris: Nourry.

———. "L'enseignement de Renan au Collège de France." In *Le Collège de France: Livre jubilaire composé à l'occasion de son quatrieme centenaire,* 345–351. Paris: Presses universitaires de France.

———. 1936. *George Tyrrell et Henri Bremond.* Paris: Nourry.

Lonergan, Bernard. 1972. *Method in Theology.* New York: Herder and Herder.

Loome, Thomas Michael. 1969. "A Bibliography of the Published Writings of George Tyrrell." *Heythrop Journal* 10:238–314.

———. 1970*a*. "A Bibliography of the Published Writing of George Tyrrell: Supplement." *Heythrop Journal* 11:161–169.

———. 1970*b*. "Tyrrell's Letters to Andre Raffalovich." *Month* 229:95–101, 138–149.

———. 1973*a*. "The Enigma of Baron Friedrich von Hügel—as Modernist." *Downside Review* 91:11–34, 134–140, 204–230.

———. 1973*b*. "Joseph Sauer—ein Modernist?" *Romische Quartalschrift 68:* 207–220.

———. 1979. *Liberal Catholicism, Reform Catholicism, and Modernism.* Mainz: Matthias-Gruenwald.

Lubac, Henri de. 1957–1965. *Maurice Blondel et Auguste Valensin: Correspondance (1899–1947).* 3 vols. Paris: Aubier.

Lyng, Stephen G., and Lester R. Kurtz. 1985. "Bureaucratic Insurgency: The Vatican and the Crisis of Modernism." *Social Forces* 63 (June):901–922.

McAvoy, Thomas T. 1957. *The Great Crisis in American Catholic History.* Chicago: H. Regnery.

———. 1963. *The Americanist Heresy in Roman Catholicism: 1895–1900.* Notre Dame, Ind.: University of Notre Dame Press.

————, ed. 1960. *Roman Catholicism and the American Way of Life.* Notre Dame, Ind.: University of Notre Dame Press.

MacCaffrey, James. 1910. *History of the Catholic Church in the Nineteenth Century.* Dublin: Gill.

McCarthy, John D., and Mayer N. Zald. 1973. *The Social Trends of Social Movements in America.* Morristown, N.J.: General Learning Press.

————. 1977. "Resource Mobilization and Social Movements: A Partial Theory." *American Journal of Sociology* 82 (May):1213–1241.

McCool, Gerald. 1977. *Catholic Theology in the Nineteenth Century.* New York: Seabury Press.

McCormack, Arthur. 1966. *Cardinal Vaughan: The Life of the Third Archbishop of Westminster.* London: Burns and Oates.

MacPherson, Duncan M. 1969. "Von Hügel on Celibacy." *Tablet* (August): 757–758.

McShane, E. D. 1967. "Heresy (History of)." In *The New Catholic Encyclopedia,* vol. 6, 1065–1069. New York: McGraw-Hill.

Madiran, Jean. 1968–1974. *L'heresie du xxe siècle.* 2 vols. Paris: Nouvelles Editions Latines.

Maignen, Charles. 1899. *Etudes sur l'Americanisme: Le Père Hecker est-il un Saint?* Paris: V. Retaux.

————. 1902a. *Nouveau Catholicisme et nouveau clergé.* Paris: V. Retaux.

————. 1902b. *La Souveraineté du peuple est une heresie.* Paris: A. Roger et F. Chernoviz.

Maistre, Joseph de. 1967. "Selections from Maistre." In *Anticlericalism,* edited by J. S. Schapiro, 129. Princeton, N.J.: Van Nostrand.

Marcilhacy, Christianne. 1962. *Le diocèse d'Orléans sous l'épiscopat de Mgr. Dupanloup 1849–1878.* Paris: Plon.

Marle, René. 1960. *Au Coeur de la crise moderniste.* Paris: Aubier.

Martin, David. 1967. *A Sociology of English Religion.* New York: Basic Books.

Martin du Gard, Roger. 1949. *Jean Barois.* Translated by Stuart Gilbert. New York: Viking.

Marty, Martin. 1972. *Protestantism.* New York: Holt, Rinehart and Winston.

Marx, Gary T. 1979. "External Efforts to Damage or Facilitate Social Movements: Some Patterns, Explanations, Outcomes, and Complications." In *The Dynamics of Social Movements,* edited by M. N. Zald and J. D. McCarthy, 94–125. Cambridge, Mass.: Winthrop.

Marx, Karl. [1843a] 1972. "Contribution to the Critique of Hegel's *Philosophy of Right:* Introduction." In *The Marx–Engels Reader,* edited by Robert C. Tucker, 11–23. New York: Norton.

————. [1843b] 1972. "For a Ruthless Criticism of Everything Existing." In *The Marx–Engels Reader,* edited by Robert C. Tucker, 7–10. New York: Norton.

Mathews, Shailer. 1925. *The Faith of Modernism.* New York: Macmillan.

May, James Lewis. 1932. *Father Tyrrell and the Modernist Movement.* London: Eyre and Spottiswoode.

Mead, George Herbert. 1936. *Movements of Thought in the Nineteenth Century.* Edited and with an introduction by M. H. Moore. Chicago: University of Chicago Press.

Mercier, Désiré Felicien François Joseph, Cardinal. 1910. *Modernism.* Translated by Marian Lindsay. London: Burns and Oates.

Merton, Robert K. [1949] 1968. *Social Theory and Social Structure.* Enlarged ed. New York: Free Press.

————. 1972. "Insiders and Outsiders: A Chapter in the Sociology of Knowledge." *American Journal of Sociology* 78 (July):9–47.

Merton, Robert K., and Elinor Barber. 1976. "Sociological Ambivalence." In *Sociological Ambivalence and Other Essays,* by Robert Merton, 1–48. New York: Free Press.

Mignot, Eûdoxe Irénée. [1914] 1969. "Mémoire de Mgr. Mignot, Archevêque d'Albi, au Card. Ferrata, secrétaire d'état, Octobre 1914." In *Intégrisme et catholicisme intégral: Un reseau secret international antimoderniste: La "Sapinière" (1909–1921),* edited by Emile Poulat, 515–523. Paris: Casterman.

Minocchi, Salvatore. 1948. "Memorie di un modernista di S. Minocchi." Edited by F. Gabrieli. *Ricerche religiose* 2:148–167.

Moltmann, Jurgen, and Hans Küng, eds. 1981. *Who Has the Say in the Church?* Published as a collection of essays, issued monthly by Concilium, Religion in the Eighties. Edinburgh: T. & T. Clark Ltd.

Montesquieu, Baron la Brede et de. [1748] 1977. *L'Esprit des lois.* Translated into English (as *The Spirit of Laws*) by Thomas Nugent, edited by David Wallace Carrithers. Berkeley, Los Angeles, and London: University of California Press.

-Moody, Joseph N. 1953. *Church and Society: Catholic Social and Political Thought Movements 1789–1950.* New York: New York Arts.

————. 1968. *The Church as Enemy: Anticlericalism in Nineteenth Century French Literature.* Washington, D.C.: Corpus.

Moore, R. I. 1975. *The Birth of Popular Heresy.* London: Edward Arnold Publishers Ltd.

Moran, Valentine G. 1979. "Loisy's Theological Development." *Theological Studies* 40:411–452.

Murri, Romolo. 1901–1904. *Battaglie d'oggi.* 4 vols. Rome: Societa italiana cattolica di cultura editrice.

————. 1908. *Lettre di un pretre modernista.* Rome: Libreria editrice Romana.

Nedoncelle, Maurice, and Jean Dagens, eds. 1968. *Entretiens sur Henri Bremond.* Paris: Mouton.

Nelson, C. N., and Norman Pittenger, eds. 1969. *Pilgrim of Rome: An Introduction to the Life and Work of Ernesto Buonaiuti.* London: Nisbet.

Neuner, Josef, and Heinrich Roos. 1967. *The Teaching of the Catholic Church: As Contained in Her Documents.* Edited by Karl Rahner, translated by Geoffrey Stevens. Staten Island, N.Y.: Alba House.

Neuner, Peter. 1977. "Religiose Erfahrung und geschichtliche Offenbarung: Friedrich von HügelsGrundlegung der Theologie." In *Beitrage zur ökumenischen Theologie,* edited by Heinrich Fries, vol. 15. Munich: Schoningh.

Newton, William L. 1946. "Sacred Scripture." In *A Symposium on the Life and Work of Pope Pius X,* prepared under the direction of the Episcopal Committee of the Confraternity of Christian Doctrine, 69–85. Washington, D.C: Confraternity of Christian Doctrine.

Novak, Michael. 1980. "Behind the Küng Case." *New York Times Magazine,* 23 March 1980, 34 ff.

Oberschall, Anthony. 1973. *Social Conflict and Social Movements.* Engelwood Cliffs, N.J.: Prentice-Hall.

O'Brien, G. J. 1967. "Integralism." In *New Catholic Encyclopedia,* vol. 7, 552–553. New York: McGraw-Hill.

O'Connor, Francis M. 1967. "George Tyrrell and Dogma—1." *Downside Review* 85:16–34.

Ozouf, Mona. 1963. *L'école, l'Eglise et la République, 1817–1914.* Paris: Colin.

Palanque, Jean-Remy. 1962. *Catholiques Libéraux et Gallicans en France: Face au Concile du Vatican 1867–1870.* Aix-En-Provence: Annales de la Faculté des Lettres.

Pastor, Ludwig Freiherr von. 1891–1953. *The History of the Popes from the Close of the Middle Ages.* 40 vols. Translated and edited by F. I. Antrobus, R. F. Kerr, E. Graf, and E. F. Peeler. London: Routledge & Kegan Paul.

Perrow, Charles. 1970. "Departmental Power and Perspectives in Industrial Firms." In *Power in Organizations,* edited by M. N. Zald, 59–89. Nashville, Tenn.: Vanderbilt University Press.

Petre, Maude D. 1912. *Autobiography and Life of George Tyrrell. Vol. 2: Life of George Tyrrell from 1884–1909.* London: Arnold.

———. 1918. *Modernism: Its Failure and Its Fruits.* London: Jack.

———. 1927. "George Tyrrell and Friedrich von Hügel in Their Relation to Catholic Modernism." *Modern Churchman* 17:143–154.

———. 1928. "G. Tyrrell et F. von Hügel. Un modernisme de croyants catholiques." In *Congrès d'histoire du Christianisme: Jubilé Alfred Loisy,* edited by P.-L. Couchoud, Vol. III, 226–239. Paris: Editions Rieder.

———. 1937a. *My Way of Faith.* London: J. M. Dent & Sons.

———. 1937b. *Von Hügel and Tyrrell: The Story of a Friendship.* Preface by Canon Lilley. New York: Dutton.

———. 1944. *Alfred Loisy: His Religious Significance.* Cambridge: Cambridge University Press.

Petruccelli della Gattina, Ferdinaudi. 1875. *Popery Exposed: An Exposition of Poppery As It Is, with a History of the Men, Manners, and Temporal Government of Rome in the Nineteenth Century.* Philadelphia: T. B. Peterson & Brothers.

Pfautz, H. W. 1961. "Near-Group Theory and Collective Behavior: A Critical Reformulation." *Social Problems* 9:167–174.

Pfeffer, Jeffrey. 1978. *Organizational Design.* Arlington Heights, Ill.: AHM Publishing.

———. 1981. *Power in Organizations.* Boston: Pitman.

Philips, C. C. 1929. *The Church in France.* 2 vols. London: Mowbray.

Pittenger, Norman. 1969. "Ernesto Buonaiuti and the Modernist Movements." In *Pilgrim of Rome: An Introduction to the Life and Work of Ernesto Buonaiuti,* edited by C. N. Nelson and N. Pittenger, 28–37. London: Nisbet.

Pius IX, Pope. [1863] 1963. "Quanto Conficiamur." In *The Papal Encyclicals in Their Historical Context,* edited by Anne Fremantle, 131–132. New York: Mentor-Omega.

———. [1864] 1968. "The Syllabus of the Principal Errors of our Times." In *Documents in the Political History of the European Continent,* edited by C. A. Kertesz, 233–244. Oxford: Clarendon Press.

————. [1910] 1967. "Form of Oath Against Modernism Prescribed by Pius X (1910)." In *The Teaching of the Catholic Church,* originally prepared by Josef Neuner and Heinrich Roos, edited by Karl Rahner, 41–44. Staten Island, N.Y.: Alba House.

Pius X, Pope. [1904*a*] 1967. "Ad diem illum." In *The Teaching of the Catholic Church,* originally prepared by Josef Neuner and Heinrich Roos, edited by Karl Rahner, 331–334. Staten Island, N.Y.: Alba House.

————. 1904*b*. "Lucunda Sane Accident." *Tablet* 103 (2 April 1904):549–554.

————. 1908*a*. "Lamentabili Sane Exitu." In *Modernism,* by Paul Sabatier, 217–230. London: Unwin.

————. [1908*b*] 1981. "Pascendi domini gregis." In *The Papal Encyclicals,* edited by Claudia Carlen, vol. 3, 71–97. Raleigh, N.C.: McGrath Publishing Co.

Pius XII, Pope. [1943] 1981. "Divino Afflante spiritu." In *The Papal Encyclicals,* edited by Claudia Carlen, Vol. IV, 65–79. Wilmington, N.C.: McGrath Publishing Co.

Pluquet, François. 1817. *Mémoires pour servir à l'histoire des egaremens de l'esprit humain, par rapport à la religion chrétienne.* Paris: A Besancon, Chez Petit, Editeur et Librairie.

Poggi, Gianfranco. 1967. *Catholic Action in Italy.* Stanford, Calif.: Stanford University Press.

Poulat, Emile. 1960. "Bibliographie Alfred Loisy et index biobibliographique." In *Alfred Loisy: Sa vie, son oeuvre,* by Albert Houtin and Félix Sartiaux, annotated and published by Emile Poulat, 301–409. Editions du centre national de la recherche scientifique.

————. 1962. *Histoire, dogme et critique dans la crise moderniste.* Paris: Casterman.

————. 1965. "Points de vue nouveaux sûr la crise moderniste." *L'Information historique* 27:110–114.

————. 1969. *Intégrisme et catholicisme intégral.* Paris: Casterman.

————. 1970. "Critique historique et théologie dans la crise moderniste." *Recherches de science religieuse* 58:535–550.

————. 1971. "Le modernisme d'hier à aujourd'hui." *Recherches de science religieuse* 59:161–178.

————. 1977. *Eglise contre bourgeoisie.* Paris: Casterman.

Powers, James Farl. 1962. *Morte d'Urban.* Garden City, N.Y.: Doubleday.

Price, Derek J. de solla. 1961. *Science Since Babylon.* New Haven, Conn.: Yale University Press.

Rahner, Karl. 1964. *On Heresy.* Translated by W. J. O'Hara. Freiburg: Herder.

Ranchetti, Michele. 1969. *The Catholic Modernists: A Study of the Religious Reform Movement, 1864–1907.* Translated by Isabel Quigly. London: Oxford University Press.

Reardon, Bernard M. G. 1966. *Religious Thought in the Nineteenth Century.* Cambridge: Cambridge University Press.

————. 1975. *Liberalism and Tradition.* Cambridge: Cambridge University Press.

Rebérioux, Madeleine. 1975. *La République radicale? 1898–1914.* Paris: Editions du Seuil.

Reddick, James A. 1950. "A Typology of Anticlericalism in France under the Third Republic 1871–1914." Ph.D. thesis, University of Chicago.

Reformkatholische, Schriften. 1908. *Programm der italienischen Modernisten: Ein Antwort auf die Enzykika "Pascendi Dominici Gregis."* Jena: Diederichs.

Reisman, David. 1976. *Adam Smith's Sociological Economics.* London: Helm.

Renan, Ernest. [1863] 1965. *Vie de Jésus.* Paris: Calmann-Levy.

Resch, Richard J. 1983. "Safe Harbor: The Use of Doctrine in the Blondel–von Hügel Correspondence, 1903–1904." In *Regarding Modernism,* edited by Ronald Burke and George Gilmore, 64–76. Mobile, Ala.: Spring Hill College.

Riding, Alan. 1984. "Brazil Tests Limits of Liberation Theology." *New York Times,* 9 September 1984.

Riet, Georges van. 1963–1965. *Thomistic Epistemology: Studies Concerning the Problem of Cognition in the Contemporary Thomistic School.* 2 vols. Translated by Gabriel Franks (vol. 1), Donald G. McCarthy, and George E. Hertrich (vol. 2). St. Louis, Mo.: B. Herder Book Co.

Rivière, Jean. [1913] 1929. *Le Modernisme dans l'Eglise.* Paris: Letouzey et Ane.

Rollmann, Hans. 1978. "Troeltsch, von Hügel and Modernism." *Downside Review* 96:35–60.

———. 1979. "Holtzmann, von Hügel and Modernism." *Downside Review* 97: 128–141, 221–244.

Root, John D. 1977. "English Catholic Modernism and Science: The Case of George Tyrrell." *Heythrop Journal* 18:271–288.

———. 1980*a.* "George Tyrrell and the Synthetic Society." *Downside Review* 98:42–59.

———. 1980*b.* "Roman Catholic and Anglican Modernist Interaction, 1896–1914." *Historical Magazine of the Protestant Episcopal Church* 49:133–156.

———. 1981*a.* "The Correspondence of Friedrich von Hügel and Clement C. J. Webb." *Downside Review* 99 (October):288–298.

———. 1981*b.* "Searching for George Tyrrell." In *Three Discussions: Biblical Exegesis; George Tyrrell; Jesuit Archives,* edited by Ronald Burke and George Gilmore, 71–79. Mobile, Ala.: Spring Hill College.

———. 1982. "William J. Williams, Newman, and Modernism." In *Modernist Uses of Newman,* edited by Ronald Burke and George Gilmore, 8–113. Mobile, Ala.: Spring Hill College.

Rousseau, Jean Jacques. [1762] 1972. *Emile.* Translated by Barbara Foxley. New York: Dutton.

Russell, J. 1963. "Interpretations of the Origins of Medieval Heresy." *Medieval Studies* 25:26–53.

Ryals, Clyde de. L. 1967. "Editor's Introduction." In *Robert Elsmere,* by Mrs. Humphry [Mary] Ward, vii–xxxviii. Lincoln: University of Nebraska Press.

Sabatier, Paul. 1906. *Disestablishment in France.* Translated by Robert Dell. New York: Scribner's Sons.

———. 1908. *Modernism: The Jowett Lectures, 1908.* Translated by C. A. Miles. London: Unwin.

Sanks, Howland. 1974. *Authority in the Church: A Study in Changing Paradigms.* Missoula, Mont.: Scholars' Press.

Sartolli, Francis. 1893. "Mgr. Sartolli's Address." In *World's Columbian Catholic Congresses,* 44–52. Chicago: Hyland.

Schapiro, J. Selwyn. 1967. *Anticlericalism: Conflict between Church and State in France, Italy, and Spain.* Princeton, N.J.: Van Nostrand.

Schillebeeckx, Edward. 1970. *Dogma and Pluralism.* New York: Herder and Herder.

Schneider, Louis. 1971. "Dialectic in Sociology." *American Sociological Review* 36 (August):667–678.

Schoenl, William J. 1974. "George Tyrrell and the English Liberal Catholic Crisis, 1900–01." *Downside Review* 92:171–184.

Schultenover, David G. 1981*a*. "George Tyrrell: Caught in the Roman Archives of the Society of Jesus." In *Three Discussions: Biblical Exegesis; George Tyrrell; Jesuit Archives,* edited by Ronald Burke and George Gilmore, 85–114. Mobile, Ala.: Spring Hill College.

———. 1981*b. George Tyrrell: In Search of Catholicism.* Shepherdstown, W. Va.: Patmost Press.

———. 1983. "George Tyrrell: 'Devout Disciple of Newman.'" In *Regarding Modernism,* edited by Ronald Burke and George Gilmore, 93–128. Mobile, Ala.: Spring Hill College.

Schweitzer, Albert. 1948. *The Quest of the Historical Jesus.* Translated by W. Montgomery. New York: Macmillan.

Scoppola, Pietro. 1957. "Il modernismo politico in Italia. Le Lega Democratica Nazionale." *Revista storica italiana* 1:61–109.

Scott, Bernard B. 1976. "Introduction." In *The Gospel and the Church,* by Alfred Loisy, edited by B. Scott, xi–lxxiii. Philadelphia: Fortress Press.

Sedgwick, Alexander. 1965. *The Ralliement in French Politics.* Cambridge, Mass.: Harvard University Press.

Semler, Johann Salomo. 1771–1775. *Abhandlung von freier Untersuchung des Canon.* 4 vols. Halle: Hemmerde.

Sheehan, Thomas. 1980. "Quo Vadis, Wojtyla?" *New York Review of Books* 27: 38–44.

Sherif, M. Harvey, O. J. White, B. J. Hood, W. R. Sherif, and C. Sherif. 1961. *Intergroup Conflict and Cooperation: The Robbers Cave Experiment.* Norman, Okla.: University Book Exchange.

Shils, Edward. 1972. *The Intellectuals and the Powers.* Chicago: University of Chicago Press.

———. 1975. *Center and Periphery: Essays in Macrosociology.* Chicago: University of Chicago Press.

Siegfried, Agnes. 1932. *L'Abbé Frémont 1852–1912: Pour servir à l'histoire religieuse.* Vol. 2: *1869–1912.* Paris: Alcan.

Simmel, Georg. [1900] 1978. *The Philosophy of Money.* Translated by Tom Bottomore and David Frisby. London: Routledge & Kegan Paul.

———. 1971. *On Individuality and Social Forms: Selected Writings.* Chicago: University of Chicago Press.

Simon, Richard. [1678] 1682. *A Critical History of the Old Testament.* 4 vols. Translated into English by a Person of Quality [Henry Dickinson]. London: No publisher.

———. 1689. *Histoire critique du texte du Nouveau Testament, Ou l'on établit la Verité des Actes sur lesque la Religion Chrétienne est fondée.* Rotterdam: Leers.

————. 1693. *Histoire des principaux commentateurs du Nouveau Testament, depuis le commencement du Christianisme jusques à notre temps.* Rotterdam.

Simons, Marlise. 1985. "Brazilian Theologian Says He Prefers to Walk with the Church." *New York Times,* 21 March 1985, 6.

Snow, David A. 1979. "A Dramaturgical Analysis of Movement Accommodation: Building Idiosyncrasy Credit as a Movement Mobilization Strategy." *Symbolic Interaction* 2 (Fall):23–44.

Snow, David A., Louis A. Zurcher, Jr., and Sheldon Ekland-Olson. 1980. "Social Networks and Social Movements: A Microstructural Approach to Differential Recruitment." *American Sociological Review* 45 (October):787–801.

Spinoza, Baruch. [1670] 1883. *Tractatus Theologico-Politicus: continens dissertationes aliquot, quibus ostenditur libertatem philosophandi non tantum salva petate, and republicae pace posse concedi, etc.* Hamburg: Kunraht. Translated into English (as vol. 1 in *The Chief Works of Benedict de Spinoza*) by R. H. M. Elwes. London: Bell.

Steinmann, Jean. 1962. *Friedrich von Hügel: Sa vie, son oeuvre et ses amitiés.* Paris: Aubier, Editions Montaigne.

Strauss, David F. 1835–36. *Das Leben Jesu kritisch bearheitet.* 2 vols. Tübingen: Osiander.

Sullivan, Francis A. 1983. *Magisterium.* Ramsey, N.J.: Paulist Press.

Swidler, Leonard, ed., tr. 1981. *Küng in Conflict.* Garden City, N.Y.: Image Books.

Szasz, Thomas. 1975. *Ceremonial Chemistry: The Ritual Persecution of Drugs, Addicts, and Pushers.* Garden City, N.Y.: Doubleday Anchor.

Talbott, John E. 1969. *The Politics of Educational Reform in France, 1918–1940.* Princeton, N.J.: Princeton University Press.

Teilhard de Chardin, Pierre. 1955. *Le Phénomène Humain.* Paris: Editions du Seuil.

Thibault, Pierre. 1972. *Savoir et pouvoir: Philosophie thomiste et politique cléricale au xixe siècle.* Quebec: Les Presses de l'Université Laval.

Thierry, Jean-Jacques. 1963. *La Vie quotidienne au Vatican au temps de Leon XIII à la fin du xixe siècle.* Paris: Hachette.

Thomas, Lucien. 1965. *L'Action Française devant l'Eglise.* Paris: Nouvelles Editions Latines.

Tilly, Charles. 1978. *From Mobilization to Revolution.* Reading, Mass.: Addison-Wesley.

Tiryakian, Edward A. 1972. "Toward the Sociology of Esoteric Culture." *American Journal of Sociology* 78 (November):491–513.

Tocqueville, Alexis de. [1856] 1955. *The Old Regime and the French Revolution.* Garden City, N.Y.: Doubleday Anchor.

Tracy, David. 1975. *Blessed Rage for Order: The New Pluralism in Theology.* New York: Seabury Press.

Troeltsch, Ernst. 1922–1925. *Gesammelte Schriften.* 4 vols. Edited by Hans Baron. Tübingen: Mohr [Siebeck].

————. 1977. *Briefe an Friedrich von Hügel, 1901–1923.* Introduction by Karl-Ernst Apfelbacher and Peter Neuner. Paderborn: Bonifacius-Druckerei.

Turmel, Joseph. 1904. *Histoire de la théologie positive depuis l'origine jusqu'au concile de Trent.* Paris: Beauchesne.

————. 1935. *Comment j'ai donné congé aux dogmes.* Paris: Herblay, ed. de l'Idée libre.

Turner, Frank Miller. 1974. *Between Science and Religion: The Reaction to Scientific Naturalism in Late Victorian England.* New Haven, Conn.: Yale University Press.

Turner, Victor. 1969. *The Ritual Process: Structure and Anti-Structure.* Ithaca, N.Y.: Cornell University Press.

Turvasi, Francesco. 1979. *The Condemnation of Alfred Loisy and the Historical Method.* Rome: Edizioni di Storia e Letteratura.

Tyrrell, George. 1897. *Nova et Vetera: Informal Meditations for Times of Spiritual Dryness.* London: Longmans, Green, and Co.

————. 1899. *Hard Sayings: A Selection of Meditations and Studies.* London: Longmans, Green, and Co.

————. 1901. *The Faith of the Millions: A Selection of Past Essays.* 2 vols. London: Longmans, Green, and Co.

————. [1902] 1907. *Oil and Wine.* London: Longmans, Green, and Co. (Printed privately 1902; Longmans' reprint 1907.)

————. [pseud. Hilaire Bourdon]. 1903. *The Church and the Future.* N.p.: By the Author. (Reprinted as *George Tyrrell, The Church and the Future,* preface by Maude D. Petre. Hampstead: Priory Press, 1910.)

————. 1904. "The Abbé Loisy: Criticism and Catholicism." *Church Quarterly Review* 58:180–195.

————. 1906a. *A Much-Abused Letter.* London: Longmans, Green, and Co.

————. 1906b. *External Religion: Its Use and Abuse.* London: Longmans, Green, and Co.

————. 1907a. *Lex Orandi, or Prayer and Creed.* London: Longmans, Green, and Co.

————. 1907b. "The Pope and Modernism." *London Times,* 30 September and 1 October 1907.

————. 1907c. *Through Scylla and Charybdis, or the Old Theology and the New.* London: Longmans, Green, and Co.

————. [1908] 1920. *Medievalism, A Reply to Cardinal Mercier.* London: Longmans, Green, and Co.

————. [1909] 1910. *Christianity at the Crossroads.* Prepared by Maude Petre, with Asistance from Friedrich von Hügel, from a handwritten manuscript. London: Longmans, Green, and Co.

————. 1912. *Autobiography and Life of George Tyrrell.* Vol. 1: *Autobiography of George Tyrrell 1861–1884.* London: Arnold.

————. 1920. *George Tyrrell's Letters.* Selected and edited by Maude D. Petre. London: T. Fisher Unwin.

Ullmann, Walter. [1955] 1970. *The Growth of Papal Government in the Middle Ages: A Study in the Ideological Relations of Clerical to Lay Power.* 3d ed. London: Methuen.

Vidler, Alec R. 1934. *The Modernist Movement in the Roman Church.* Cambridge: Cambridge University Press.

————. 1945. *The Orb and the Cross: A Normative Study in the Relations of*

Church and State with Reference to Gladstone's Early Writings. London: Society for Promoting Christian Knowledge.

———. 1954. *Prophecy and Papacy: A Study of Lamennais, the Church and the Revolution.* New York: Scribner's Sons.

———. 1964. *A Century of Social Catholicism 1820–1920.* London: Society for Promoting Christian Knowledge.

———. 1965. *Twentieth Century Defenders of the Faith.* London: SCM Press.

———. 1970. *A Variety of Catholic Modernists.* Cambridge: Cambridge University Press.

———. 1977a. "An Abortive Renaissance: Catholic Modernists in Sussex." In *Renaissance and Renewal in Church History,* edited by Derek Baker, 377–392. Oxford: Blackwell.

———. 1977b. "Last Conversations with Loisy." *Journal of Theological Studies* 28:84–89.

———. 1977c. *Scenes from a Clerical Life: An Autobiography.* London: Collins.

Voltaire, Jean François Marie Arouet. [1758] 1960. *Candide.* Translated by John Butt. Baltimore, Md.: Penguin.

Walker, James. 1944. "Maude Petre." In *Alfred Loisy,* by Maude Petre, i–xxiii. Cambridge: Cambridge University Press.

Wallace, Lillian Parker. 1966. *Leo XIII and the Rise of Socialism.* Durham, N.C.: Duke University Press.

Ward, Mrs. Humphry [Mary]. [1888] 1967. *Robert Elsmere.* Lincoln: University of Nebraska Press.

———. 1911. *The Case of Richard Meynell.* London: Smith, Elder.

Weaver, Mary Jo. 1978. "Wilfrid Ward, George Tyrrell and the Meanings of Modernism." *Downside Review* 96:21–34.

———. 1981. *Letters from a Modernist: The Letters of George Tyrrell to Wilfrid Ward.* Shepherdstown, W. Va.: Patmos Press.

Weber, Eugen. 1962. *Action Française: Royalism and Reaction in Twentieth Century France.* Stanford, Calif.: Stanford University Press.

Weber, Max. [1925] 1968. *Wirtschaft und Gesellschaft.* Tübingen: J. C. B. Mohr. Translated into English (as *Economy and Society*), edited by Guenther Roth and Claus Wittich. New York: Bedminster Press.

———. [1946] 1958. *From Max Weber: Essays in Sociology.* Translated, edited, and with an introduction by H. H. Gerth and C. Wright Mills. New York: Oxford University Press.

———. 1947. *Gesammelte Aufsätze zur Religionssoziologie.* Tübingen: Mohr.

Whelan, Joseph P. 1971. *The Spirituality of Friedrich von Hügel.* New York, Paramus, Toronto: Newman Press.

White, Andrew Dickson. 1896–97. *History of the Warfare of Science with Theology in Christendom.* 2 vols. New York: Appleton.

Whitehead, Alfred N. 1929. *Science and the Modern World.* New York: Macmillan.

Wilkes, Keith. 1969. *Religion and the Sciences.* Oxford: Religious Education Press.

Wilson, John. 1977. "Social Protest and Social Control." *Social Problems* 24 (4): 469–481.

Zald, Mayer N., and Michael A. Berger. 1978. "Social Movements in Organizations: Coup d'Etat, Insurgency and Mass Movements." *American Journal of Sociology* 83 (January):823–861.

Zurcher, Louis A., Jr., R. George Kirkpatrick, Robert G. Cushing, and Charles K. Bowman. 1971. "The Anti-Pornography Campaign: A Symbolic Crusade." *Social problems* 19 (Fall):217–238.

Zurcher, Louis A., and David A. Snow. 1982. "Collective Behavior: Social Movements." In *Social Psychology: Sociological Perspectives*, edited by Morris Rosenberg and Ralph H. Turner, 447–482. New York: Basic Books.

Index

Abelard, Peter, 20
Abercrombie, Nigel, 220 n. 46
Academie Française, 78
Action Française, 81, 142, 161, 164–165;
condemnation of, 226 n. 37, 223 n. 85.
See also Integralism
Acton, John, 37
Acts of the Apostles, 21, 33
Ad diem illium, 151
Aeterni Patris, 33, 35, 38–42, 53, 150,
209 n. 13
Albert, Prince of Monaco, 65
Albrow, Martin, 176
Alfieri, Antonio Aiace, 58, 88, 113, 124,
153, 221 n. 57, 221 n. 59
Ambivalence: of Catholic scholars, 56–
59; concept of, 54–55; construction of,
54–59; and contradictory behavior, 94,
96, 101, 138; Loisy's, 61, 91–97; socio-
logical, 2, 15, 91–108, 134, 212 n. 2;
of young Catholics, 80
Amelli, Don, 58
American Church Review, 24
Americanism, 33, 35; condemnation of,
45–48, 50, 117
Amiaud, Arthur, 61
Ancien régime, 7, 13, 21, 38; and Action
Française, 161; and Vatican, 25
Annales, 76–77, 79, 122, 130, 214 n. 38

Anticlericalism, 7–11, 13, 17–18, 21, 30,
52 53, 55, 178; concept of, 209 n. 7;
and conservative Catholic alliance, 25–
32; and criticism, 18–19; in England,
108; and evolution, 24; in Italy, 35
Antimodernism, 10, 12, 17, 125, 141,
185, 226 n. 35; characteristics of, 142–
144; in France, 67, 162–163; oath,
142, 158–159; official, 147–165 pas-
sim; suppression of, 164–165
Apollinaire, 42
Apostolic succession, 13
Appelbaum, Richard P., 176, 227 n. 4
Aquinas, Thomas, 9, 14, 37–43, 48–50,
57, 73, 104, 106, 116, 146; influence
of, 83–84; *Summa Theologica* of, 60
Arconati-Visconti, Marie-Louise, 132,
223 n. 84
Arianism, 146, 213 n. 21
Aristotle, 20, 38, 40, 57
Arnold, Matthew, 74, 121
Aron, Raymond, 13
Association catholique internationale des
oeuvres de protection de la jeune fille,
226 n. 31
Attwater, Donald, 3, 159, 216 n. 7, 225
n. 14
Aubert, Rogert, 28
Augustine, Saint, 4, 123, 146, 151

Designer: U.C. Press Staff
Compositor: Janet Sheila Brown
Printer: Cushing-Malloy, Inc.
Binder: John H. Dekker & Sons
Text: Sabon 10/12
Display: Sabon